GRAVEYARD OF THE ATLANTIC

GRAVEYARD

OF THE

ATLANTIC

BY DAVID STICK

Illustrated by Frank Stick

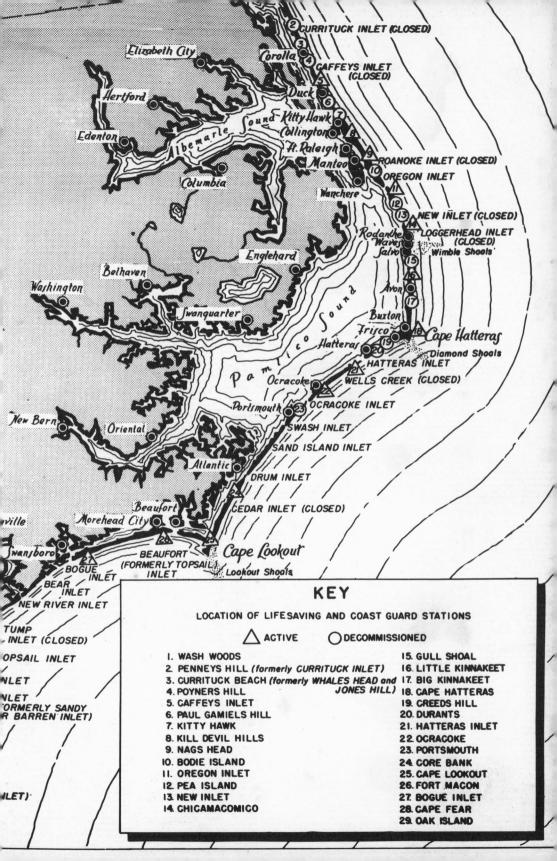

CURRITUCK INLET (CLOSED)
Corolla
CAFFEYS INLET (CLOSED)
Duck
Elizabeth City
Hertford
Kitty Hawk
Collington
Ft. Raleigh
Edenton
Manteo
Albemarle Sound
Wanchere
ROANOKE INLET (CLOSED)
OREGON INLET
Columbia
NEW INLET (CLOSED)
LOGGERHEAD INLET (CLOSED)
Rodanthe
Waves
Salvo
Wimble Shoals
Englehard
Belhaven
Avon
Washington
Buxton
Swanquarter
Frisco
Hatteras
Cape Hatteras
Pamlico Sound
Diamond Shoals
HATTERAS INLET
Ocracoke
WELLS CREEK (CLOSED)
New Bern
Portsmouth
OCRACOKE INLET
Oriental
SWASH INLET
SAND ISLAND INLET
Atlantic
DRUM INLET
New Bern
Beaufort
Morehead City
CEDAR INLET (CLOSED)
...ville
Swansboro
BEAUFORT (FORMERLY TOPSAIL INLET)
Cape Lookout
BOGUE INLET
Lookout Shoals
BEAR INLET
NEW RIVER INLET
TUMP INLET (CLOSED)
OPSAIL INLET
NLET
NLET
ORMERLY SANDY R BARREN INLET)
NLET)

KEY

LOCATION OF LIFESAVING AND COAST GUARD STATIONS

△ ACTIVE   ○ DECOMMISSIONED

1. WASH WOODS
2. PENNEYS HILL (formerly CURRITUCK INLET)
3. CURRITUCK BEACH (formerly WHALES HEAD and JONES HILL)
4. POYNERS HILL
5. CAFFEYS INLET
6. PAUL GAMIELS HILL
7. KITTY HAWK
8. KILL DEVIL HILLS
9. NAGS HEAD
10. BODIE ISLAND
11. OREGON INLET
12. PEA ISLAND
13. NEW INLET
14. CHICAMACOMICO

15. GULL SHOAL
16. LITTLE KINNAKEET
17. BIG KINNAKEET
18. CAPE HATTERAS
19. CREEDS HILL
20. DURANTS
21. HATTERAS INLET
22. OCRACOKE
23. PORTSMOUTH
24. CORE BANK
25. CAPE LOOKOUT
26. FORT MACON
27. BOGUE INLET
28. CAPE FEAR
29. OAK ISLAND

Shipwrecks of the North Carolina Coast

CHAPEL HILL

The University of North Carolina Press

To my wife,

PHYLLIS,

*who shared equally in the tiring
work of research for this book, but
not in the pleasure of writing it.*

MEN LIKE CAPTAIN HAND,
the only survivor of the loss of the sloop *Henry* at Ocracoke in
1819; and Ensign Lucian Young, hero of the wreck of the U.S.
gunboat *Huron* at Nags Head in 1877; and Dunbar Davis of Southport, who devoted most of his life to saving mariners wrecked on
the North Carolina coast, deserve the bulk of the credit for this
book. For without the detailed information on disasters recorded
by these and other participants, factual accounts of bygone shipwrecks could not now be written.

Even so, it has been necessary to eliminate a major share of the
thousands of shipwreck accounts examined in the compilation of
material for this book, for only those vessels which are definitely
known to have been total wrecks are listed here. Many other ships
were lost before accurate records were kept; hundreds more just
disappeared, with no trace of ship or crew, or have been surrounded
by such confusion and conflict as to dates, places, and circumstances
that they had to be eliminated.

The material included here comes from newspapers, magazines,
books, pamphlets, official records, and personal interviews. Special
thanks are due my father, Frank Stick, for taking time out from his
busy schedule to do the fine pen and ink drawings that enliven the
accounts to follow; and John L. Lochhead and the staff of the
Mariners' Museum at Newport News, Virginia; Mary Brown and
her co-workers in the Norfolk Public Library; the United States

Hydrographic Office, the United States Coast Guard, the United States Navy, the National Archives, and the Library of Congress; L. F. Small, Huntington Cairns, John C. Emmerson, Jr.; A. W. Drinkwater, Aycock Brown, Ben Dixon MacNeill, Levene Midgett, T. S. Meekins, W. H. Lewark, Marianne C. Small, Joseph Hergesheimer, and the friends and members of my family who have encouraged and assisted during the days when the task seemed never ending.

Limitations of space have made necessary the abbreviation of some wreck accounts which, in the opinion of this writer, have already received more than their proportionate share of publicity and recognition. In other instances there is no mention at all of supposed wrecks about which the old-timers speak because exhaustive research has failed to substantiate the stories handed down from past generations. And finally, except in special cases, losses in inland waters, and of vessels of less than fifty tons, have been eliminated.

Even so, more than six hundred wrecked vessels are mentioned in the pages that follow. All were totally lost in the Graveyard of the Atlantic.

David Stick

Kill Devil Hills, N.C.
September 12, 1951

CONTENTS

GRAVEYARD OF THE ATLANTIC

OU CAN STAND on Cape
Point at Hatteras on a stormy day and watch two oceans come together in an awesome display of savage fury; for there at the Point
the northbound Gulf Stream and the cold currents coming down
from the Arctic run head-on into each other, tossing their spumy
spray a hundred feet or better into the air and dropping sand and
shells and sea life at the point of impact. Thus is formed the dreaded
Diamond Shoals, its fang-like shifting sand bars pushing seaward
to snare the unwary mariner. Seafaring men call it the Graveyard
of the Atlantic.

Actually, the Graveyard extends along the whole of the North
Carolina coast, northward past Chicamacomico, Bodie Island, and
Nags Head to Currituck Beach, and southward in gently curving
arcs to the points at Cape Lookout and Cape Fear. The bare-
ribbed skeletons of countless ships are buried there; some covered
only by water, with a lone spar or funnel or rusting winch showing
above the surface; others burrowed deep in the sands, their final
resting place known only to the men who went down with them.

From the days of the earliest New World explorations, mariners
have known the Graveyard of the Atlantic, have held it in under-
standable awe, yet have persisted in risking their vessels and their
lives in its treacherous waters. Actually, they had no choice in the
matter, for a combination of currents, winds, geography, and eco-
nomics have conspired to force many of them to sail along the
North Carolina coast if they wanted to sail at all.

A great number of the craft lost in the Graveyard of the Atlantic were engaged in coastal trade, transporting cargoes from north to south or back again in the days before the advent of airlines, highways, and fast railroad service. They were small vessels, mainly, and a constant stream of them connected the vast productive lands of the South with the cities on the Chesapeake and the manufacturing centers of the Central Atlantic States and New England.

For all their numbers and the frequency of their losses, the vessels of the coastal trade were no more a factor in the over-all history of Carolina shipwrecks than were the larger craft engaged in trade with South America, the West Indies, and our own Gulf Coast. For they, too, were forced to pass the Carolina outer banks if their cargoes were to be delivered to the northern markets, and many a shipload of coffee and sugar, of salt and spice, of logwood and phosphate, has been consigned to the depths off Frying Pan and Lookout and Diamond Shoals as a result.

More difficult to understand is the reason for the loss here of so many vessels engaged in transoceanic trade, ships of many nationalities, of almost every shape and size, bound to and from the ports of Europe, Africa, and even Asia. What reason could there be, for example, for a seventeenth-century Spanish frigate, en route from Central America to her home country, purposely sailing a thousand miles out of her way to pass within sight of dreaded Diamond Shoals; or for an English brigantine of the eighteenth century travelling by such a circuitous route from the British Isles to New York as to end up on Ocracoke Bar, pounded to pieces in the surf, a total wreck?

The Gulf Stream figures in the answer to both questions, for the Spanish explorers learned, even before our coast was first settled by Europeans, that they could save considerable time on their return voyage from the Caribbean to Spain by taking advantage of the Gulf Stream current, travelling northward along the coast until they sighted Cape Hatteras, then bearing east for the shorter trip across the Atlantic. And, by the same token, the vessels bound to this hemisphere soon devised a system of sailing southward along the coast of Europe and Africa until they reached the Canary Islands, then crossing in the Equatorial Current to the West Indies, and finally moving up the coast with the aid of that same Gulf Stream.

In either case the first land jutting out across their path on the run northward was the section of the Carolina outer banks extending like a huge net from the South Carolina border to Cape Hatteras, a long, sweeping series of shoal-infested bights and capes and inlets, laid out as if by perverted human design to trap the northbound voyager.

These are the reasons so many vessels have been lost on the North Carolina coast; yet every bit as important as the reasons are the changes which have come about as the result of the shipwrecks. For, the past history and the present day life of the entire coast of North Carolina are closely integrated with shipwrecks; so closely integrated, in fact, that much of the outer banks might yet be a barren, uninhabited sand reef but for the ships that have been lost there.

A great many of the present residents can trace their ancestry back to individuals who were shipwrecked there. These were seafaring men, mainly, who soon discovered that life on the narrow sand spit separating sound and sea was the next closest thing to treading the deck of a sailing vessel; and so they decided to build homes, marry, and raise families on the banks instead of moving on to their intended destinations. Others of the early settlers went there in the first place as the direct result of shipping and shipwrecks; some, in tiny sailboats, served as pilots for the larger cargo vessels attempting to cross the bars and pass through the inlets to the sounds and inland ports beyond, and others came as customs inspectors or militia sent down by the Colonial government.

There were pirates, too—Blackbeard, Stede Bonnet, Anne Bonny, and Calico Jack Rackam, to name a few—who rendezvoused behind the isolated islands of the outer banks, sailed out from there to attack merchant vessels, then returned again to celebrate and fight over their loot and maybe even bury some of it behind the ever-shifting dunes. Between them, the pirates were as much a menace for a time as the winds and tides and shoals.

Maintenance of law and order at the scene of shipwrecks was long a problem for the authorities. As early as 1678 the Lords Proprietors of Carolina appointed a man named Robert Houlden to "looke after, receive and recover all wrecks, ambergrice or any other ejections of the sea," but Houlden and the agents who fol-

lowed him were never able to exercise any real control over the
disposition of wrecked vessels and cargoes. The situation became
so bad, in fact, that Governor Johnson, receiving reports in 1750
that a Spanish ship driven ashore at Ocracoke had been plundered,
found it necessary to dispatch an armed vessel to recover the property from the bankers, whom he referred to as "a people so called
from inhabiting near the banks of the sea shoar."

The Governor later described these same bankers as "a set of
indigent desperate outlaws and vagabonds," and though his choice
of words may have been a bit on the harsh side, there is no question
that the early bankers were both strong-willed and independent—
still are, for that matter. It can be said in their defense, however,
that they frequently risked their own lives in the attempt to rescue
unknown mariners cast adrift on their shores; and later, when the
first lighthouses were built near the beginning of the nineteenth
century and the Lifesaving Service was extended to the Carolina
coast in the 1870's, the lifesaving records established by the bankers
were enviable.

As for wrecked property that drifted ashore, it has been said of
the people of Ocracoke Island, for example, that they would drop
a corpse on the way to a burial if they heard the cry of "Ship
Ashore!" But it was more than idle curiosity that prompted this
kind of interest, for many a stranded cargo has brought wealth to
the finder, and even today the person who first locates cargo drifting on the beach shares in the proceeds at the auction sale or
"vendue" that follows.

There are houses in almost every coastal community in North
Carolina built wholly or in part from lumber salvaged from wrecked
vessels; there are villages today largely populated by descendants
of shipwrecked mariners; and there are countless coastal families
whose main source of income still is a monthly pay check for
service, past or present, in guarding our shores.

Thus shipwrecks have resulted not only in populating the outer
banks, but in providing income for the people living there. And the
rarity of shipwrecks today probably has a lot to do with the fact
that the village of Portsmouth, once a thriving community of
approximately five hundred souls, now numbers less than ten
residents; and that the county of Dare, despite a greatly intensified

year-around tourist business, is less densely populated now than it
was ten years ago. And for the first time since the earliest residents
settled along North Carolina's outer banks a new generation is
growing up which has never seen a surfboat full of survivors coming through the breakers, or watched a rescue in the breeches buoy,
or listened to the sound of the auctioneer at a vendue of salvaged
cargo on the beach.

This new generation, and the ones to follow, might still succeed
in finding remnants of the earliest known wrecks on this coast,
though there is little to help in locating them. There was, for example, the Spanish brigantine of the fleet under command of Lucas
Vasquez de Ayllon which was lost on the treacherous reaches of
Cape Fear in June, 1526, while en route to the Spanish colony of
Chicora on the Cape Fear River; and the *Tiger*, flagship of Sir
Richard Grenville's fleet, which stranded in Ocracoke Inlet while
attempting to reach Roanoke Island with Sir Walter Raleigh's
colonists in June, 1585; and Sir John Yeamans' fly-boat, sunk on
Frying Pan Shoals in November, 1665; and the vessels of Don Juan
Manuel de Bonilla's Spanish flotilla, which were scattered along the
coast all the way from Currituck to Topsail Inlet by the tempest
of 1750.

Or, if they are really lucky, they might uncover some new evidence that would aid in solving one of the most intriguing shipwreck mysteries of the Carolina coastland—the fate of the passengers
and crew of the schooner *Patriot*, which is generally assumed to
have drifted ashore at Nags Head in January, 1813, with no one
on board. For there are few known facts about the disappearance
of the *Patriot*, the available information being a mixture of rumor,
legend, and conjecture.

The *Patriot*, a former New York pilot boat and privateer, left
Georgetown, South Carolina, December 30, 1812, bound for New
York. One of the passengers for that fateful journey was Theodosia
Burr Alston, wife of Governor John Alston of South Carolina and
daughter of former vice-president Aaron Burr. At twenty-nine she
had become, under her father's constant supervision, one of the
most gifted gentlewomen of her day. At the time of her departure
from Georgetown she was in ill health, partly because of the recent
loss of her only child and partly because of the stigma surrounding

her father as the result of his fatal duel with Alexander Hamilton and his trial for treason in the alleged plan to take over the government of Texas and Mexico.

When, in early 1813, the *Patriot* failed to arrive in New York, extensive efforts were made to learn her fate. Investigations were carried on as far away as Nassau and in most of the ports along the Atlantic seaboard. It was definitely known that a severe storm had struck in the vicinity of Cape Hatteras at about the time that the *Patriot* was due to pass there, though strangely enough there is no indication that either the father or husband—both men of great influence—carried their investigations to the wreck-strewn sand bank of which Hatteras is the hub.

At length all hope of survival was abandoned and Theodosia and her companions were presumed to have been lost at sea. In subsequent years, however, a number of additional facts and purported facts have been unearthed, shedding considerable light on the fate of Theodosia Burr Alston. No attempt will be made here to draw conclusions; rather, the evidence will be presented, chronologically, so that the reader himself can make his own deductions.

In 1833 an Alabama newspaper, the *Mobile Register*, reported that a man "residing in one of the interior counties of this state" made a deathbed confession that he had participated in the capture of the *Patriot*, the murder of all those on board, and the scuttling of the vessel "for the sake of her plate and effects."

Fifteen years later another confessed pirate told a similar deathbed story, adding that one of the passengers on board the captured vessel was a woman named "Odessa Burr Alston," who had, when given the alternative of sharing a cabin with the pirate captain, chosen death.

In 1869, a Dr. William G. Pool, of Elizabeth City, spending his summer vacation at Nags Head, was called to the bedside of an old banker woman named Mann. On the wall of her cottage was an oil portrait of a young woman, expertly done and in the doctor's mind completely out of keeping in the banker shack. When asked about the picture Mrs. Mann said that it was given to her by her first husband, a Mr. Tillett, before their marriage. One winter morning "when we were fighting the British," a boat was discovered ashore two miles below Nags Head. She stated that all sails were set on the vessel, the rudder was lashed, and the craft seemed to be in good condition, but entirely deserted. In the cabin were several fancy silk dresses, a vase of beautiful waxed flowers, and the portrait.

Dr. Pool is reported to have successfully treated the old woman but, knowing her financial condition, would accept no payment. Accordingly Mrs. Mann presented the picture to him.

Soon after this an author named Charles Gayarre published a novel entitled "Fernando de Lemos," in which he devoted a chapter to the purported confession of an infamous pirate, Dominique You. According to the story, You admitted having captured the *Patriot* and murdered Theodosia Burr, and since Gayarre represented his story as being both "truth and fiction" there was considerable speculation that this part of his novel might have been based on fact.

Meanwhile, it was publicly suggested that the portrait in Dr. Pool's possession might be of Theodosia, and in 1878 this possibility was mentioned by Colonel J. H. Wheeler, eminent North Carolina historian, in an address before the North Carolina Historical Society.

In the years that followed, considerable publicity was given this theory, and in 1888 editor R. B. Creecy, of the Elizabeth City *Economist*, reported that he had interviewed a woman named Stella E. P. Drake, a descendent of the Burrs, who had come to Elizabeth City to see the portrait. "We were startled by her close resemblance to the portrait in question," he said.

The following year Mrs. Drake wrote a letter to the Washington (D. C.) *Post*, recounting the details of her visit to the home of Dr. Pool. Describing her entrance into the Pool home, she said: "As I turned to go through the door I saw upon the wall above the mantelpiece a portrait of a young woman in white."

" 'That is the picture,' I exclaimed. 'I know it is, because it bears a strong resemblance to my sister.' "

The picture she saw was approximately twelve by eighteen inches in size and painted on mahogany. It has been reproduced many times, and is, together with the accounts of the pirate confessions and the story of Mrs. Mann, the strongest link in the thread of evidence concerning the fate of Theodosia.

There have been other supposed revelations since then, and undoubtedly still more will appear as the years go by. But unless one is satisfied with the evidence assembled here, the fate of Theodosia Burr Alston will probably remain a mystery for all time; a mystery which might never have been, if the former vice-president of the United States or the Governor of South Carolina had dispatched an investigator to the coast of North Carolina where, during the winter "we were fighting the British," a vessel came ashore containing a twelve-by-eighteen-inch portrait of a woman who may well have been Theodosia Burr Alston.

AVAILABLE ACCOUNTS of
early shipwrecks on the North Carolina coast are fragmentary, for
neither the participants who figured in them, nor the bankers who
witnessed them, seemed to care whether even the names of the lost
vessels were preserved for posterity. Soon after the end of the War
of 1812, however, newspapers began featuring news of ship losses,
and from that time on the record of North Carolina shipwrecks is
both detailed and fascinating.

The following letter, written at Ocracoke Island, December 10,
1819, is an excellent example of the type of information handed
down to us by shipwreck survivors of that period. The letter was
written by the captain of the sloop *Henry*, of Albany, bound from
New York to Charleston, and is reprinted verbatim from the *Norfolk Beacon and Portsmouth Advertiser* of January 15, 1820.

"I have," the Captain's letter begins, "a melancholy
affair to relate. I am the only one living of the crew and
passengers of the sloop *Henry*. We left New York on
Monday, 30th November. On Wednesday following experienced a heavy gale, but received no damage, only
split our jib, which after the gale, was unbent and re-

paired. On Friday afternoon following, took the wind from the southward, blowing fresh. Saturday morning made Cape Lookout lighthouse, hove about and stood off, wind canting in from the southeast, and the gale and sea increasing so fast that we were obliged to heave to.

"Lay to until 5 o'clock p.m., then began to shoal water fast, and blowing, instead of a gale, a perfect hurricane. We set the head of the foresail to try to get offshore, but to no use, it blowing away in an instant; likewise the jib. We then lay to under the balance of the mainsail until we got in 10 and 9 fathoms water, when the sea began to break and board us, which knocked us on our beam ends, carried away our quarter, and swept the deck. She righted, and in about five minutes capsized again, which took off our mainsail. We were then left to the mercy of the wind and waves, which were continually raking us fore and aft. With much exertion we got her before the wind and sea, and in a few minutes after run her ashore on the south beach of Ocracoke Bar, four miles from land.

"She struck about 10 o'clock at night, bilged in a few minutes, and got on her beam ends, every sea making a fair breach over her. At 12 o'clock her deck blew up and washed away altogether, and broke in two near the hatchway. The bow part turned bottom up, the stern part righted. Mr. Kinley (passenger) and Wm. Bartlett (seaman) washed off. The remainder of us got on the taffil rail, and that all under water. About 2 o'clock a.m., Mr. Campbell (the other passenger) and Wm. Shoe-maker (cook) expired and dropped from the wreck. About 4 o'clock, Jesse Hand (seaman) became so chilled that he washed off. At daylight, Mr. Hawley (mate) died, and fell from along side of me into his watery grave, which I expected every moment would be my own lot. But thro' the tender mercy of God, I survived on the wreck 24 hours alone.

"On Monday morning, about 2 o'clock, the stern broke away and I went with it. At sunrise I was taken off, so much mangled and bruised that few persons thought I could survive. I, however, am gaining, having received the kindest treatment, and every possible care from the inhabitants. My chest has been picked up, but it had been opened, and all my clothes of value taken out. I am here almost naked and shall try to get home as soon as I am able.

"The vessel and cargo are a total loss. The fragments have drifted into Albemarle Sound. I have heard of some barrels being picked up some distance from the sound, but the heads all out. I have noted a protest, and shall have it extended according to law. I wish this published. It is the first of my being able to write. There is no way of conveying letters from this place except by water.

"The bodies of Wm. Bartlett and Jesse Hand have been picked up and decently buried."

Signed: Captain Hand

ENTERPRIZE

There are several recorded instances in which dogs played valiant parts in effecting the rescue of shipwrecked mariners, but so far as can be determined the horse which was led aboard the schooner *Enterprize* at Bristol, Rhode Island, in early October, 1822, was the first and only one of that species who guided his shipmates to safety when stranded on the Carolina coast.

The *Enterprize* was bound for Charleston with a cargo of rum, lime, crockery ware, and lumber, and carried fifteen passengers in addition to her crew.

She was favored with a fair wind after leaving Bristol and made excellent time on the voyage south until, shortly before dawn the morning of October 27, she struck without warning and bilged. Captain Ephriam Eldridge knew that he was somewhere to the north of Cape Hatteras, but he had no more idea than did the horse as to which of the sandy coastal islands he had struck, or how far the vessel was from shore.

In this state, the passengers, roused from their berths, immediately took to the rigging, and the crewmen soon followed their example as the waves began breaking over the stranded craft. But when it was determined that she was not breaking up, and that so far she did not seem completely filled with water, the men came down from the rigging and attempted to pump her out. Their efforts were fruitless, however, and in the process the lime somehow caught on fire. Thus they were threatened, at one and the same time, with the prospect of being drowned or burned to death.

"The general exclamation was we must all perish," wrote William Gardiner, a passenger. "I told them not to despair, that the Lord was a prayer hearing and prayer answering God, and that I still cherished the hope we should escape." Accordingly, the majority set about praying, an activity no doubt alien to many of them in the past.

The result of this sudden turn to religion was not exactly in the best church tradition; for the upshot was that the horse was led to the side and pushed overboard, with the thought that if he could reach land, then no doubt the rest of them could also.

The horse did reach land; in fact, the vessel was so close that he almost waded ashore, followed soon after by a long procession of passengers and crewmen. In this way all were saved, and as the sky lightened and the tide fell an effort was made to land some of the cargo. Meanwhile, some of the passengers had discovered the marks of a cart's wheels in the sand on the beach. "It was like the soft beams of the moon which kindly illumines the path of the benighted traveller, and guides into a place of shelter," Gardiner wrote. They then followed the cart tracks and soon met three men on horseback who informed them that they were on Chicamacomico Banks, some thirty miles north of Cape Hatteras Lighthouse.

There were about twenty-four families living on the island, and when the survivors of the *Enterprize* reached the village of Chicamacomico (now Rodanthe), they made arrangements with Captain Edward Scarborough of Kinnakeet (now Avon) to hire his schooner the *Thomas A. Blount* for the passage across the sound to Ocracoke.

Apparently the valiant horse was left there on Chicamacomico Banks—its descendents may still be there among the banker ponies for all that's known—for when the *Thomas A. Blount* left Chicamacomico the next day with the survivors of the *Enterprize*, the horse was not on board. Neither, by nightfall, was Captain Edward Scarborough, for in mid-afternoon the *Blount* ran into bad weather and the Captain was washed overboard. His body never again was seen.

Thus the wreck of the *Enterprize*, in addition to occasioning the complete loss of the vessel, resulted also in the death of one of the prominent residents of the outer banks, and the addition of one more horse to the number already residing on the sandy islands off the Carolina coast.

HARVEST

Lieutenant Grimke of Norfolk boarded the schooner *Harvest* in that city November 17, 1825, accompanied by his wife, their only child, and the child's nurse. In addition there were five other passengers and a crew of six on the schooner, which was bound to Charleston with a mixed cargo. Soon after passing Cape Henry that afternoon, however, the *Harvest* ran into a strong northwest gale, and at two o'clock the next morning she stranded. Both anchors were immediately let go and her stern swung around toward the distant beach, though not until her hatches had washed off and water had begun to pour into her hold. In the darkness the passengers were herded onto the quarter deck, where the women and child were wrapped in the mainsail to protect them from the wind and the waves which were by then sweeping all the way across the vessel.

At dawn the ship's boat was launched, and the captain, mate, two crewmen and several passengers succeeded in reaching shore; later some residents of the area—presumably Nags Head—attempted to row out to the wreck in a fishing dory, but they were overturned in the surf. Not until the sea had subsided in mid-afternoon were they able to get through to the stranded vessel. By then, however, Lieutenant Grimke was stretched out on the deck, suffering from the effect of injuries and exhaustion. He was immediately lowered into the dory and was followed by the remaining survivors, but the Lieutenant died before the small craft reached the breakers. There was little chance he would have lived much longer, in any

event, for the dory was swamped in the surf and four more persons
—Lieutenant Grimke's child, the child's nurse, and the cabin boy
and cook of the *Harvest*—were all drowned.

Mrs. Grimke reached shore safely, suffering from severe shock;
and a second passenger, an unnamed German, was so moved by the
experience that he was reported in a deranged condition. While
Mrs. Grimke and the German were being escorted to Norfolk by
a physician, the captain of the *Harvest* superintended the removal
of the cargo and managed to save approximately two thirds of the
material aboard the vessel, including 348 barrels of flour, 5 pipes of
brandy, 38 kegs of butter, 16 quart casks of wine, and 103 barrels
of whiskey, all of which was sold at a vendue on the beach two
days later. The bodies of Lieutenant Grimke, the child, and the
nurse were not recovered.

CAPE HATTERAS LIGHTSHIP

From the very first, the lightships anchored off Cape Hatteras
at the tip of Diamond Shoals to warn passing vessels away from the
Graveyard of the Atlantic have had a stormy time of it.

Lightships as a rule are comparatively small vessels, pointed at
both ends like a cigar, and ungainly and top-heavy in appearance;
they are floating tubs, really, with thick hulls and a top speed not
much greater than that of a sick caterpillar walking backwards.
Beauty, speed, and comfort, qualities usually sought in a ship, are
purposely forgotten when designers get around to lightships, for
they are built for the sole purpose of remaining at anchor in the
most turbulent seas, at the very danger spots which other ships
instinctively try to by-pass.

A lighthouse had been in operation on the point at Cape Hatteras
for almost twenty years when the first lightship took up her position fourteen miles away, on the outer Diamond Shoals, June 15,
1824. Constructed in New York, she was a vessel of upwards of
320 tons, with two lights, one 60 feet high and the other 45 feet
high, and was under the command of Captain Jesse D. Elliott of
the Navy. During the first six months of her active career the vessel
ably fulfilled her mission, but in January, 1825, she broke her moorings, drifted a considerable distance up the coast, and was finally

picked up off Currituck and towed into Hampton Roads by steamboat.

When next heard from she was heading back to her station again
just before Christmas of 1825, and though Christmas on a lightship
is considered by many the very essence of loneliness, those aboard
the Cape Hatteras Lightship that Christmas probably had as merry
a time as if they had remained ashore.

There had been changes on board the vessel. Captain Elliott had
been transferred to another assignment, and his place taken by
Captain Life Holden, a teacher of navigation and maker of nautical
instruments, who had previously been captain of the steamboats
Powhatan and *Albemarle*. Captain Holden, a married man with
three daughters, had made other changes; in fact, he had turned the
lightship into a home, taking all four of his womenfolk along with
him.

For two years the Holden family and crew lived aboard the
vessel anchored out there in the most feared spot on our coast.
There were storms and calms; they fished and talked and read, and
partied too, on occasion; and through it all the lights continued to
shine, constantly warning mariners away from danger. Then, in
late August of 1827 a hurricane moved up from the Windward
Islands to strike the Hatteras coast, and the lights went out.

At the height of the storm a tremendous wave struck the vessel,
throwing her into what was described as "a perpendicular position,"
but she weathered that one and returned to an even keel again. Then
a terrific cross sea hit her broadside, she rolled deep in the trough
of the wave, then bounced back to the surface like an apple tossed
into a bobbing-bucket. "The concussion," Captain Holden said,
"was equal to the report of a cannon." The cable parted under the
strain, and the vessel drifted toward the dangerous shoals. The
mainsail was hurriedly hoisted in an attempt to keep her off, but
she passed into the shoals nonetheless, the breakers making a clean
breach over her.

That first Hatteras light vessel was a stout ship; she must have
been, for she passed through those breakers, drifted to the south
of the shoals and along the coast toward Ocracoke. The companion
slide and doors had been swept away, and now canvas was nailed
over the openings to keep out the seas, still breaking over her.

Fourteen hours later, in the darkness, she grounded; this time her binnacle and hatches were washed away and the chief mate and carpenter were carried overboard to certain death. Captain Holden, his wife, the three daughters, and the remaining members of the crew, survived the trip and the night, and found themselves the next morning hard aground near old Whalebone Inlet just west of Portsmouth. They were exhausted, and for the most badly bruised, but all were alive, and with the help of local residents reached shore safely.

Repeated unsuccessful attempts were made to launch the lightship in the ensuing months, and for a number of years afterwards the warning lights were absent from the station on the outer edge of Diamond Shoals.

WILLIAM GIBBONS

Captain E. L. Halsey was an experienced seaman. He had, by 1836, made an estimated four hundred trips past Cape Hatteras, the great majority of them as master. For the last two years of his active career he had commanded the steam packet *William Gibbons* on a regular schedule between the ports of New York and Charleston; he had, in fact, been standing on deck warming his feet beside the steam chimney of that vessel when the chimney exploded in New York harbor in January, 1836, killing two passengers and three of the crew. Soon after that, having experienced his full share of adventures at sea, Captain Halsey retired.

On October 8 of that same year, 140 passengers, among them 32 women and 14 children, boarded the *William Gibbons* in New York for the passage to South Carolina. Shortly before the time of departure, Captain Spinney, the new master, was taken sick, and old Captain Halsey was hurriedly called out of retirement by the owners to sail again on the *Gibbons*.

It was Captain Halsey's understanding that he was not expected to take charge of the navigation of the craft, since First Mate Joshua Andrews and his navigator, T. W. Winship, both were experienced in that department. Rather, Captain Halsey understood that he was "to preside at the table, and to assist in having every necessary attention paid to the comfort and convenience of passengers during the passage; and also to advise with Mr. Andrews, if necessity required."

Thus, under a sort of split-command arrangement, the *William Gibbons* sailed from New York at four o'clock that afternoon, steamed southward along the coast that night and all of the next day at a steady pace of about 10 miles per hour, and the second night was off the outer banks of North Carolina. At that time, after passing Cape Henry on the trip south, there were no other lighthouses to guide them until they reached Cape Hatteras.

Visibility was poor that night of October 9, and it was impossible for Andrews or Winship to take observations. Instead, they relied on soundings, taking them every quarter hour, and finding at midnight some eleven fathoms of water; just what was expected in that locality.

Captain Halsey presided at the table that evening and saw to the comfort of the passengers in the saloons thereafter; then he made his appearance on the bridge, where he remained for a considerable time. At approximately 2:30 A.M. a light was seen bearing on the northwest, which Andrews identified as Cape Hatteras Lighthouse. This opinion was further borne out during the next hour as the water deepened—to fifteen, then seventeen and nineteen fathoms —and Andrews, looking through his spyglass, said he could distinctly see the breakers on outer Diamond Shoals. At 3:45 A.M. the leadsman reported no bottom, and fifteen minutes later Andrews told Captain Halsey they had passed Diamond Shoals and he was going to change to a westward course and head for Cape Lookout.

So far all had gone well, or at least it had seemed to go well. There was, however, one slight mistake; for the light Andrews saw was not Cape Hatteras, as he thought, and instead of heading westward through deep water toward Cape Lookout, they were actually headed straight for the outer banks of North Carolina approximately forty miles further north.

The *William Gibbons* struck at 4:40 A.M., lurched over one bar, slipped across a gully, and ended up in shoal water close to shore. Captain Halsey, realizing too late that the captain who sits at the head of the table should be in charge of the ship as well, now proceeded to take over. He ordered the engines reversed and repeated efforts were made to back the vessel off the shoal, but when she did move at last it was discovered that the rudder was out of commission, and she soon grounded again.

At daylight some people were seen on shore, and one of the small boats was dispatched to find out where they were and what accommodations could be secured on the beach for the comfort of the passengers. The report that came back was that they were in New Inlet, at the north end of Chicamacomico Banks, and that there were two small deserted houses less than a mile away. Four miles distant, it was reported, stood "Mr. John Midyett's residence, containing a boun iful supply of provisions."

The two ship's boats were immediately pressed into shuttle service, transporting passengers ashore six and eight at the trip; but by the time 116 had been removed the wind and tide had risen to such an extent that the remaining passengers refused to budge from the deck of the stranded vessel.

Thus, that afternoon, more than a hundred men, women and children—without a crewman among them—were crowded into the two small houses ashore, with only a very limited supply of water, and with the bountiful provisions of Squire Midyett still several miles away; while on the *William Gibbons*, the remainder of the passengers and the entire crew were in equally bad straits.

For three days that situation continued, a strong northeaster and high tides marooning those who were on the vessel and at the same time confining the other 116 to the two small houses on Chicamacomico Banks. By Tuesday morning—the second day aground in the inlet—Captain Halsey noticed that some of the crewmen had been partaking of hard liquor and were no longer obeying his commands with alacrity, so he ordered the bartender to destroy all of the liquor, an act which was promptly accomplished. But some of the crewmen—the firemen especially—had already stolen enough gin to keep them in the desired state for a considerable time, and Andrews had joined them below decks in their inebriety. Whereas the passengers on shore had not enough to drink, the crew of the *Gibbons* had too much, and before it was over practically every bag and trunk on the vessel had been broken open and the more valuable contents stolen, the mail which the steamboat carried was pilfered by the firemen, and poor old Captain Halsey found himself even less in command of the vessel than when his sole duty had been to preside over the dinner table.

The wreck of the *William Gibbons* must certainly be classed as major, for few vessels lost on our coast have carried so many human beings aboard; yet, for all the confusion, danger, lack of discipline, and privation the wreck of the *William Gibbons* ended without the loss of a single life.

When the storm finally let up Captain Halsey went ashore in one of the boats and assisted in making arrangements to transport the passengers and crew back to Norfolk.

Mate Andrews and his buddies among the firemen had meantime commandeered the other boat and set out for Elizabeth City, where they were reported two days later to have tried to sell the miscellaneous trinkets, items of clothing, and jewelry which they had stolen. Yet, the first mention of the loss of the *Gibbons* in the newspapers of the day included a card, signed by a number of the passengers, censuring old Captain Halsey for his negligence; a charge which he vehemently refuted, and of which he was proved innocent some time later when Andrews and four of the firemen were arrested and clapped into jail in New York.

The five were later tried at Raleigh. The firemen got off free, and Andrews received only a token fine, which he immediately paid from the proceeds of the very crime with which he was charged. As for Captain Halsey, it can be assumed that he once more retired; this time for good.

CARROLL

The brig *Carroll*, Captain Mitchell commanding, set sail from New Orleans on Wednesday, January 25, 1837, bound for Baltimore. She was loaded with a mixed cargo of cotton, pork, hides, lard, castor oil, and madder, and in addition to her crew carried two passengers and a mascot, a dog named Pillow.

Leaving New Orleans the brig picked up the Gulf Stream currents, rounded Key West, moved north along the Florida, Georgia, and South Carolina coasts, and on the night of February 8 approached Cape Lookout—after two weeks at sea.

Throughout that period it is reasonable to assume that the passengers had entertained themselves by watching flying fish in the Gulf Stream and by talking long hours of New England—the *Carroll* was a Maine craft, from Bangor—and of the imminent prospect of war in Mexico, a country which one of the passengers, a Mr. S. Bangs, had just visited. In all, it had been a lazy and uneventful voyage, and no doubt the laziest of all those on board had been the dog Pillow, who probably just lay in the sun, or on a bunk below, and slept.

The beam of the lighthouse on Cape Lookout was obscured by fog that February night in 1837, and the first indication Captain Mitchell had of the proximity of Lookout Shoals was when, at 10 P.M., the *Carroll* suddenly struck a submerged sand bar, ground to a stop, and careened over on her side. Sailors standing on deck were knocked down at the moment of impact, and no doubt Pillow was fully awakened for the first time on the entire voyage.

Almost as quickly as the brig struck, she now drifted over the bar and into deep water again. A quick investigation showed that she was shipping relatively little water and to outward appearances was not badly damaged, but when the helmsman attempted to carry out a command he found that the wheel had lost contact with the rudder; even worse, it was soon obvious that the rudder had been completely torn loose from the ship, leaving her practically unmanageable.

They might have anchored there, put all hands at the pumps, and attempted to ride out the night, but the wind, from the southeast, was rapidly increasing in intensity, and Captain Mitchell decided to make every effort to get his vessel ashore before she foundered at sea with the imminent prospect of death for all of them.

"Finally," Mr. Bangs reported later, "the light of Cape Look Out came in sight, distance about one mile. We endeavored by shifting the position of the sails to gain the light, but it was impossible to do so as the wind headed too much, and we struck the shore one mile to the south of the Cape. We remained beating on the shore all night, with a tremendous sea breaking over us every minute, looking forward with the greatest anxiety for daybreak, to see and get ashore if possible.

"The looked-for hour arrived," Bangs continued. "Orders were given to clear the boat and all hands get in. The boat, however, no sooner touched the water than was filled, capsized, and dashed to pieces in the surf. It was fortunate for us all it so happened, for it was impossible a boat of any kind could live on such a sea, much less gain the shore with the wind ahead and the tide making out."

Throughout this period of great anxiety there is no mention whatsoever of poor Pillow, though it is safe to assume he did little sleeping, if any at all.

As the morning wore on Captain Mitchell, his crew, and passengers made every sort of attempt to get a line to the beach some forty or fifty yards away, but without success; and when people arrived on shore opposite the wreck they were as powerless to get a line out to the *Carroll* as Mitchell and his cohorts were to get one in to them. To make matters worse the sky had clouded up, and shortly after dawn rain had begun to fall. This had turned to sleet, then to hail, and finally to snow, and by noon, according to Mr. Bangs, "we had been exposed for 14 hours and almost chilled to death."

There was, at that time, no prospect of a let up in the force of the huge breakers crashing down on the doomed vessel. The snow continued to fall, interspersed with hail, and the tide, having reached the ebb, was now starting in again.

It was at this seemingly helpless stage of affairs, when the prospect of high tide threatened to engulf them all, that someone thought of Pillow. No one had attempted to swim to shore for fear of the terrific surf, but in a way that humans have, a consultation was held among Captain, crew, and passengers, and it was unanimously decided to try to swim ashore with a line. It was further decided that the one to do the swimming should be their inarticulate companion, Pillow!

Quickly a line was made fast around the dog's neck, the would-be rescuers on shore were pointed out to him, and he was carried to the extreme forward part of the vessel and tossed overboard.

Picture the irony and pathos of the scene there at Cape Lookout that cold and stormy Thursday afternoon in February, 1837. Strong and able men, experienced in the ways of the sea, clinging helplessly to the violently pitching hull of the wrecked brig; other men, no less able and experienced in their way, standing equally as helplessly on the snow-covered shore; while between the two, more frequently covered over by the seething waters than above them, the dog, Pillow, half choked by the rope around his neck, swam with all of his fast ebbing strength toward the low lying beach.

Did Pillow make it? Of course he did, for how else would the details of the wreck now be known? He made it, the line still tight around his neck, and soon afterwards his former shipmates, nearly dead from the cold and exposure, were safely drawn ashore. All of them saved, because a dog accomplished what they were afraid even to try.

AURORA

In June, 1837, at Ocracoke, the schooner *Aurora* of New York stranded on the bar and was lost. To the people of the section there seemed nothing out of the ordinary about the wreck, for the *Aurora* was a small vessel, she had come ashore in moderate weather, and her crew had been saved through their own efforts and with little difficulty.

The real story behind the loss of the *Aurora* finally came to light in January of the following year, when the New York *Courier* published the following brief news item: "On Thursday last, Mr. Waddell, the United States Marshal, arrested Richard Sheridan, late master of the schooner *Aurora*, of New York, John Crocker, mate, and James Norton, seaman, on a charge of the most serious nature, and which, if proved, will place the lives of the offenders in jeopardy. The prisoners are charged with wilfully wrecking, and losing on Ocracoke Bar, the schooner *Aurora*, bound from Havana to New York, in June last, and they are also charged with stealing from the vessel after she was wrecked $4000 in doubloons, which had been sent on board in Havana, consigned to Don Francis Stoughton, Spanish Consul in New York."

The Marshal specifically charged that Captain Sheridan had enlisted the aid of the two crewmen, and together they had carefully planned the shipwreck and stolen the 264 doubloons, which had then been entrusted to the Captain by his henchmen for transfer to the north where they could be converted into American money.

But at about the time this charge was being made public it must have become obvious to Mate Crocker and Seaman Norton that they had joined forces with the wrong man, for on meeting the Captain in New York he told them that he had been robbed of the doubloons and consequently there was no loot to divide.

Somewhere along the line Captain Sheridan made a serious mistake. It may have been in picking the time and place for the shipwreck, for Ocracoke was far off his course and there was little excuse for losing a vessel under sailing conditions as they then existed; or it may have been the fact that the doubloons were not found on the vessel after she was wrecked; or maybe Crocker and Norton turned him in to the authorities.

In any event, when the Captain was brought to trial in New York in February he was found guilty—the doubloons had been discovered in the hands of yet another accomplice—and he was ordered to pay costs and to repay the Spanish Consul, in all an amount of $4,919. In addition, Captain Sheridan was kept in jail for an undetermined period as further punishment.

HOME

In late September, 1837, a particularly violent hurricane known as "Racer's Storm" blew up south of Jamaica, crossed Yucatan, struck the Gulf coast of Texas, and then curved back to the east, moving over Louisiana, Mississippi, Alabama, Georgia, and South Carolina, and arriving off the North Carolina coast on October 9. Before Racer's Storm passed on into the expanses of the Atlantic it was credited with taking something like ninety lives in one of the worst marine disasters in North Carolina's history—the wreck of the proud new steamboat *Home*.

This was only the third voyage for the *Home*, yet already she was a record breaker. She was a 550-ton craft hailing from New York, an "elegantly constructed vessel" built at a cost of $115,000, with a 198-foot keel, a 220-foot overall length, and a 22-foot beam. Sleek and trim, designed for the river trade, she had been converted to the coastwise run—was even being considered for transatlantic crossings—and had been referred to generally as the finest packet afloat.

On her first passage to Charleston the *Home* proceeded cautiously, but on the second trip, encountering clear weather, she

rounded Cape Hatteras in thirty-six hours after leaving New York
and reached Charleston in a total elapsed time of sixty-four hours.
As reported in the press as late as October 6, this was "a quicker
passage than was ever before performed by any steam packet or
other ship . . . and she has thereby established an enviable reputation
as a packet."

This reputation accounts in part, for the large list of passengers
—approximately ninety—on board the *Home* when she sailed from
New York for the third time on October 7. So great was the interest, so high the hopes for further record-breaking voyages, that
several passengers boarded her at the last minute, too late even to
turn in their names to the shipping agent or notify relatives of their
departure.

The *Home* was dogged by ill luck from the very start of that
third trip. She grounded for three hours at the entrance to New
York harbor, and by the time she reached the Carolina coast the
next night had experienced so much rough weather that water already stood ankle deep in her hold.

On the morning of October 9 the *Home* was off Cape Hatteras,
bucking the tremendous hurricane seas of Racer's Storm and shipping water at an alarming rate. The pumps could not keep ahead
of the flow of water, so Captain Carleton White ordered the cabin
floor scuttled and called on the passengers to aid in bailing. Kettles,
buckets, pans, and pails were pressed into service, and even the
women joined in the frantic effort to lighten her, but still the water
gained. Shortly after noon, figuring he had passed Cape Hatteras,
Captain White changed the *Home's* course, heading westward with
the intent of beaching the vessel at the first opportunity. By this
time the packet was pitching so violently that the paddle wheels
were more often than not churning air, and on each wave the bow
fell, independently of the stern, as much as five feet. In mid-afternoon, the water had reached the fires, the engines had stopped
completely, and the *Home*, now under short sail, continued toward
shore, finally striking the beach at 10 P.M. at a point approximately
six miles northeast of Ocracoke village.

There were published statements, later, that Captain White had
been drunk throughout the voyage, though members of the crew
testified that he was cold sober and that "the intoxicated captain"

was a passenger who had been mistaken for White by many of the people on board. In any event, the actions of all involved seemed to have been level-headed throughout the harrowing experience and until the actual moment of striking; then, with full realization that the vessel could not long hold together, crewmen and passengers alike were overcome by panic.

Most of the women and children had been herded together on the high forecastle, the nearest point to the land, some one hundred yards distant. One of the boats had been crushed at sea, and as soon as the *Home* struck an attempt was made to launch another, but this too was dashed to pieces before it ever reached the water. The third and last boat was then lowered, with fifteen to twenty people in it, but the small craft had hardly cleared the ship when it overturned, spilling the occupants into the surf.

There were only two life preservers on the entire vessel; two life preservers and three frail lifeboats for something like 130 men, women, and children. And even as the helpless women and children clung together on the forecastle the life preservers were commandeered by two men—able-bodied, strong men—both of whom were subsequently washed overboard and reached shore alive.

Suddenly the forecastle broke loose and washed into the surf, carrying with it the assembled women and children, most of whom almost immediately disappeared beneath the frothing, teeming sea, never to be seen again. One woman, Mrs. Schroeder of Charleston, had tied herself to one of the braces, and now found herself in the water, held under most of the time by the weight of the brace, yet unable to untie the lines with which she was held. Miraculously she reached the beach, crawled beyond the water mark dragging the brace with her, and then collapsed.

An aged and portly woman, Mrs. Lacoste, was tied to a settee, and she drifted ashore also, though the settee was too much for her to handle, and time after heart-breaking time she was washed back into the surf, until finally some of the residents of the island, who had gathered on the beach opposite the wreck, managed to pull her to safety.

Until the very moment when the vessel finally disintegrated, breaking into three different sections, Andrew A. Lovegreen of Charleston had remained on the upper deck, tolling the ship's bell in an attempt to signal shore for assistance. When the deck parted he fell into the sea and after a lengthy struggle managed to swim to shore.

Phillip S. Cohen and Isaac S. Cohen, brothers of Columbia, South Carolina, had been passengers on the ill-fated steam packet *William Gibbons*, when that vessel stranded at New Inlet and was lost the year previous. Once again Isaac survived, but this time his brother was drowned in attempting to gain the safety of the beach.

A final count showed that only forty persons were saved— Captain White, nineteen crewmen, and twenty passengers. Some ninety others were lost, including most of the women and children and a large percentage of the male passengers. Among the prominent people lost were former Senator Oliver H. Prince of Georgia, and Mrs. Prince; James B. Allaire, nephew of the owner of the *Home;* Professor Nott and Mrs. Nott of Columbia, South Carolina; William H. Tileston of New York, who had on his person upwards of $100,000 in notes to be collected in Charleston; Mrs. Boudo and Mrs. Riviere, both well-known storekeepers in Charleston, and the Reverend and Mrs. George Cowles of Danvers, Massachusetts.

The survivors were cared for by the people of Ocracoke; Captain Pike and Mr. Howard opened their homes for this purpose. The day following the disaster bodies and wreckage were scattered along the Ocracoke beach for miles, while only her boilers remained above water to mark the spot where the finest steam packet afloat had ended her third and last voyage.

As a direct result of the disaster, Congress passed legislation requiring all seagoing vessels to carry a life preserver for each person on board. For every one of the ninety people lost on the *Home*, if you care to look at it that way, scores of others have been saved in later years as the result of this requirement.

1838

HOLIDAY MOOD prevailed aboard the steam packet *Pulaski* as she made her way out of Charleston Harbor and headed up the coast. For one thing, summer had arrived at last, and with it the prospect of sunny days and warm nights. For another, accommodations aboard the *Pulaski* were of the finest—elegant, was the word some used to describe her fittings—and the food was both expertly prepared and handsomely served. And to round it off, there was a congenial group aboard, evenly enough divided as to age and sex so that anyone who had a mind to, man, woman, child, or servant, could make new and interesting acquaintances before the vessel reached Baltimore.

It was June 14, 1838, a Thursday. The 680-ton *Pulaski*, a sleek 206-foot side-wheeler with a narrow 25-foot beam, had been in service for less than eight months. She had been built at Baltimore by Messrs. Ross along the lines of the older coastwise packets, *South Carolina* and *Georgia*. She was equipped with three cabins with berths for 116 passengers, and four staterooms for family use. Her steam cylinders were capable of developing close to two hundred horsepower, and steam-navigation men considered her one of the finest such vessels afloat.

The *Pulaski* had left Savannah on June 13 with ninety passengers aboard and had steamed into Charleston Harbor just short of dusk that evening. Some sixty-five additional passengers boarded the *Pulaski* there, and now, fully loaded, she was beginning the long run up the Carolina coast.

Young Mr. Ridge of New Orleans, who was somewhat reticent

by nature, had remained by himself on deck after boarding the vessel, not mixing with the other passengers. But shortly before the departure from Charleston his attention had been drawn to one of the young ladies who boarded the vessel there, and he now entertained hopes of arranging an introduction before the voyage was over.

Major Heath of Baltimore was no doubt pleased with the arrangements aboard the *Pulaski*, for he had been assigned a berth in the section aft, beyond the large cabin, where he had considerably more privacy than he would have had up forward.

First Mate Hibbert of the *Pulaski*, long since accustomed to the routine of departure, remained in the wheelhouse with Captain Dubois as they cleared the harbor, then went below. He was due to take over the watch that night, and he figured to catch up on some sleep beforehand.

Captain Dubois held his vessel within sight of shore until Cape Romain was passed, then changed to a more easterly course and turned the command over to Mr. Pearson, his second captain. Dubois would be available if needed throughout the voyage, but the Captain's job was as much that of genial host to the passengers as it was master of the vessel.

Cape Romain disappeared astern, and throughout the day no other land was sighted. The wind soon came up from the east, throwing up fans of spray each time the vessel's bow plowed into a wave. Despite the turbulent sea the passengers assembled on the lower deck remained comfortable, for the *Pulaski* was equipped with interchangeable windows for use when the weather was rough. Just to be on the safe side, Second Captain Pearson kept well to sea as he passed Cape Fear and the dangerous Frying Pan Shoals.

By dusk the holiday mood had disappeared for the most. The wind had slackened somewhat, but was still strong enough to retard the *Pulaski's* progress and keep her in a constant state of pitching and wallowing. Many of the fifty-seven women and fourteen children aboard had to make frequent and hurried trips to the rail —and some of the men, too, for that matter. Expert preparation and handsome serving had not been able to make the evening meal palatable to most of the passengers.

At 10:30 that night First Mate Hibbert, an old steam hand, took over the watch and began pacing back and forth across the fore-castle. Captain Dubois was asleep in the wheelhouse, curled up on a mattress he kept there for that purpose. Most of the lights on the vessel were dimmed, and the passengers dozing.

Young Mr. Ridge was lounging in a deck chair, thinking no doubt of the young lady who had come aboard at Charleston, and apparently not in the least bothered by the rough weather.

Major Heath, en route to his berth, passed by the starboard boiler and noticed that the gauge showed almost thirty inches of steam pressure. He stopped to ask the second engineer about this and was informed that the boilers could safely bear forty inches. He then walked aft, holding to the railings as he went along, moved gingerly through the aft cabin so as not to disturb the passengers who were stretched out there on the settees, and reaching his own berth, began making preparations for bed.

Half an hour later First Mate Hibbert heard the second engineer turn the water cock on the starboard boiler, and from the shrill whistle which ensued, he was quite certain that the water in the boiler was too low. He was on the verge of warning the second engineer not to add fresh water until the temperature could go down, when the boiler suddenly blew up, knocking Hibbert to the main deck below.

On hearing the noise of the explosion, Major Heath jumped from his berth and ran for the aft cabin, only to be met there by a spray of deadly steam. He fell back and got underneath the steps where he was soon joined by Mr. Lovejoy, of Georgia, and there the two remained, safely shielded, until the steam subsided. Again Major Heath made his way gingerly through the aft cabin, but this time it was not for fear of disturbing the passengers who had been doz-ing on the settees, but to keep from stepping on those same pas-sengers, now dead, sprawled in grotesque positions about the floor where they had crouched in a futile attempt to escape the scalding steam which gushed through the cabin. There was not, the Major reported later, a single living person in the aft cabin.

Meanwhile, Mate Hibbert found himself lying between the mast and the side of the vessel, in a dazed condition. When his faculties returned to him, Hibbert made a quick appraisal of the damage. He discovered that the boat amidships was blown entirely to pieces;

that the head of the starboard boiler was gone and the top torn open, that the timbers and planks on the starboard side were forced asunder, and that the boat took in great quantities of water whenever she rolled in that direction. In short, the *Pulaski* was done for.

Mate Hibbert was aware immediately of the horrors of the situation and the danger of letting the passengers know that the ship was sinking before lowering the four lifeboats which she carried. He therefore proceeded to the side with haste, loosened the lines holding the starboard yawl, and lowered it into the water, climbing in himself and taking in two other men at the same time.

Perceiving the mate in the lifeboat, a group of excited passengers assembled at the rail above and demanded to know his object, to which he replied that he intended to pass around the stern of the steamer to determine the amount of damage. Before doing this, however, he ordered the other boats lowered, and Elias N. Barney, a crewman, with the assistance of several passengers, shortly had the larboard yawl in the water also; and others threw over one of the small boats on deck, but it soon filled with water and sank.

During this time other passengers and crewmen were being dragged from the water into the two yawls, until Barney announced that his boat was filled and proposed to Mate Hibbert that they strike out for shore. This the Mate declined to do, saying that he intended to stay by the wreck until daybreak and pick up as many people as he could.

Major Heath, meanwhile, had reached the main deck and found that all was dark and surprisingly quiet. He called for the Captain but received no answer, and perceiving that the vessel was sinking, he attempted to move forward to the mast. But before he could secure himself the sea burst over the bow and carried him overboard, fortunately dragging him against a loose line with which he was able to gain the deck again.

Just then the mast fell, crushing a Frenchman named Auze who was clinging to it. With a great splintering noise the vessel broke completely in two, and the forward section, almost submerged, began drifting away.

Young Mr. Ridge, immediately following the explosion of the boiler, had assisted Mate Hibbert in launching the yawl, and then observing the young lady who had previously attracted his attention, he attempted to help her into the boat. But in the confusion they were separated, and while he was searching for her the mast fell, the vessel parted, and he was thrown overboard.

In short order he succeeded in lashing together a couple of settees, some pieces of torn sail and a large cask, thus forming a raft capable of sustaining his weight. But no sooner had he accomplished this purpose than he discovered someone struggling in the water a short distance away, and without hesitation he plunged into the sea, swam twice his length through the darkness, and returned with the other survivor to his raft.

It was then that he realized the person he had saved was a woman, a young woman. Her name, she said, was Onslow. And on hearing the soft sound of her voice he realized that she was the same young woman he had noticed earlier and had attempted to assist into the yawl. Fate had arranged the introduction he sought.

Meanwhile, a majority of the other passengers, including the Reverend Dr. J. L. Woart, his wife, and child were now huddled on the promenade deck, fervently praying. And as they prayed the after part of the vessel, on which the promenade was located, slipped more and more to the larboard side, until, with a dreadful crash, it turned over completely, drowning most of the passengers assembled there. Less than thirty, including the Reverend Dr. Woart and family, were able to regain that small portion of the promenade which remained afloat.

Forty-five minutes had passed since the starboard boiler exploded, and already almost half of those aboard the *Pulaski* were dead: drowned, scalded to death, or crushed by falling masts and spars.

Of those remaining, nine people, including First Mate Hibbert, were in the starboard yawl; eleven others were in Elias Barney's larboard yawl; approximately twenty were on the small bow section with Major Heath; some twenty-five others were on a piece of the promenade deck with the Woarts; and young Mr. Ridge, Miss Onslow, and between thirty and forty of the remainder were clinging to furniture and scattered fragments of the wrecked vessel.

Again the occupants of the two boats urged First Mate Hibbert to direct their course to shore, a distance of some thirty miles, but as before he insisted on remaining in the vicinity until daylight.

Accordingly, when the first rays of dawn showed through the
eastern sky, the two small boats began the slow trek toward the
low-lying sand banks along the North Carolina coast, while behind
them they could still hear the wailings of the hopeless beings who
remained alive.

With daylight Hibbert took stock. His two yawls were equipped
with oars, there were ample able-bodied men to row, and despite a
strong wind from the south the small boats were shipping comparatively little water.

In his own craft were Boatswain Gideon West, a New Bedford-
man; a Negro steward named Brown, from Norfolk; Mr. Bird of
Bryan County, Georgia; an elderly man, Judge Rochester, from
Buffalo; a German named Zeuchtenberg; Charles B. Tappan, of
New York; W. C. N. Smith of New Bedford, and a Mr. Swift. Nine
men, all except Judge Rochester, fully able to take their turns at the
oars and share in other manual tasks.

The other boat was in worse condition, for its occupants were
mainly women and children. In addition to Barney there was another seaman, named Soloman; Mr. J. H. Cooper, of Glynn,
Georgia; Mrs. Nightengale, of Cumberland Island, and her seven-
month-old child; Mrs. Fraser, of St. Simeons, and her small child;
Senator R. W. Pooler, of Savannah, and his son R. W. Pooler, Jr.;
and two Negro women, Priscilla, a *Pulaski* stewardess, and Jenny,
a servant.

Mr. Cooper took the steering oar of the larboard boat, and the
Mate that of the starboard boat. With two men rowing in each
they headed for the distant coast, travelling in a northwest direction
to take full advantage of the wind and current. Throughout the
day there were frequent changes, the men alternating at the oars
of the two boats, which remained close together at all times.

In the late afternoon, after thirteen grueling hours of rowing,
they approached close enough to shore to get a fairly good idea of
the geographical arrangement of the coastline. They were opposite
a wide sandy beach, with no inlets immediately in evidence, and
Hibbert suggested that they should travel further along the coast
in search of an opening through which they could pass to the sound
waters beyond. Because of the approach of darkness, however, and
the constant exposure of those in the two boats, especially of the

women, the majority decided against this course, preferring not to remain a second night on the open sea.

The Mate finally agreed to attempt a landing, though he was not at all certain it could be effected successfully because of the huge breakers pounding down on the shore. Before he started, the two Negro women were transferred to his boat, and it was agreed with Mr. Cooper that upon landing Hibbert should walk along the beach until he saw a good spot for the other boat to come in and wait there with the remainder of the survivors from his boat to help the women and children ashore.

The two Negro women might just as well have remained in the Cooper boat, and certainly Judge Rochester, Mr. Bird, and Steward Brown would have done better to have sided with the Mate when he voted against attempting a landing; for no sooner had Hibbert steered his craft into the breakers than it capsized, and though six men reached shore, the five mentioned above were drowned.

Because of the disastrous results of his own landing attempt Mate Hibbert was more skeptical than ever over the chances of the second boat coming through the surf with its cargo of women and children, but after repeated signals from Cooper he finally located a spot where the surf seemed not so heavy, gathered the five other survivors about him, and gave the pre-arranged sign for Cooper to make the attempt.

Cooper had already supervised the lashing of the Nightengale infant to its mother. He now began sculling with the stern oar, at the same time motioning for Barney and the other crewman to put their weight on the oars. The boat rose without difficulty upon the crest of the first breaker, and for a brief moment those on shore thought she might come through safely. Then the second one, coming on with great violence, struck the oar from the hands of one of the rowers, the boat turned sideways in the trough of the sea, and the next breaker hit the craft with full force and flipped it upside down.

Upon regaining the surface Cooper took hold of the side of the boat, and drawing himself up as best he could, discovered that all of the others in the party, with the exception of Mrs. Nightengale, were making good headway for shore. He was still searching the near-by waters for some sign of Mrs. Nightengale and her child when he felt something drag against his leg. Diving down, he discovered it was the woman's clothing. He came to the surface just long enough for a gasp of fresh air, then dove again, grasped her hair, and pulled her clear of the water. The men on shore came out through the surf to meet him, and together they were able to reach the sandy beach, all of them completely exhausted.

Fortunately, all nine of those in the Cooper boat, including the two children, had come through alive; so that of the twenty persons who had left the scene of the disaster in the yawls, fifteen had now made their way to shore. However, with darkness it turned very cool, and the women and children, especially, were suffering from the effects of the exposure. It was decided that several of the men should go in search of some habitation, while the others sought out a protected spot behind one of the dunes. Here the ladies lay down, and the men covered them and their children with sand to protect them from further exposure.

It was not long before the searchers returned with information that they had landed near the east end of Stump Sound, in Onslow County, North Carolina, and that they had safely reached the house of a Mr. Siglee Redd, who had kindly consented to take them all in. And so, at 10:30 that night, just twenty-four hours after the starboard boiler of the *Pulaski* exploded, fifteen of the survivors were safely sheltered ashore and provided with food, drink, and dry clothing.

Major Heath was not so fortunate.

The forward section of the *Pulaski*, he discovered at dawn the morning following the explosion, was fast breaking up. The mast, which had killed the Frenchman when it fell, now lay along the forward section, its weight keeping the deck almost a foot under water.

Among the twenty-one persons who shared this submerged raft with Major Heath was Second Captain Pearson, who had been blown out into the sea by the force of the initial blast. He had caught hold of a plank and succeeded in reaching the forward section sometime during the night. He now proposed that they attempt to lash the timbers together so that they would not all be cast into the open sea, and this the survivors promptly did with the aid of ropes attached to the mast. By dropping the end of a piece of rope

overboard and letting it drift underneath the raft they were able
to secure it on the other side. Thus, in time, they managed to form
a sort of net over and around the raft, and before it was over they
had even salvaged a couple of large boxes floating by and lashed
these down as seats.

All that day, Friday, they drifted before the wind, twenty-two
of them sitting there in knee-deep water, without food or drink.
The heat of the sun was oppressive, its rays pouring down on their
bare heads and blistering their faces. Some did not even have shirts
for protection, and none had more than thin summer wear.

Their thirst now became intense, and Heath and Pearson had
difficulty keeping some of the others from drinking the salt water.
A Major Twiggs had saved his child, a boy of about twelve, and now
kept him in his arms at all times, for the boy was delirious. When
he would call on his mother, who was safe at home, and beg for
water, his father would seek in vain to comfort him by words of
kindness and by clasping him closer in his arms.

And so it went throughout that first day and the second night,
and not until dawn Saturday was there any perceptible change in
their circumstances. But as the morning light filled the sky they
could make out a dim, purplish line on the horizon which Second
Captain Pearson said was land.

At about the same time a floating object was spotted in the distance, and throughout the morning it drew closer until human
beings were easily discernible upon it. This, it developed, was a
small section of the wreck with the first engineer—a man called
Chicken—and three others upon it.

At first Major Heath and his companions on the forward section
were cheered by this discovery, thinking that there might be food
or water on the other raft, or at least room to transfer some of the
twenty-two from the overcrowded forward section. But when at
last it came alongside they realized that those clinging to it were in
worse straits than they themselves, and so four more people joined
the twenty-two aboard the submerged bow.

By this time they had approached within less than a mile of
shore, and many were anxious to make an attempt to land. But
Major Heath, observing the huge breakers which were visible even
from that distance, urged that they make every attempt to keep off

from shore until a better landing place could be found, or help should arrive from the sea. A Mr. Greenwood, of Georgia, came forward then with an offer to attempt to swim to shore for aid, saying that he was one of the best swimmers in his home community.

"No," replied Major Heath. "You'd certainly lose your life." And even as they argued, the decision was taken from them, for the wind shifted, and a slight shore breeze was now carrying them out to sea again.

This was almost beyond endurance for some, to have come so close to safety, only to have fate step in and deprive them of it. They had been almost forty-eight hours on the open sea without sustenance, and in despair one member of the party suggested that if relief did not come soon it would be necessary to cast lots.

Again it was Major Heath who raised vehement objections. "We are Christians," he said, "and we cannot imbue our hands in the blood of a fellow creature. We have still life left; let us not give up all manliness, and sink to the brute. I will risk my life now for the safety of any of you; but I will never stand by and see another's sacrificed, that we may eat his flesh."

And so, for the second time that day, the Major's firmness put an end to a proposal which could have proved only disastrous.

Another speck was sighted on the horizon that afternoon, probably the makeshift raft on which young Mr. Ridge and Miss Onslow were attempting to reach land, but it soon disappeared from view.

Rain came early Sunday morning, but with the rain came also a stiff breeze from the northeast, which soon increased to gale proportions. Every effort was made to catch some of the water in a piece of canvas which the survivors had taken from the mast and now held between them, but the sea ran so high that the little they did catch was nearly as salt as the water in the ocean. Still, each of the twenty-six persons aboard the raft was able to catch enough of the rain on his tongue to ease a burning throat.

When darkness settled Sunday evening Major Heath made a determined effort to sleep, but for the third successive night he was unable to do so except for a few moments at a time. The following morning, since the rain had stopped and the high winds had somewhat abated, he and his companions were once again subjected to the torture inflicted by the burning sun; and several among them began to exhibit the peculiar signs of madness attendant on starvation.

Four vessels were sighted during the day, and though a flag was attached to a pole and hoisted on high each time, none of the four came to their rescue, and the castaways watched with sinking hearts as each in turn passed from sight. One of these was the steam packet *New York*, which docked at Norfolk two days later and reported that the raft had been sighted from a distance but that there was no sign of life on board. The plain facts were that Captain Allen of the *New York*, intent on maintaining his schedule, had not bothered to alter his course for a closer examination of the wreckage.

It was Monday night. The survivors had spent four days and nights on the raft. Again Major Heath tried to sleep, but with his own pain and torment, the continued necessity of holding on at all times to keep from being washed overboard, and his constant efforts to succor and encourage the others, he passed another sleepless night.

The first light of morning always held promise, and was eagerly awaited by those on the raft. Tuesday morning revealed to them another section of wreckage in the distance, but hardly had their eyes focused on this than a ship was seen on the horizon. This, like the others sighted the day previous, was so far off that it was doubtful its occupants could see the tiny flag or the submerged raft with its cargo of dying human beings. But it continued on in their direction, and as it came closer the pole and flag were waved with increased vigor, and some, even, raised their voices in feeble shouts. Then suddenly she tacked and turned away again.

"She's gone," cried a crewman who was suffering from dreadful burns and scalding, and with this he lay down on one of the boxes, his last hope gone.

But Second Captain Pearson had not taken his eyes from the vessel, and now he too shouted, but his, unlike the scalded seaman's, was a shout of joy. "She sees us! She's coming toward us!" And so she was, with all sails set before the wind.

The vessel was the schooner *Henry Camerdon*, bound from

Philadelphia to Wilmington, North Carolina, Captain Davis commanding. She hove to near the raft and lowered her boat. Strong
and eager hands lifted the twenty-six survivors aboard. Those who
were able to walk, stumbled toward the water casks, the others
dragging behind them. But Captain Davis was firm in ordering
them away, and he instructed his crew to guard the casks as he sank
to his knees to give thanks that his prayers had been answered; for
Captain Davis had spotted wreckage the day before and had been
on a constant search for survivors ever since.

Captain Davis then doled out to each of the occupants of the
raft a half pint of water, sweetened with molasses, repeating the
dosage at short intervals; while for those in need of stimulants he
provided heated vinegar, for there was no strong drink aboard
Captain Davis' vessel.

Later, when the schooner's Captain was told of the other raft
which had been sighted that morning, he resumed the search, and
shortly afterwards the remains of the promenade deck came into
view, but there were only four persons clinging to it.

The four survivors told a harrowing story. Twenty-three of
them had been crowded together on the promenade deck the morning following the explosion, including the Reverend Dr. Woart
and family and Mr. G. B. Lamar, of Savannah, and his children, en
route to England for the coronation of Queen Victoria.

On the surface these people were more fortunate than those who
had drifted away on the bow, for though the remaining part of the
promenade was almost submerged and the survivors were without
food or water, still the remaining deck boat was lashed to the
wreckage, not visibly damaged. For two days the twenty-three
remained on the piece of wreckage, and then it was decided that
six of the most able-bodied should attempt to make shore in the
boat and summon help.

Mr. Lamar took charge of the boat, assisted by the second mate
of the *Pulaski*, and with four others they took their departure
Saturday. From that time on, the seventeen remaining on the
promenade suffered acutely. Sunday morning, when the rain and
heavy winds struck, the raft was tossed about so violently that the
survivors had difficulty holding on. Throughout this time of peril
the Reverend Dr. Woart and his wife held their child close to them

and prayed fervently, until a great wave washed them overboard and they sank from sight, still clasping their child between them.

Each day and night the number was lessened, and Monday morning only five remained aboard the wreckage: Mr. and Mrs. Noah Smith, of Augusta, Mr. Robert Hutchison, Miss Rebecca Lamar, and Master Charles Lamar. It was then that Major Heath's raft was sighted, at about the same time apparently that those with the Major saw the wreckage of the promenade deck. But there was a decided difference in the reaction aboard the two rafts, for whereas Second Captain Pearson and Major Heath recognized the promenade for what it was, Mr. Smith and Mr. Hutchison took the Major's raft to be a sail. They waited for a time, in hope that it would near them, but at length Mr. Smith announced that the only hope was to swim to it for aid. He quickly stripped off his tattered clothes, embraced his wife, and plunged into the water. For a brief time it looked as if he might make it, for he pushed onward with powerful strokes; but suddenly those on the wreckage saw him stop swimming, and in a moment's time he sank beneath the waves. It was supposed later, that he had gone close enough to see that the Major's raft was not a rescue craft, and with all incentive gone, had given up hope. Had he waited but an hour more he would have been saved with his wife and the other three.

As for the six men who took to the deck boat, they rowed and paddled and sculled and bailed and prayed throughout Saturday night, Sunday, Monday, Tuesday, and finally on Wednesday morning, they safely reached shore at New River Inlet, North Carolina, near where the two yawls had landed five days earlier.

Thus of the nearly two hundred persons aboard the *Pulaski* when her boiler exploded Thursday night, fifty-one had so far been saved: fifteen reached shore in the two yawls; thirty were picked up on the two rafts by the schooner; and six others landed safely in the tiny deck boat.

Still unaccounted for were thirty or forty people last seen clinging to wreckage at the scene of the explosion, including young Mr. Ridge, of New Orleans, and Miss Onslow.

That young lady had been rescued from the waters and found herself safely aboard the small raft which her rescuer had put together. She recovered sufficiently to realize that it was large enough for one, but too small for two. She thanked him for saving her life, showing great emotion as she did so. "But," she added, "you will have to let me go to save yourself."

According to a statement published shortly after the *Pulaski* disaster, Ridge would have none of it. "We live or die together," he said, and so Miss Onslow remained.

In a short time they discovered a larger piece of wreckage, on top of which they managed to haul their settees and cask and canvas, the young lady sharing equally in the task. When this was accomplished one of the yawls came near, and though it was already overcrowded, Ridge begged that the occupants take the young lady with them.

Again Miss Onslow expressed her feelings with certainty and conviction, saying that he had saved her life, and she could not leave him there alone. And so the two remained on their improvised raft, floating day after day before the wind. They almost reached land once but were borne seaward again by the same shifting wind which had saved Major Heath's raft from the breakers.

Among all of the survivors of the *Pulaski*—six others reached shore on fragments of the wreckage—these two young people were the last to be saved. But though they had gone without food or drink, they had, between them, an added incentive to live; for there on their raft on the stormy seas they pledged themselves, each to the other, in sickness and health, in life and in death.

A fairy-tale ending, that, to a disaster from which only fifty-nine of nearly two hundred persons survived. But that was not the ending, for though they lived and were saved, the pledge was not immediately fulfilled.

When they were fully recovered from the effects of their experience, and had once again returned to the safety of land, the gallant Ridge made a confession to his betrothed. He told her that he had lost everything in the disaster; that he was penniless. "In poverty to my very lips" was the way he phrased it. And he offered to release her from her verbal bond if she so chose.

The young lady is reported to have burst into tears, to have proclaimed that poverty could never drive them to a more desperate extremity than that which they had suffered together, and to have, once again, repeated her expression of complete love for him.

So, it ended in fairy-tale style after all; their engagement became official, and shortly afterwards they were married. And only then, it might be added, did Ridge learn that his bride was heiress to an estate valued at two hundred thousand dollars.

FROM THE TIME of the loss of the *Pulaski* in 1839 until the beginning of the Civil War in 1861 the North Carolina coast was the scene of so many shipwrecks that the majority rated no more space in the newspapers of the day than do routine automobile accidents in the contemporary press. A total of eighty-five vessels are listed as having been totally lost during this period, but there were many more—hundreds, probably—about which there is only such sketchy information that they cannot be listed here. The following accounts are of a few of the more interesting and unusual shipwrecks about which factual information is available for this period.

NORTH CAROLINA

It did not take long for the railroads to cut in on the new steamboat business; witness the Wilmington and Roanoke Railroad Company, which was maintaining its own steamboat schedules between Wilmington and Charleston by the summer of 1840.

Using two fast steamboats, the *North Carolina* and the *Governor Dudley*, the company was able to provide overnight passenger service between the two ports. And in July of that year, business was booming.

Late in the evening of July 24 the *Governor Dudley*, loaded with passengers and carrying a considerable quantity of government mail, left Charleston for the northward run. A short time afterwards the *North Carolina,* also carrying passengers and mail, pulled away from the company's wharf at Wilmington and headed down the Cape Fear River.

It was, to all outward appearances, an ideal night for an ocean voyage. The sky overhead, emblazoned with stars, cast a pleasant glow over the calm surface of the sea. A soft breeze occasionally stirred ripples in the water—just enough to keep down the July heat.

By midnight, when Captain Smith of the *Governor Dudley* turned the watch over to his first mate, most of the passengers were in their berths, asleep. The shoal water outside Charleston had long since been passed, but as was his custom Captain Smith lay down in the wheelhouse, fully clothed, instead of retiring to his cabin for the night. On board the *North Carolina,* at that moment some twenty-five miles to the northward of the *Dudley,* a similar change of watch had taken place, and there, too, most of the passengers had long since sought their berths.

At 1 A.M. the next morning the mate of the *North Carolina* sighted a moving light to the south, almost dead ahead, and about two miles away. It was the *Governor Dudley.*

The two vessels continued onward, moving at a steady rate of between twelve and fourteen miles per hour, each headed slightly to the right of the other, as was custom. On they came, throwing up starlit froth as their bows cut through the still water, each leaving behind a wake of churning white foam. They had passed at sea many times before, but never when conditions were more perfect or the night more beautiful.

Closer and closer they moved, two slim sidewheelers, the latest and trimmest marvels of man, carrying their human freight in excursion fashion between two of the South's leading ports. There was no blowing of whistles, for each was aware of the other's presence. A mile separated them, then a half mile, a quarter mile. Still they came on, a thousand feet, five hundred, passing close and to the right. Then, suddenly, the *Dudley* changed her course, swung over to the left; the mate, confused at the moment of passing, had thrown his wheel hard over, to pass to the left of the other vessel.

It was too late, then, for the mate of the *North Carolina* to avert disaster. He released steam, tried to halt his ship, but not in time; for the *Governor Dudley* drove on, straight at her sistership, and struck her amidships between the ladies' and gentlemen's cabins, a crunching, sickening, splintering blow that tore four feet from the *Dudley's* bow and cut the *Carolina* almost in two.

Quick work saved lives after that, for within ten minutes the *North Carolina* had settled to her decks and soon after disappeared. But in that ten minutes every person on board the *Carolina*, many of them without clothes or belongings of any description, were transferred to the *Dudley*. Tarpaulins and blankets were stretched across the hole in the *Dudley's* bow, and for the remainder of the night she remained near by, searching the silvery surface of the sea for mail and baggage. Two trunks, only, were picked up; thousands of dollars in cash—$15,000 belonging to just one passenger—was lost; but the important thing was that the crippled *Dudley*, double-loaded with the crew and passengers from her sistership, reached Wilmington safely the following day.

THE GREAT STORMS OF 1842

A bottle washed ashore at Shelby Bay, Bermuda, October 27, 1842, with the following note inside: "Schooner *Lexington*, off Cape Hatteras, July 15, 1842. This morning at half past two o'clock A.M., it commenced blowing a strong North Wester, which increased to such a degree that it was certain my vessel could not stand it. At 5 I tried the pumps and found that she made eleven inches. She being an old vessel, worked in her joints. At half past eleven, I determined to leave her with my crew (three men and myself) in our launch; but before leaving sounded the pumps, and found she had increased the water in her hold three feet. I write this and enclose it in a bottle, so that if we should not be saved and the bottle be found, it may be known what became of the vessel and us. At 1 P.M. got into the boat with provisions and water sufficient for six days, having beforehand offered up our prayers to God to protect and save us. Signed Wm. H. Morgan, Captain; John Rider, Mate."

Newspapers of the day made no more mention of the *Lexington* or her crew, but the storm which Captain Morgan referred to was one of the most destructive ever recorded on our coast. Its center seemed to strike Ocracoke and Portsmouth Islands, but great losses were reported all the way from the Virginia line to Cape Lookout.

Captain Etheridge of Chicamacomico said that he saw large numbers of dead horses and cattle drifting down the sound. Two unknown vessels were capsized and beaten to pieces in the breakers on Diamond Shoals, their entire crews lost, and seven men who went out later to try to salvage some of the wrecked goods were also drowned.

Fourteen vessels were reported ashore between New Inlet and Ocracoke, including a large English schooner, with the owner and one of his daughters on board, both of whom lost all of their personal belongings when the vessel was destroyed. Fourteen more ships were reported aground on the sound side of Ocracoke Island, and another six were swept out to sea from Ocracoke Inlet and presumed lost. A store owned by William Howard, at Ocracoke, "was blown down and floated away"; another store at the same place owned by Tilman Ferrar was also destroyed; while at Portsmouth, according to a man who left there the day after the storm, there was only one house left standing.

Unfortunately, at this writing, no authentic information has come to light which would give the names of the many vessels totally lost or the number of persons drowned; it is sufficient to say that the hurricane of July 12, 1842, was one of the worst in the history of coastal Carolina.

Hardly had the residents begun clearing up the debris from this hurricane, however, when another storm, hardly less severe, struck the same area. This one swept in from the sea August 24, and by the time it was over three vessels were known to have been lost, a number of others were reported aground, and at least eight mariners were dead.

The brig *Kilgore*, en route from Trinidad to Baltimore in ballast, went ashore on Currituck Beach, bilged and became a total wreck, but her captain and crew managed to reach shore safely. Meanwhile, the brig *Pioneer*, carrying a load of salt from Turks Island to Norfolk, stranded on Ocracoke Island with the loss of one crewman; and the ship *Congress*, also loaded with salt from Turks Island, was wrecked on Cape Hatteras and seven on board were lost. Thus, within one month, two storms had ravaged the coast, taking a terrific toll in shipping, lives, and property.

F. A. TUPPER

Captain Parkinson and the crew of the bark *Mary Ballard*, which sailed from Boston March 2, 1843, bound to New Orleans with a cargo of ice, did not reach their destination and almost failed to make it back home again!

On March 12 the *Ballard* was cast away on Berry Island in the Bahamas. Fortunately the Captain and crew were picked up by wreckers, who took them to Nassau. There they met up with the crew of the ship *Algonquin*, of Philadelphia, which had also been wrecked on one of the near-by islands, and together the two crews of shipwreck survivors took passage on the schooner *F. A. Tupper*, which was bound from Nassau to Baltimore. They had a pleasant enough trip of it until they reached the vicinity of Cape Hatteras; but then, on March 27, they ran into a severe gale, and that night struck the beach southeast of Chicamacomico.

The three crews—from the *Mary Ballard*, the *Algonquin*, and the *F. A. Tupper*, numbering thirty-one men in all—spent the night in the *Tupper's* rigging, expecting every moment to be cast into the seething surf beneath them. At 4 A.M. the next morning the vessel finally broke in two, and at five o'clock she completely disintegrated in the breakers, casting the men into the sea. But by then most of them were old hands at that sort of thing, and though the vessel proved a total loss, all thirty-one of the men managed to gain the safety of the beach. There is no record of how they proceeded on the remainder of the return trip to Boston, but it is an even bet they travelled by railroad.

EMILIE

The French bark *Emilie*, of Bordeaux, having crossed the greater part of the Atlantic without mishap, was nearing land. Her destination was Norfolk, Virginia, where she was slated to pick up a cargo, but thick and foggy weather had prevented Captain Sauvestre from taking observations for twenty-four hours, and at sunset, December

3, 1845, he was not at all certain how close he was to land. By dead reckoning he figured, however, that he was sufficiently far north to make Cape Henry, and a sharp watch was kept for the light there throughout the early evening.

At 8 P.M. that night, not having seen the light, the Captain became apprehensive and decided to wear ship and stand off from shore until daybreak. He should have thought of that earlier, for even as he gave the necessary commands the vessel struck, and so violent was the impact that her rudder, sternpost, and part of her stern frame were torn off, and she immediately sank in two and a half fathoms of water. Captain Sauvestre did not know it, but his vessel had stranded at a point near the boundary line between the states of Virginia and North Carolina, less than 150 yards from shore.

Efforts were quickly made to get the vessel's launch overboard, but she was stove in before striking the water and soon sank alongside. All hands—ten in number—then took refuge in the rigging, where they remained throughout the night, while the vessel beneath them was constantly swept by tremendous breakers.

Dawn the next morning brought no respite and no prospect of rescue, for the coast was shrouded in a dense covering of waveborne spray so thick that they could not see shore.

Their clothes soaked, and the masts beneath them swaying wildly in the wind and threatening to fall each time a wave rolled over the deck, the ten men held on until mid-afternoon. Then one crewman climbed down, jumped into the tumultuous surf, and attempted to swim to shore for help. He was drowned soon after striking out from the ship.

The weather by then had cleared sufficiently for the coastline to be visible, and all hands pitched in to make a raft from the sails and spars left dangling. This was finally completed and launched, the nine remaining men taking positions on the unwieldly craft. Even as the last man got on board, however, the line holding the raft to the wrecked bark parted, the raft was swept into the breakers, and six of the nine men were washed overboard. The three yet remaining—the Captain, mate and one crewman—succeeded in holding their positions on the raft while it was driven through the breakers and washed up on the beach.

The three French survivors were soon discovered by residents of the area; all were in desperate shape, especially the mate, who was not expected to live. As for the six other men who had been washed off the raft, all of them were later recovered from the surf, their lungs filled with water, dead. Seven of ten lives lost, and another ship consigned to the sands of the Carolina coast.

ORLINE ST. JOHN

The loss of the New England bark *Orline St. John* off Cape Hatteras, February 21, 1854, provides the only case which has come to the attention of this writer where cannibalism was actually resorted to by shipwreck survivors on the Carolina coast.

The *Orline St. John*, built in 1848, was owned by William Bradstreet of Gardiner, Massachusetts. Under command of a Captain Redbird the 250-ton bark left Norfolk in mid-February, 1854, bound for Barbados, B.W.I., but was dismasted in a severe gale off Hatteras on February 21. That night a heavy sea swept the wallowing vessel, almost completely filling the cabin and drowning a colored seaman named Martin.

Mrs. Hannah Redbird, recent bride of the Captain, was caught in the cabin at the same time but was extricated by the Captain and crewmen through a small window. She was carried out on deck and hauled up into that part of the rigging still standing, where she was securely lashed to a spar. The Captain and crew had meanwhile sought positions of safety near by, for the entire deck of the vessel was regularly swept by storm-driven seas.

The next afternoon, February 22, Mrs. Redbird died in her husband's arms, and her body was subsequently lowered into the sea. That same night the second mate, who had been drinking salt water, became delirious and, against the advice of the Captain, tried to enter the cabin in search of fresh water. He was never seen again.

The following day another colored seaman, a man named Douglass, died in the rigging from exposure and want. His body was left hanging there.

For a full week the survivors, including the Captain, first mate and several seamen, remained in the rigging of the derelict, without access to food or water, and suffered constantly from cold and exposure. As a last resort, according to a report published in Boston the following month, "they were compelled from necessity to feed on the body of the colored sailor named Douglass."

During this period several vessels came within sight of the wreck and attempted to reach it, but they were driven off by the extreme state of sea and weather. On the first of March, ten days after the vessel was wrecked, the bark *Saxonville*, bound from Calcutta to Boston, appeared near by, and through the diligence and persistence of her master and crew, remained there until a rescue could be effected.

On arriving in Boston it was found necessary to amputate both feet of one of the survivors, a sailor named Thomas Grant, described as "being in horrible condition from frostbite and continually in salt water." All of the other survivors, as well, were in bad condition from these same causes, but none seemed to have suffered ill effects from eating human flesh taken from the dead body of their shipmate, Douglass.

HE CIVIL WAR came early
to the North Carolina coast and departed late. The capture of
Forts Hatteras and Clark at Hatteras Inlet, August 29, 1861, was
the first successful naval operation for the Federal forces; the
capture of Fort Fisher, at the mouth of the Cape Fear River below
Wilmington, January 15, 1865, was the last. During the intervening
three and a half years there was no normal ship traffic in the area,
for the merchant carriers were supplying either North or South,
and thus were as much a part of the fight as were the warships
which engaged in numerous skirmishes on the coast, as well as in
the sounds and rivers.

The resultant ship losses fell into two broad categories. First were
those vessels lost in actual naval combat, or as a direct result of
such combat. Second were the merchant vessels lost while attempting to run the Federal blockade of Wilmington. In this volume the
two types will be treated separately.

CIVIL WAR NAVAL LOSSES

The capture of Hatteras Inlet in late August, 1861, was accomplished with a minimum of effort and no ship losses or serious
damage to the Federal Navy. Even while that battle was in progress,
however, a second Federal fleet was being outfitted at Hampton
Roads, this one for an attack on Port Royal, South Carolina. Approximately twenty-five schooners, loaded with coal for the steamers of the fleet, left Hampton Roads on October 29 for Port Royal,

followed the next day by more than fifty other craft; in all, the largest flotilla ever assembled under an American commander up to that time.

Some of them never got to Port Royal, for a terrific gale was encountered off Cape Hatteras, the vessels of the fleet were promptly scattered, and by the time it was over at least two of them had foundered. One was the transport *Peerless*, loaded with stores, whose crew was rescued by the *Mohican*. The other was the old steamer *Governor*, carrying a landing force of six hundred marines in addition to some fifty naval officers and crewmen. At the height of the storm her smokestack was washed away, her engines failed, and she wallowed helplessly in the rough sea, sinking. The steamer *Isaac Smith* attempted to come to her assistance, but shipped so much water that her commander was forced to order the *Smith's* guns thrown overboard to keep his vessel afloat; and it was left to the sail frigate *Sabine* to effect the rescue of the 650 persons aboard the *Governor*, a feat which was accomplished finally with the loss of only seven men.

Ironically, none of the remaining vessels was sunk in the successful campaign against Port Royal; demonstrating once again that the sea itself—especially the shoal-infested sea off Cape Hatteras—is the naval man's most formidable foe.

At the conclusion of the Port Royal campaign a third and even larger fleet was assembled in Hampton Roads. The destination this time was Roanoke Island and the other fortifications held by the Confederates in the North Carolina sounds.

This fleet sent out to capture eastern North Carolina was a motley collection of ferry boats, side-wheel steamers, and river craft, hurriedly got together for the purpose. Some, armed with a gun or two, were designated as gunboats; the others were used for transporting troops, horses, and supplies. It was, however, far superior to anything possessed at that time by the Southern defenders.

This improvised Federal battle flotilla reached Hatteras Inlet January 12, 1862, found the coast buffeted by strong winds and a rough sea, and was forced to anchor offshore until the tempest died down sufficiently to effect a crossing of Hatteras bar. While anchored, a number of the vessels grounded and at least one, the steamer *City of New York*, was lost.

It took almost a month for the fleet to cross into the sounds and prepare for the actual attack on Roanoke Island; but once Admiral Goldsborough's forces got there they made quick work of it: engaging the small Confederate force in Croatan Sound on February 7; sinking the flagship, *Curlew;* and forcing the others—which had expended most of their ammunition—to retreat up the Pasquotank River that night.

The *Curlew,* which sustained a direct hit and sank near Fort Forrest (Manns Harbor) was an iron-hulled, side-wheel, river steamboat. The *Seabird,* which took her place as command ship of the Confederate fleet, was a wooden vessel, also a side-wheeler. The other six were converted canal tugs, averaging about ninety-five feet in length.

This pitiable little force, manned for the most by foreign-born, non-English-speaking seamen, formed a second defensive line below Elizabeth City on the Pasquotank, augmented by a large armed schooner, the *Black Warrior.*

On February 10, a portion of the Federal fleet, consisting of fourteen vessels mounting thirty-three guns—as against six smaller Confederate vessels with a total of eight guns—steamed up the Pasquotank to attack, and it took them exactly thirty-nine minutes to capture Elizabeth City and the small fort near by at Cobbs Point, and sink most of the defending craft.

The *Seabird* was rammed and cut completely in two by the Federal gunboat *Commodore Perry* before the former hardly had a chance to sight her two guns; the *Fanny,* a former tugboat captured from the Federals at Chicamacomico in December, was run ashore and blown up by her commander; the schooner *Black Warrior* kept up a sharp fire until she was set afire and abandoned; the *Appomattox* attempted to flee through the canal, only to find that the vessel was "about two inches too wide to enter," and so it too was set on fire and blown up; the *Forrest,* damaged at Roanoke Island, was destroyed on the ways; and the *Ellis* was captured. Only the *Beaufort* escaped, making her way through the canal to Norfolk, at that time still in Confederate hands.

Thus in short order the Federal forces eliminated the Confederate fleet guarding the North Carolina sounds, and thereafter it was a fairly simple mopping-up operation to take Edenton, Winton,

South Mills, Nags Head, Oregon Inlet, and Plymouth. The next month New Bern was attacked and captured, then Havelock Station, Morehead City, and Beaufort fell into Federal hands, and on April 26 the heavily fortified works at Fort Macon, guarding Beaufort Inlet, were captured. No further ship losses were reported, however, until September 6, when the Federal gunboat *Pickett* was sunk while attacking Washington, North Carolina.

In November the small gunboat *Ellis*, captured at Elizabeth City, was dispatched on a daring reconnaissance mission up New River, going as far as Jacksonville; but on the return she ran aground near the mouth of the river, was attacked by Confederate forces, and on November 25 she was finally destroyed by the Federal sailors manning her.

By the end of 1862 the day of the improvised gunboat was on the wane, for both sides were now actively engaged in turning out specially designed ships of war. The first of these put into service by the Confederates was the former schooner *Merrimac*, transformed into an iron-clad ram and renamed *Virginia*. The first for the Federals was a new type of gunboat equipped with a revolving turret and named *Monitor*. These basic designs were followed throughout the remainder of the war, the Federals completing more than thirty of the monitors, and the Confederates commissioning several iron-clad rams.

The first of each—the *Virginia*, most frequently referred to in history by its previous name, the *Merrimac*, and the original *Monitor*—engaged in their now famous battle at Hampton Roads, March 9, 1862, and though the result was indecisive, later engagements between other monitors and rams gave a decided edge to the little Federal craft. But the original *Monitor* did not last long enough to take part in these subsequent tests.

On her only previous sea voyage, from New York to Hampton Roads three days before the *Merrimac* fight, the *Monitor* had almost foundered. A radically different type of craft from any previously constructed, 172 feet long and 41 feet wide at the water line, she was built so low that only her revolving turret and small pilot house were visible above the surface in even a moderate sea, thus earning for her the nickname of "cheesebox on a raft."

One deficiency in the original *Monitor*, corrected in later vessels of the same design, was that she shipped large quantities of water at the point where the turret joined her hull, whenever rough seas were encountered; and on December 30, 1862, while off Cape Hatteras, the seas she encountered were rough to an extreme.

After she had successfully defended the wooden vessels of the Federal fleet against attack by the *Merrimac* in Hampton Roads and participated later in a limited campaign on the James River, the *Monitor* was no longer needed in Virginia waters, and so the ship had been ordered to proceed to South Carolina for action against the remaining Confederate strongholds there.

She departed from Fort Monroe, Virginia, the morning of December 29, 1862, with a total of sixty-five officers and men on board and was accompanied by the powerful side-wheel steamer *Rhode Island*. The weather was heavy at the time, with dark, stormy-looking clouds and a westerly wind. To hasten the *Monitor's* speed the *Rhode Island* took her in tow with two long twelve-inch hawsers, and throughout that afternoon and night the vessels proceeded southward toward Cape Hatteras.

At noon the next day, December 30, the wind shifted to the southwest and increased to gale force, and shortly before dark that evening the two vessels attempted to round Cape Hatteras. "The sea pitched together in the peculiar manner only seen at Hatteras ... and rolled over us as if our vessel were a rock in the ocean only a few inches above the water," said Helmsman Francis B. Butts, who was on duty at the time. "The wheel had been temporarily rigged on top of the turret.... The vessel was riding one huge wave, plunging through the next as if shooting straight for the bottom of the ocean, splashing down upon another with such force that her hull would tremble, while a fourth would leap upon us and break far above the turret, so that if we had not been protected by a rifle-armor that was securely fastened and rose to the height of a man's chest, we should have been washed away."

Because the *Monitor* had no mast on which to hoist the regular naval code signals, a method of communication had been established in which a message was written with chalk on a blackboard and held up to view. But with the approach of darkness this system was of necessity abandoned, the last chalk message from Commander

J. P. Bankhead informing the *Rhode Island* that a red light would be burned as a signal if the crew of the *Monitor* was forced to abandon ship.

On board the *Monitor*, meanwhile, the water had gained steadily, the coal was so wet that the engineer found it impossible to keep up full steam, and he was ordered to slow down the engines and use all power that could be spared on the pumps. The water still gained, the forward momentum of the *Monitor* was practically stopped, and for fear of striking the *Rhode Island* Commander Bankhead ordered the tow lines cut. James Fenwick, a gunner, volunteered to go forward for this purpose, but was washed overboard and drowned almost as soon as he had gained the deck; Boatswain's Mate John Stocking, though succeeding in reaching the bow and cutting the line, was also swept away by the seas before he could return to the comparative safety of the turret. Anchors were then let go, striking bottom in about sixty fathoms, and for a while the *Monitor* rode more easily. But then the small pumps drowned out, the main pump came to a virtual standstill for lack of power, and it became necessary for all hands to start bailing, an operation described by one crewman as being akin to "bailing out the ocean."

Water was pouring into the *Monitor* from two main leaks. The first was at the juncture of the turret and hull; the second was through the anchor well, where the packing had been torn away by the cable as the anchor was let go. By this time, also, the two lines cut loose from the *Monitor* had become entangled in the *Rhode Island's* wheel. From the deck of that vessel the lights of the *Monitor* were clearly visible; white lights, shining up from the openings in the turret. Then, suddenly, a red light was seen; the *Monitor* was being abandoned.

Two boats were lowered away from the disabled *Rhode Island*. Brave men, volunteers, manned the oars and headed for the smaller iron-clad vessel, half submerged beneath the towering seas. By the time these boats reached the *Monitor* most of her officers and crewmen were crowded in the turret or on deck. The two boats pulled up alongside, were held there as the *Monitor's* crewmen jumped on board; then, fully loaded, they headed back for the *Rhode Island*, leaving a handful of men still trapped inside the sinking cheesebox.

The task of getting on board the *Rhode Island* proved harder than had been that of getting off the *Monitor*. Crewman Butts described the perils in graphic style:

"We were carried by the sea from stem to stern," he said, "for to have made fast would have been fatal. The boat was bounding against the ship's side; sometimes it was below the wheel, and then, on the summit of a huge wave, far above the decks. Lines were thrown to us from the deck of the *Rhode Island*, which were of no assistance, for not one of us could climb a small rope; and besides, the men who threw them would immediately let go their holds, in their excitement, to throw another—which I found to be the case when I kept hauling in rope instead of climbing.

"Two vessels lying side by side, when there is any motion to the sea, move alternately; or, in other words, one is constantly passing the other up or down. At one time, when our boat was near the bows of the steamer, we would rise upon the sea until we could touch her rail; then in an instant, by a very rapid descent, we could touch her keel. While we were thus rising and falling upon the sea, I caught a rope, and rising with the boat, managed to reach within a foot or two of the rail, when a man, if there had been one, could easily have hauled me on board. But they had all followed after the boat which at that instant was washed astern, and I hung dangling in the air over the bow of the *Rhode Island*, with Ensign Norman Atwater hanging to the cat-head, three or four feet from me, like myself, with both hands clinching a rope and shouting for someone to save him.

"Our hands grew painful and all the time weaker, until I saw his strength give way. He slipped a foot, caught again, and with his last prayer, 'O God!' I saw him fall and sink, to rise no more. The ship rolled, and rose upon the sea, sometimes with her keel out of water, so that I was hanging thirty feet above the sea, and with the fate in view that had befallen our much-beloved companion, which no one had witnessed but myself. I still clung to the rope with aching hands, calling in vain for help. But I could not be heard, for the wind shrieked far above my voice.

"My heart here, for the only time in my life, gave up hope, and home and friends were most tenderly thought of. While I was in this state, within a few seconds of giving up, the sea rolled forward,

bringing with it the boat, and when I would have fallen into the
sea, it was there.

"I can only recollect hearing an old sailor say, as I fell into the
bottom of the boat: 'Where in _____ did he come from?' "

Butts now found himself right back where he had started, but
fortunately, while he was hanging from the rope dangling over the
side of the *Rhode Island*, preparations had been made for lowering
heavier ropes, and by this means the survivors were hauled to the
deck. One boat crew refused to be drawn aboard, however, for
they remembered the men still trapped on the *Monitor*. Casting off
again they set off for the sinking craft, by then more than two miles
distant from the side-wheel steamer. From the deck of the *Rhode
Island* the boat's progress was observed for a while; then it disappeared in the gloom, just as the lights of the *Monitor* were seen for
the last time.

The two vessels were then about ten miles offshore directly opposite Cape Hatteras. When finally the tow lines were untangled
from the wheel of the *Rhode Island* and that vessel got underway,
no trace of the *Monitor*, or of the lifeboat, could be found, and
after searching the area for some time the following morning, the
Rhode Island returned to Fort Monroe with forty-nine survivors
of the *Monitor*.

The lifeboat from the *Rhode Island* was picked up at sea by a
passing vessel and returned to Philadelphia. Local rumor has it that
several bodies, supposedly some of the four officers and twelve men
lost from the *Monitor*, drifted ashore near the Cape later. There
have been recent claims that the remains of the *Monitor* have
been discovered, and a plan has even been advanced to salvage
the craft and move her bodily ashore as a museum piece. That may
be, but even if she is never again in a position where men can tread
her decks, people the world over will long remember the gallant
little vessel which helped so dramatically to revolutionize the con-
cepts of naval warfare, only to meet an ignominious end in the Atlantic Graveyard.

During the period following the original attacks on the North
Carolina coastal fortifications other ships foundered, stranded, and
were sunk. The 329-ton Federal steamer *R. B. Forbes* went down

at about the time of the battle of Roanoke Island; the *Frying Pan Shoals Lightship*, removed from its station by the Confederates and anchored in the Cape Fear River just above Fort Caswell as a sort of floating fortress, was burned by a raiding party; and the brig-of-war *Bainbridge*, which normally carried a crew of about forty, foundered off Hatteras, August 21, 1863, with all hands but one being lost.

In early February, 1864, the Federal steamer *Underwriter* was sunk at New Bern, and in April of that year the Confederate ram *Albemarle* came down the Roanoke River, attacked the small Federal garrison at Plymouth, captured the town, and sank the gunboat *Southfield*. The presence of the powerful *Albemarle*, patterned after the *Merrimac* but much improved over that first ram, made the North Carolina sounds untenable for the Federals, and they were therefore faced with the alternatives of retreating from the area or of destroying the ram. The latter course was decided on, and a small fleet of powerful naval vessels was sent out for the purpose, encountering the *Albemarle* in the sound for which she was named and coming off second best. Then a daring young officer, Lieutenant W. B. Cushing, volunteered to attempt to sink the *Albemarle* with a torpedo-like bomb while she was at anchor at her new home base in Plymouth, and despite general skepticism as to the feasibility of the plan, Cushing succeeded in destroying the vessel.

Fort Fisher, Wilmington, and the Cape Fear River still were in possession of the Confederates, and many millions of dollars worth of badly needed supplies had passed through this single open avenue into Southern hands since the other coastal ports had been closed. Accordingly, in December, 1864, approximately sixty warships and numerous transports and auxiliary craft, then the largest naval force ever assembled in American waters, was got together at Hampton Roads, an army of eight thousand men boarded the troop carriers, and the mighty flotilla headed south for Cape Fear. Like the earlier fleets attacking Port Royal and Roanoke Island, this one encountered stormy weather on the North Carolina coast; but the vessels anchored off Beaufort, successfully rode out the gale, and on Christmas Eve the naval bombardment of Fort Fisher began.

Fort Fisher, located between Carolina Beach and Cape Fear, was an exceptionally strong fortification with a normal defending garrison of something under two thousand, but in anticipation of the Federal attack, a large body of additional troops was made available.

General B. F. Butler, in command of the attacking Federal troops, had already figured out a scheme whereby he thought the fort, its defenders, and the handful of Confederate ships aiding in the defense could all be levelled at the same time without incurring any loss of life on the part of the attacking forces. In carrying out this plan the old Federal gunboat *Louisiana* was filled with three hundred tons of gunpowder, a special fuse and firing mechanism was rigged out, and the *Louisiana* was towed to Cape Fear, though the other vessels of the fleet were careful to remain a safe distance away while this floating bomb was in transit.

Finally, late on December 23, the *Louisiana* was towed in close to shore opposite the fort, the time fuse was ignited, and the brave men attending to this hazardous enterprise were removed from the scene at top speed in the same vessel which had towed the *Louisiana* to her place of attack.

General Butler, apprehensive of the disastrous effects of the impending explosion, had anchored his fleet off Beaufort, better than fifty miles away. The sixty vessels of the naval force had proceeded seaward, where most had let their fires die down and let off steam so that the concussion would not cause further explosions. The poor Confederate defenders, meanwhile, had heard rumors that a powder boat was being sent to the attack, but having no inkling of the magnitude of General Butler's undertaking they continued about the normal work of preparation for the more conventional attack which they expected momentarily.

The *Louisiana* blew up at 1:30 A.M. December 24, 1864. The resultant explosion was heard as far away as Wilmington, but even in Fort Fisher it was more like the sound of a large cork being expelled from a bottle of champagne than anything else, and the Confederates continued their work without delay. The Navy men on the warships heard it too and came in soon after to see what damage had been done; but General Butler, the originator of the awesome plan, was not aware that the ship had exploded until a dispatch vessel reached him later that morning with the news that the operation had gone off as planned, except that about the only thing destroyed was the *Louisiana!*

The naval vessels took up the work then, bombarding the fort throughout most of the day, and on Christmas three thousand of General Butler's troops landed on the beach near by. But on close examination the defenses were deemed too solid for a ground attack and Butler's army withdrew. Two weeks later, however, an even larger fleet and a ground force under a new commander made a second attack on Fort Fisher, this one culminating in success for the Federals. No further losses were sustained by the attacking vessels, but the Confederate gunboat *Tallahassee* was blown up by the defenders; the gunboat *Raleigh*, abandoned up the river, was destroyed; and the gunboat *North Carolina*, her bottom eaten out by worms, was found sunk.

Thus, on January 15, 1865, the last remnants of the Confederate Navy in North Carolina waters were lost, the strongest of the coastal fortifications was captured, and the last open port was finally closed. So far as the North Carolina coast was concerned, the Civil War was ended.

THE BLOCKADE RUNNERS

By 1863 most of the Atlantic coast seaports as far south as Florida were in Federal hands or effectively neutralized by Federal forces. The lone exception was Wilmington, North Carolina, which remained until January, 1865, the main port of entry for foreign goods consigned to the Confederate States of America.

Wilmington, before the war, was a small though prosperous town, noted primarily for its exports of tar, pitch, turpentine, and lumber. Suddenly, through the peculiar exigencies of war, it became the sole port from which badly needed southern cotton could be shipped abroad.

Economists have long attributed the relatively poor condition of our southern states to the centralization in agriculture by which cotton became king. Yet, ironically, this very concentration on cotton production was a prime factor in enabling the Confederacy to hold out as long as it did; for the world needed cotton, and the only place from which it could be secured in quantity was the South.

Thus cotton became, in effect, the medium of exchange between the money-poor Confederates and the rest of the world; and the northern states, as well as the countries of Europe, paid dearly for it.

Cotton, at Wilmington, was worth something like eight cents a pound; in Europe it sold for nearer eighty cents, and in the northern states for as much as a dollar. Thus a thousand dollars worth of merchandise, traded for cotton in Wilmington, brought ten thousand dollars or more when delivered abroad.

At the outset the same vessels which had been engaged in the delivery of lumber and other peacetime exports, were employed in shipping cotton from Wilmington and returning with the military stores and merchandise needed in the South. These were sailing vessels, schooners for the most, and the Federal government quickly put a crimp in their activities by dispatching a small fleet of coal-burning steamers to blockade the port. The sailing ships were no match for the steamers and so withdrew from this lucrative traffic, but they were replaced shortly by small, fast steamers, able to run past the blockading vessels under cover of darkness.

On the River Clyde, in Scotland, there began then a veritable shipbuilding boom; for Clyde-built steamers were recognized as among the fastest in the world, and many of them, being of small size and shallow draft, were admirably suited for the job of navigating the shoal-infested waters in the vicinity of Cape Fear.

In short order most of the available Clyde-built steamers were purchased by firms, individuals, or governments anxious to cash in on the cotton bonanza. Premium prices were paid for the older vessels, usually amounting to more than their original cost, and construction of additional craft was speeded up. So great was the exodus of steamers from the Clyde to blockade-running activities that the *Times*, of London, said in 1863: "Should the demand continue at this rate, there will soon be scarcely a swift steamer left on the Clyde."

The introduction of the Clyde steamers brought an intensification of the Federal blockade. At one time there were three separate lines of blockading vessels past which the steamers had to go; one some forty miles at sea, a second approximately ten miles out, and a third close to shore.

The blockade runners soon evolved a system whereby they approached close to land as much as forty or fifty miles away from Cape Fear, waited for night, and then ran at full speed for Wilmington, hugging the shoreline in the process. A great number of these steamers stranded, and when unsuccessful in getting clear of the sand bars, were discovered at dawn the following morning by the Federal blockading vessels. In most cases a dramatic contest then ensued between the blockading vessels on the one hand and the Confederate shore-based troops on the other for possession of the valuable cargo. The most frequent result, however, was that neither one salvaged any appreciable amount before the stranded vessel was set afire by the blockaders' guns or by demolition squads sent out by the Confederates.

Thus, today, the coastal waters extending from Topsail Island to Shallotte are littered with the remains of these iron-hulled steamers, and though most are buried in the sands, a few are still visible above the water—rusted reminders of the days when King Cotton reigned.

The newspapers of that day, and books, magazine articles, and pamphlets since published, contain numerous accounts of these strandings, but only the highlights can be mentioned here.

One of the first steamers lost in attempting to run the blockade was the *Modern Greece*, a large English vessel registered at about one thousand tons, which was chased ashore by the blockaders in the early morning of June 27, 1862. The crew of the *Modern Greece* escaped, and later the troops from near-by Fort Fisher succeeded in removing a large part of her valuable cargo, including several badly needed Whiteworth guns, considerable clothing, and enough liquor to keep most of the Fort Fisher garrison in high spirits for more than a week.

It was more than a year later, however, before the blockade was sufficiently strengthened to take an appreciable toll of the vessels bound in and out of Wilmington; and in the interim, that town was subjected to a severe plague of yellow fever, in which more than four hundred lives were lost.

In the last six months of 1863 at least ten blockade runners were destroyed on the coast, one of the finest of which was the *Hebe*, described by observers as "a beautiful little steamer," her hull and smoke funnels camouflaged with a coating of grayish green paint, and carrying at the time of her loss a cargo of drugs, coffee, clothing, and foodstuff.

In attempting to enter the Cape Fear River through New Inlet (located at the northern end of Smiths Island but now closed), the *Hebe* was intercepted by a Federal vessel and was run ashore the morning of August 18 to prevent her capture. Even as the passengers and crew put off for the beach in the *Hebe's* boats a boarding party from the blockading vessel approached the stranded steamer. Meanwhile a Confederate battery set up in the sand dunes opposite the wreck opened fire, and before the would-be boarding party reached the *Hebe* their boats were sunk, the Federals were forced to swim through the breakers in order to save their lives, and were captured the moment they reached shore. Finally, the following day, the blockaders bombarded the *Hebe* and set her on fire, destroying both vessel and cargo.

The *Atlantic*, a converted Gulf coast steamer renamed *Elizabeth*, was stranded and burned at Lockwoods Folly September 24, 1863, supposedly through the activities of a Federal spy who was later found to have been on board. And the *Douro*, which left Wilmington the night of October 11, 1863, and was lost between Fort Fisher and Masonboro Inlet, had once before been captured by Federal vessels, sold as a prize in Canada, purchased by the Confederate Government, and put right back in the blockade running business again.

Only one case is recorded of the Federals losing a ship in their blockading activities, and that came about during an attempt to float a stranded blockade runner. The vessel lost was the gunboat *Iron Age*, one of five craft attempting to haul off the steamer *Bendigo* which had stranded at Lockwoods Folly Inlet, January 4, 1864. The *Iron Age* likewise stranded on January 11, was set afire, and destroyed; and though this was the Federals' only such loss, few of the other attempts at salvage netted more than what the boarding sailors could carry off on their persons.

The blockade runners, for the most, operated from Nassau and Bermuda to Wilmington, and those which were successful averaged at least one round trip a month. They were required by Confederate law to provide at least one-third of their cargo space for government stores, but the law was not strictly enforced, and at the same time that Southern troops were deserting by the thousands because of hunger and lack of clothing and munitions, many steamship agents—and even some army officers in Wilmington—were accumulating fortunes through the sale of delicate perfumes, silks, tea, and other non-essentials brought in by the blockade runners in which they owned part interest.

There must, therefore, have been considerable mourning among the speculators in Wilmington in early February, 1864, for during the first nine days of that month a total of six blockade runners were lost. One was the little Clyde steamer *Spunkie*, which had made a number of successful runs before grounding a short distance west of Fort Caswell, February 9. The others were the *Wild Dayrell*, which accidentally ran ashore near Stump Inlet on February 1; the *Nutfield*, which stranded and was burned at New River Inlet, February 4; the *Dee*, grounded off New Inlet, February 6; and the *Fanny and Jenny* and the *Emily of London*, both of which were lost north of Wrightsville Beach on February 9.

The last blockade runner lost was the *Ella*, which was wrecked off Baldhead, or Smiths Island, in December, 1864, shortly before the Federal forces attacked Fort Fisher. The *Ella* was owned by the Bee Company of Charleston, and her cargo belonged to "private parties and speculators." Chased ashore by blockading vessels, she was abandoned by her crew; but a company from the Edenton Battery, commanded by a Captain Badham, boarded the vessel in the face of strong enemy fire and successfully removed thousands of dollars worth of food, whisky, and other stores. So impartially were the salvaged items distributed throughout the garrison that even the Chaplain was reported, in an article in *Harper's Magazine* some time later, to have "said some very queer graces at the head-quarter's mess-table."

The *Ella* was the last of more than thirty blockade runners to become total losses in the vicinity of Cape Fear. But for every one thus destroyed there was at least one other captured at sea by the Federal naval vessels, which preferred to capture if possible because of the large prize money involved. The acting ensigns of one blockading vessel received $9,589.67 each as their share of the proceeds from the sale of just one captured vessel, and the cabin boy of another got the equivalent of six years pay. Blockading, as well as blockade running, paid off well along the North Carolina coast in the Civil War.

CATCHING UP ON LOST TRADE

1866-1877

COASTAL TRADE flourished in the period immediately following the Civil War, for peace brought with it a great demand for the civilian goods so long denied the participants in the struggle between the North and South. One immediate result was that a large number of war craft were hastily converted to commercial use; another was that coastal Carolina was soon littered with the remains of ships lost in this scramble to catch up on lost trade.

THAMES

The 560-ton passenger steamer *Thames*, on its regular run between Galveston and New York, rounded Cape Hatteras, April 6, 1869, and headed north along the coast. When still within sight of the lighthouse on the cape a frenzied cry was heard from amidships: "Fire!" By the time Captain Pennington could organize his fire-fighting crew, the flames had spread so rapidly that there was no hope of bringing them under control, and all hands—nine crewmen and nine passengers—were driven from the cabin.

With the wind blowing strong from the west Captain Pennington ordered the three aft boats removed from their davits and carried forward; then, with passengers and crew gathered on the bow, he headed his vessel into the wind, toward shore.

The flames continued to spread, however, and soon afterwards Pennington was driven from the pilothouse, leaving the vessel in an unmanageable state. Hurriedly the three boats were then lowered over the side, the passengers and crew crowded in them, and the *Thames*, by then almost completely engulfed in flames, was abandoned in the sea off Hatteras.

Two of the boats reached shore that night. The third, containing the ship's cook, two cabin boys, a seaman, and a coal heaver, either drifted to sea or overturned on Diamond Shoals, the five crewmen being given up for lost.

KENSINGTON

On January 27, 1871, the bark *Templar* and the steamer *Kensington* were involved in a collision sixty miles northeast of Diamond Shoals. The *World Almanac* lists this as one of the worst maritime disasters in history and claims a total of 150 lives were lost; but the plain facts are that no one was lost on either the *Templar* or the *Kensington*, though the steamer did go to the bottom.

The *Kensington*, with a crew of thirty and eighteen passengers, left Savannah, January 25, 1871, for Boston carrying a full cargo of cotton, rice, and lumber. Two days later, January 27, the *Templar* sailed from Hampton Roads, bound for Rio de Janeiro.

About 7:30 that evening, while tacking to the eastward, Captain Wilson of the *Templar* made out a steamer on his starboard beam. "Saw her mast head and red light plain," the Captain said, "and supposing that the steamer would pass under our stern we held our course to the eastward. Finding then that the steamer did not alter her course, several of the crew hailed her as loud as they could. No attention was paid to the hail, the steamer holding her course."

Realizing that the steamer would, on that course, cut his own craft in two, Captain Wilson ordered his wheel hard over. Slowly the bark turned aside as the *Kensington* passed under her bow, taking away the "bowsprit, jibboom, fore and main topgallants, foretopmast, and all attached." A moment later the bark crashed into the side of the steamer.

A sailor, who at the time of the accident was perched in the forward rigging of the bark, was thrown to the deck of the *Kensington*. The two vessels then drifted apart, and since Captain Wilson claimed he "heard no sound or indication from the steamer, of distress," he quickly sounded his pumps and ordered the debris cleared away on the *Templar*.

Meanwhile, the sailor who had fallen from the bark to the deck of the steamer found all confusion there. The *Kensington*, with a large hole in her side, was already filling with water, and the crewmen were even then in the process of lowering away her boats. The sea being comparatively calm, this was accomplished in a short time, and the thirty members of the steamer's crew, the eighteen passengers, and the lone sailor from the *Templar* managed to row clear before the vessel sank.

They were picked up late the next morning—fifteen hours after the collision—by the steamer *Georgia*, which transported them to Charleston. Complete details of the disaster, as recounted by the crew and passengers of the *Kensington* and the sailor from the *Templar*, were printed in the newspapers there and sent by telegraph to other parts of the country, together with a statement that the *Templar* and the remaining members of her crew were presumed lost.

Two days later, however, the steamer *Yazoo*, en route from Havana to Philadelphia, sighted the *Templar* off the Virginia Capes, partly filled with water and moving slowly northward under improvised sails. The *Yazoo* took the bark in tow, reaching Norfolk the following day, and subsequently the vessel was repaired and made ready for sea duty again.

The above facts are gleaned from interviews with the Captain of the *Templar*, the passengers and crewmen of the *Kensington*, and the crews of the *Georgia* and *Yazoo*, as published in contemporary newspaper accounts. It is definitely stated in several of these articles that there were forty-eight persons on board the *Kensington* and that all were saved; and in none of them is there mention of so much as a single life being lost on the *Templar*, thus completely refuting the published reports in more recent times that 150 lives were lost and that this was one of the worst maritime disasters in history.

HENRIETTA

The clipper ship *Henrietta* left Puerto Rico in late October, 1873, loaded with a cargo of molasses, sugar, and syrup. The 950-ton vessel carried a crew of sixteen, including the master, and was bound for the port of Philadelphia.

While en route north the *Henrietta* came upon a schooner, disabled and lying low in the water. In order to lighten the schooner, most of her cargo of coffee was transferred to the larger clipper. Then the two vessels parted, and the *Henrietta*, now heavily loaded, continued on her way up the coast.

The morning of November 4 the clipper encountered a strong northeast gale, and before it was over the vessel's main topsail was carried away, her foremast fell with it, and the mizzenmast was wrung off six feet above the deck, leaving the ship little more than a log drifting upon the angry waters.

After that the wind let up, but the waves seemed to grow even larger as the vessel drifted toward shore. Subsequently all of her boats were swept away except one which was lashed amidships; one man, the steward, was washed overboard; and by the time she appeared off the Carolina coast she was a complete derelict, at the mercy of wind and wave.

She struck, finally, on the southern end of Frying Pan Shoals, lodging briefly on a bar in about three fathoms of water, then drifting clear and sinking in a deep gully beyond. The fifteen remaining crewmen put off in the lone boat, but two hours later the small craft capsized, throwing all fifteen into the raging surf. Two, the captain and mate, managed to regain the boat; the other thirteen drowned. And for five more days the two surviving officers, without food or water, drifted aimlessly on the open sea until they were finally picked up by a passing vessel.

NUOVA OTTAVIA

Spencer D. Gray, like most residents of coastal Carolina in 1875, was a man of most trades and of none, an individual of diverse talents—carpenter, fisherman, farmer, hunter—who could and would do just about any kind of work that might bring in a living for himself and his growing family.

In 1875, Spencer D. Gray, a balding man with a slight middle-age stoop, took on something entirely new; Spencer Gray left his home at Church's Island and moved over to Currituck Lighthouse on the beach, there to become a member of the new United States Lifesaving Service.

He was listed on the payroll—at $20 a month—as a surfman; his job was to patrol the barren beach north and south from Jones Hill Station (later, Whales Head; still later, Currituck Beach) on the lookout for ships in distress. And at those times when a ship did come on shore he and his fellow surfmen were charged with the task of saving the lives of unknown castaways—even at the peril of their own.

By March 1, 1876, Spencer Gray had become accustomed to the job—to the long hikes along the beach in the worst of weather; the handling of his particular oar in the station lifeboat; the method of operation of the mortar gun, the breeches buoy, and the life car. And he had grown accustomed, almost, to separation from his wife and two children back at Church's Island, though a third child was six months on the way, and that would make it harder later on.

Soon after dusk on March 1, a vessel appeared just north of Jones Hill Station, a large sailing vessel, a bark, stranded on the bar a couple of hundred yards from shore.

Keeper John G. Gale, who had taken command of the Jones Hill Station when it was first put in operation, mustered his crew. One man, John Chappell, was absent, having been sent to Tulls Creek for supplies. The others—Gale, Spencer Gray, Lemuel Griggs, Lewis White, Malachi Brumsey, and Jerry Munden—hauled the lifeboat down to the surf and made preparations to go to the aid of the crew of the distressed vessel.

Neighbors appeared on the beach at this time—J. W. Lewis, H. T. Halstead, George W. Wilson, and others—and offered their assistance. Keeper Gale asked for one volunteer to take the place of Chappell in the boat. Halstead stepped forward, actually climbed in the boat, but was replaced by Wilson, a younger, larger, stronger man.

The wind that night was from the southeast, light, but the

weather was thick and the sea was rough, with the surf pounding on the beach. Offshore, in the haze, the stranded vessel was barely visible. The sound of her flapping sails came across the water dimly. But it was impossible to see, from shore, whether she was a stout ship or frail; whether she was in the breakers or beyond them; whether her decks were above water or swept by the seas. Keeper Gale could have set up his beach apparatus and fired a line aboard; but there was no certainty, there in the darkness, that a rescue could be effected until morning—and morning might be too late. So the seven men, six lifesavers and volunteer Wilson, launched their lifeboat through the surf and rowed out toward the stranded bark.

Spencer Gray, at his oar, was bent over even more than usual; the others, near him, pulled with equal strength and willingness. Lifesavers at stations all along our coast have gone out since, many times, under just such conditions as those; but that night of March 1, 1876, at Jones Hill one thing was different, for the surfmen, inadvertently or otherwise, had neglected to put on the cork life jackets which the service had provided for them.

The group of observers on the beach, augmented now by other neighbors from the community near the lighthouse, watched as the lifeboat passed through the breakers, reached the calmer water beyond, then moved off into the darkness. A lantern on the stern of the little boat, bobbing up and down with the heavy ground swells, marked the position of the craft; the only sounds were of the wind and the surf and the flapping of the sails against the masts. Then, suddenly, another sound came to them across the water, a shrill scream, terrified. And then the bobbing light disappeared from view.

A constant watch was kept on the beach then, and soon after one of the lifeboat oars drifted ashore, then a second, a third, and a fourth. After that the boat itself, turned bottom upwards, empty; and still later, one of the lifesavers, Malachi Brumsey, all life gone from his body.

Throughout the night the friends and neighbors and kinfolk waited, and at dawn the bark was still there; masts still standing, sails still flapping, and men clustered together on her deck. Eight of them were counted, but Keeper Gale was not among them. His body was found on the beach with the bodies of Lemuel Griggs,

Lewis White, George Wilson, and five unidentified Italian sailors, members of the crew of the ill-fated vessel on the bar. As for the others, only one thing was certain: Spencer Gray was one of the eight still on board the vessel, for his stoop, his bald head, stood out even at that distance.

If it was a period of trial for the eight men yet alive on board the Italian vessel, it was no less trying for the neighbors on shore. The craft was within easy range of the lifesaving mortar, and ample shot and line were available. But the trouble was that the lifesavers, the men trained in the use of the equipment, were all gone; at Tulls Creek, or drowned, or still out there on the ship.

The neighbors tried. They fired time after time after time, until the shot was exhausted and the vent in the mortar was clogged by sand. Forty-one rockets were sent up throughout the day and night, as encouragement for the men stranded on the vessel; for at least one of them was a native man, a neighbor: Surfman Spencer D. Gray.

It was all in vain, for at noon that second day of March the vessel began to go to pieces, and by 2 P.M. she had completely disappeared. Four men drifted ashore on a piece of wreckage, strangers all, Italians; they were exhausted, bruised, two with open gashes in their feet where spikes on the breaking deck had cut them. In the days that followed the Italians told, as best they could with signs and motions, what had happened. But it was never determined how or why the bark—her name was *Nuova Ottavia*—had stranded there. Fragments of the wreck which drifted ashore (one large section of the stern came in twenty miles down the beach near Kitty Hawk) were charred, leading to speculation that the vessel had caught fire at sea. But it was only speculation, never substantiated.

At Church's Island, across the sound, meanwhile, Molly Berry Gray was left a widow, with two children to support and a third on the way; for her husband, Spencer D. Gray, who had somehow managed to reach the deck of the *Nuova Ottavia* after his lifeboat capsized, did not live long. Like his six brave companions, he drowned before ever again reaching shore.

AT 11:35 A.M., SATURDAY,
November 24, 1877, the Signal Service in Washington received an
urgent and foreboding message from the operator at Kitty Hawk,
North Carolina: "The United States man-of-war steamer *Huron*
struck two miles north of Number 7 station at 1:30 A.M. The foremast and maintopmast have gone. The steamer is a total wreck. Assistance is needed immediately. The sea is breaking over her, and
several bodies have already washed ashore drowned. The number
on board is about 135. No cargo."

In Norfolk, Virginia, where this message was relayed, the news
was not such a shock as might have been expected; for rumors had
been making the rounds in Norfolk all morning that the *Huron*,
which had left that port the day previous in the face of a heavy
southeast gale, had grounded on the treacherous North Carolina
outer banks.

The *Huron*, en route from New York to Key West, the Gulf of
Mexico, and the Caribbean on a leisurely survey expedition, had
put in at Norfolk several days earlier for coal, and on the eve of
her regularly scheduled departure had received orders to remain
there until a draftsman from Washington could join the expedition.

For three days the *Huron* lay at anchor in Hampton Roads while
her 16 officers and 115 crewmen waited and fretted and groused,

navy style, over the delay. Late Thursday, John J. Evans of Washington—the draftsman—reported aboard, and the following morning the *Huron* was inspected and made ready for sea.

Old salts, the superstitious kind, will not put to sea on a Friday; bad luck, they say. And it is worth noting that on this particular Friday the *Huron* was the only vessel which cleared Hampton Roads for sea duty, for storm warnings were flying at Norfolk and Cape Henry—had been flying, in fact, since Wednesday afternoon —and the merchant masters, even the unsuperstitious ones, remained where they were.

Commander George P. Ryan, Captain of the *Huron*, was an experienced seaman and navigator; his officers and crew were among the best disciplined in the entire Navy; his vessel, only two years old and built of five-eights inch iron, had been referred to on occasion as "the strongest hull in the Atlantic waters." Storm warnings might hold merchantmen in port, but Commander Ryan's orders were to put to sea as soon as draftsman Evans arrived, and with no subsequent orders of a contradictory nature it was his job to do just that.

With the addition of Evans there were 132 of them on board the *Huron* when she moved out of Hampton Roads shortly after noon that Friday, a full crew, right down to a small contingent of United States Marines. The only conspicuous absentee was Lieutenant Arthur H. Fletcher, who had served previously as her executive officer. He had been plagued by a premonition that the *Huron* was destined to disaster, and being refused repeated requests for a transfer, he had simply jumped ship and deserted. His place had been taken by Lieutenant S. A. Simmons, a man less concerned over what the future might hold.

Ensign Lucian Young, who had on occasion come face to face with disaster, was another who seemed to experience no such fears as those which had bothered his former superior officer. Ensign Young, a short, stout young man of twenty-five, born in Lexington, Kentucky, and trained at Annapolis, looked anything but the hero. Yet in his locker box he carried a medal awarded by the Humane Society of the City of New York and a letter of commendation from the Secretary of the Navy, for distinguished bravery in jumping overboard in the middle of the Mediterranean Sea, at the height of a severe gale, to rescue a seaman who had fallen out of the rigging. On second thought, a man like that might not recognize fear even if it slipped up and kicked him from behind.

Once past the mouth of Chesapeake Bay that afternoon it was obvious to all on board the *Huron* that the weatherman had known what he was talking about, for the wind was at gale force and a heavy sea was running. The *Huron* was not alone out there, for one vessel passed close by, a schooner, and another was seen in the distance; but whereas the *Huron* was steaming toward the open sea the other two were shoreward bound, scurrying for the safety of Hampton Roads.

Every ship's captain, heading south from Chesapeake Bay as Captain Ryan of the *Huron* was doing, is faced with an immediate decision; there are three courses from which he must choose. The warm greenish waters of the Gulf Stream, passing slowly up the Atlantic Coast, come in so close at Hatteras that they almost touch the outer fringes of Diamond Shoals, then bear away from the land again as their northward movement continues past the mouth of the Chesapeake. Always the movement is northward, at a steady pace of about four miles an hour, carrying tropical fish and plant life far beyond their normal habitat, and providing north-bound mariners with a sort of watery conveyor-belt on which they can travel.

For south-bound ships it is a different proposition, for then the movement of the Gulf Stream is against the vessel, and a craft whose engines pushed her at a steady four miles an hour, say, would get no place at all. That is where the decision comes in; whether to travel in the Gulf Stream, bucking that four-mile current all the way; to move beyond the Gulf Stream a couple of hundred miles from shore, thus losing the time it takes to get out that far; or to sail right down the coast, close in between the Gulf Stream and the fearful sand reefs along the Carolina coast.

Commander George P. Ryan of the 541-ton barkentine-rigged screw-steamer *Huron*—putting faith, no doubt, in his own ability, in the experience of his crew, and in his sturdy vessel—chose the last course, ignoring the repeated warning that the seaman who hugs the land always courts death.

At 6:30 P.M., with Currituck Light on the starboard beam, the
gale increased in intensity and carried away the *Huron's* jibstay.
Lieutenant W. P. Conway, in charge of the deck at that time, took
a single reef in his fore-trisail, a double reef in his main-trisail,
brailed up the spanker, and set the fore-storm-staysail. Currituck
Light was then approximately eight miles off, and ordering soundings taken, Conway learned that the vessel was in fifteen fathoms
of water.

Lieutenant James M. Wright relieved Conway of the watch at
8 P.M. and in turn reported nothing out of the ordinary when he
handed the duty over to Lieutenant W. S. French at midnight.
Currituck Light had by then disappeared astern, and the beam from
the new light at Bodie Island was not yet visible ahead. So far as
Wright and French knew, the vessel was a safe distance from shore,
and no changes were made in her course. What they failed to take
into consideration is that the coast, almost straight from the Virginia
line to Caffeys Inlet, makes a slight bend eastward between the
villages of Duck and Kitty Hawk (standing on top of the dunes
north of Duck, the Wright Memorial, fifteen miles to the south, is
today visible over the cove thus formed) so that a minor change in
course is necessary.

No such change was made, and as the fog by then obscured the
Bodie Island Light, the earlier premonitions of Lieutenant Fletcher
were on the verge of realization, yet it is probable that that gentle-
man, safely ashore in custody of the naval authorities, was at the
moment sleeping soundly and without fear; for it was his successor,
Simmons, and not Fletcher, who was destined for a watery grave
aboard the *Huron* that cold November morning.

An hour and a half later—at 1:30 A.M., Saturday—the lookout
sang out that he had sighted breakers to starboard. Lieutenant
French immediately ordered the helm hard over, and at the same
time shouted for the leadsman to take soundings. The orders came
too late, for the ship suddenly jarred to a stop, swung around
toward the beach, and heeled over on her port side.

Lieutenant Conway, awakened by the shock of the ship striking,
thought she had collided with some other vessel. Commander
Ryan, apparently dressed and prepared for any emergency, quickly
appeared on deck with charts in hand, checked the approximate

location with Lieutenant French, and ordered all hands on deck. Ensign Young had already taken his place near the Captain, awaiting further orders. There was considerable movement throughout the vessel, as officers and crew members ran to their stations, but the moment was marked by a complete absence of confusion and hysteria; the discipline was paying off.

Already the seas were breaking over the vessel from the port side, sails and spars were scattered over the deck, and she was partly filled with water flowing down the open hatches. Orders were now given to batten down the hatches, throw the guns overboard, and take in the sails. None of these orders was ever carried out, for the hatch covers were washed away or broken, the guns were too firmly attached to the deck to be dislodged, and those men who climbed aloft were unable to make headway with the sails.

When the command was given to launch the boats, Lieutenant Conway assembled a crew and directed efforts to get the cutter overboard. Even before the boat cleared, however, she was partly stove in by the forward davit; and as she struck the water a huge wave carried her away. But she rode back on the next swell, this time smashing into a stanchion and tearing another hole in her side. Conway and his helpers were able to secure her, however, and a line was attached to her bow with the thought that if the cutter reached shore the line might serve as a means of rescuing those left behind. But the whole effort was doomed to failure, for water poured in through the holes in her side, and the small craft filled and sank from sight.

The shore, by this time, was dimly visible through the haze and darkness—though many questioned whether it was really the shore they saw—and Ensign Young, having gone below in search of signals, returned with two boxes of Coston lights and an armful of rockets. He sent up five rockets and burned more than a hundred of the signals, but no response was observed from shore.

In the engine room, meanwhile, every effort had been made to keep up the fires, and for half an hour after the vessel struck, her engines continued a fruitless attempt to back her off the reef. At 2 A.M. Chief Engineer Olsen ordered the fires hauled, the engines were stopped, and shortly afterwards the fastenings of the starboard boilers gave way and the massive boilers drifted across the sloping

fireroom floor and lodged on the port side. At that point, with
water pouring down the engine-room hatches, Olsen ordered his
engine-room crew on deck.

Ensign Young, having exhausted his supply of rockets and Coston
signals, returned to the poop for further orders from his captain.
"The ship was lying on her port, bilged, broadsides inclined about
ten degrees and seas breaking clear over her," he said. "I heard the
order given for all hands to go forward as quick as possible. As I
passed the cabin door Mr. French asked me if that was all. I stopped
and told him 'Yes.' Then he said: 'We must go quick.' We all
started together. I had hold of the Gatlin gun, when a very heavy
sea came over and washed myself and about five others down to
leeward. All but myself went under the sail, and they were
drowned. I was caught in the bag of the sail and hurt both legs
against the gaff, but worked myself forward and succeeded in
getting on the top gallant forecastle."

It still was not light, though a faint glow had appeared in the east.
The tide was rising, and the stern of the vessel was almost completely submerged. A few men were huddled together in the main
rigging, but most were forward, clinging to the bowsprit and
grouped together on the gallant forecastle with Ensign Young. It
was bitter cold, and those with extra clothing shared it with others
near them. Lieutenant Conway had located a blanket somewhere,
and he and Ensign Young and two others tried to use it as a shield
against the cold wind and spray. It did little good.

Suddenly a light appeared off the starboard bow, a moving light,
apparently on shore. The survivors, some by now lashed to the
bowsprit with halyards, cheered at the prospect of help from that
quarter.

But if the remaining crewmen aboard the *Huron* were looking
for assistance from shore they were in for bitter disappointment.
The light they saw was carried by a fisherman, one of several who
had come over from the soundside village of Nags Head to see the
wreck. They were men who lived by the water—fishing provided
their livelihood—but they had no boats with them, and no lifesaving
apparatus, and all they could do was stand there and watch and
wait and maybe pray, if any among them felt so inclined. A life-

saving station, one of several recently established on the outer banks, was located two and a half miles south of the scene of the disaster. But Congress had provided meager funds for operation of the stations, and at that particular season Station Number Seven at Nags Head was inactive, the keeper was at his home on Roanoke Island across the sound, and none among the Nags Head fishermen knew how to use the lifesaving apparatus stored in the station, or dared to break in and get it if they did.

It had taken some time, even, for most of the Nags Head people to realize that there really was a vessel ashore, and more time, still, for them to decide whether it was worthwhile going out in the storm to offer what little assistance they could.

Patti Tillett, a young girl living with her stepfather up in the woods, said later that she was the first to hear the boom of the rockets fired by Ensign Young. She was up at that hour preparing breakfast for her stepfather, but when she woke him and told him there was a vessel ashore, he considered the story a figment of her imagination, turned over on his side, and went back to sleep again. Shortly afterwards Patti saw Evan O'Neal, another fisherman, passing by en route to the sound landing and tried to get him to "get up a crowd and go for the beach apparatus, but there were no men in the station, and nobody dared to break in, they stood that much in fear of the Government."

Finally, O'Neal and Patti and several of their neighbors did walk over to the beach, and it was their light which the shipwrecked sailors saw and cheered.

More than fifty men were crowded on the forecastle of the *Huron* when it became light enough to see, and others were hanging on to spars and rigging and railings—to anything that was stationary—all over the forward part of the vessel.

One boat remained intact, but when Captain Ryan and one of the crewmen attempted to launch it the boat crashed down on them, capsizing the craft and throwing both men into the water. Neither was seen alive again.

Thus at daybreak the survivors of the shipwreck found themselves confined to a small forward section of the wreck; each successive series of waves was breaking higher and higher on that part of the vessel which was still above water; the boats had all been washed away or dashed to pieces in their davits; and their captain was drowned.

With almost every wave someone else disappeared. Executive Officer Simmons was washed overboard three times, regained the comparative safety of the ship twice, but was drowned the third time. One particularly large wave swept completely over the vessel, carrying at least a dozen men to their death.

Cadet Engineer E. T. Warburton had secured a position by the pinrail on the starboard side. "I protected my head for some time by a tarpaulin, which several of us held around us," he said, "but the seas came heavier and by every one I was dashed against the pinrail, bruising my limbs and taking my breath away."

Dennis Dasey, a sailmaker, had clung to the starboard fore-chains, but he relaxed his grip momentarily and was washed overboard. "I swam back to the ship," he said, "and Peter Duffey swung me a line and pulled me back into the chains." Both Dasey and Duffey later reached shore.

Ensign Young and Lieutenant Conway had been taking periodic soundings over the vessel's side. At first they found six feet of water, then seven, then seven and a half, and finally eight. That was when Ensign Young decided to leave the shelter of his blanket and take some definite action to save himself and the others.

The *Huron* carried, in addition to its cutter and other small boats, several rubber balsas, or life rafts. These were oblong in shape and similar in design and size to those used as emergency rafts by airmen in more recent times. At dawn only one remained on board the *Huron*, the last visible means of communication with shore; a small, frail, unwieldy contraption, more suitable for child's play in an indoor pool than the purpose Ensign Young had in mind. But Ensign Young, remember, was a man experienced in saving life. "He can swim like a duck, and knows no such thing as fear," it was said of him later. And so Ensign Young made his way along the littered deck to the tiny balsa, calling for volunteers to help him get it into the sea.

"A three-inch line was made fast to the balsa," he said, "and the same was lowered overboard, but it fouled with the jibboom fore-guard and other spars. I got down on the torpedo spar and worked about ten minutes to clear the balsa, and called for someone to help me. Mr. Danner (Ensign Fred Danner, who was drowned) came down part of the way and said he was too weak and could not get on."

At this point a seaman, Antonio Williams, crawled down to Young's side and offered his assistance. It took them fifteen minutes to get the balsa clear of the spars, but then they found that the line held it close to the ship. Their shipmates, gathered on the forecastle, shouted for them to cut the line and get on shore for assistance. "I had a small penknife but could not open it because my hands were so numbed," Young said. "Williams opened it, and I succeeded in cutting the rope. Was then struck several times by the spars, once in the small of the back and across the hips. We thought the beach ran perpendicular to the ship. It was foggy and we could not see the shore. When the line was cut the balsa went towards the stern of the ship, and we thought we were going to sea. We paddled the balsa with pieces of panelling, and near the stern of the ship a heavy surf struck us and capsized the balsa end for end."

That was almost the finish for both of the brave men. Williams said his neck was caught between two spars and he was almost choked to death before he could free himself and gain the surface. As for Ensign Young, his leg was jammed tight and he too was held under water far beyond the time he thought his breath could hold out. But, miraculously, both he and Williams managed to regain the balsa.

"I told Williams to get on the end," Young continued, "and we would swim and steer the balsa in for fear of another capsize. We were thrown over again, and this catastrophe threw Williams about ten feet. My arm being jammed I was thrown on my back. When we came up again it was rather still water. I swam and pushed the balsa toward Williams and he got on top and stood up and looked around, and said that he saw the masts of fishing vessels ahead, which proved to be the telegraph poles on shore. I told him we'd steer for it. We capsized twice more, and before we knew it were on the beach."

They had reached the shore about three-quarters of a mile north of the wreck, and immediately pulled the balsa out of the surf so it would be available if needed later. Despite his ordeal on the balsa

and the injuries he had received, Ensign Young did not hesitate
then, for his task had just begun.

Two men, washed off the *Huron* earlier, were lying in the comparatively calm water inside the surf, too weak to get up. Young
pulled both on shore, then hurried down the beach, pausing at the
first building he came to—probably a fisherman's temporary shack
—but finding it empty. Opposite the wreck he met O'Neal and
Patti Tillett and a dozen or so of their neighbors and told them to
go up the beach where the men were washing ashore and try to
render what aid they could. He himself assisted in this, but only
after he had dispatched a man on horseback to the telegraph station
at Kitty Hawk with a message for assistance to be sent to Washington.

It was then shortly after seven o'clock in the morning. The sea
was so high that many of those aboard the *Huron* at the time Young
and Williams left in their balsa had been washed overboard; among
them was Lieutenant Conway, who reached shore safely.

Learning that the lifesaving station at Nags Head was closed and
the fishermen were afraid to break in, Young induced five of them
to accompany him to the station. "I then walked and ran down the
beach with these men to the station," he said. "Found no one there
but saw a team coming down the beach, which proved to be that
of Sheriff Brinkley of Dare County. I broke open the door, got the
mortar and line; broke open a locker and found powder and balls,
which Sheriff Brinkley brought up in his team."

But by the time Lucian Young and Sheriff Brinkley and the
fishermen returned to the scene of the wreck with the lifesaving
apparatus it was nearly noon, the *Huron* was almost completely
submerged, and not a single living person remained on board the
vessel.

Survivors, bruised and exhausted, suffering from the cold and
exposure, some completely naked, were stretched out on the beach
or searching for their shipmates in the surf. The bodies of several
others were laid in a neat row on top of the bank. Of 132 men
aboard the *Huron* when she left Hampton Roads twenty-four hours
earlier, only thirty-four remained alive.

In Washington and Norfolk, meanwhile, Ensign Young's message, transmitted by the signal service operator at Kitty Hawk, was

setting in motion extensive rescue operations. The Secretary of the Navy telegraphed Baker Brothers, Norfolk wrecking firm, to send their steamer *B & J Baker* to the scene; Admiral Trenchard, flag officer of the North Atlantic squadron based in Norfolk, dispatched the government steamers *Powhatan*, *Swatara*, and *Fortune*, taking passage himself on the first of these. Captain J. J. Guthrie, superintendent of the newly formed Sixth Lifesaving District, took the steamer *Lady of the Lake* from Portsmouth to Old Point Comfort and boarded the outbound *B & J Baker* there. Mr. Henry L. Brooke, reporter for the *Norfolk Virginian*, also secured passage on the wrecking steamer.

The *B & J Baker* arrived off the Nags Head beach at 7:45 Sunday morning. The sea was still rough, though the wind had moderated (it had been recorded at sixty-eight miles per hour at Cape Henry the morning of the wreck), and the *Baker* lay off the coast for some time attempting to establish contact with the survivors on shore. Captain Stoddard of the *Baker* considered it too rough to attempt a landing through the surf at that time, but in the early afternoon a boat was lowered over the side containing Captain Stoddard, Superintendent Guthrie, reporter Brooke, six seamen, and Stoddard's pet dog. The official report of this landing attempt stated that the boat "came shoreward in good style up to the surf on the outer bar, 100 yards south of the *Huron* and 200 yards from shore. The first breaker, a huge mound of tumultuous water, was gallantly surmounted by the boat, which then swept swiftly down the long valley of the subsiding wave, when another tremendous breaker arose aft, and, although the crew pulled for their lives, it overtook the boat, caught it under the quarter, whirled it broadside to, and flirted it up, ten feet in the air, spilling every one on board into the sea."

Captain Stoddard, Mr. Brooke, and one of the crewmen regained the overturned craft and clung to it until it was dragged through the surf. Another crewman swam to shore unaided. Stoddard's dog, taking a dim view of the whole proceedings, swam back to the *B & J Baker* and was hoisted on board. But Superintendent Guthrie and four of the crewmen were not seen again until their bodies were washed up on the beach some time later. Thus five more deaths were added to the *Huron's* toll, bringing the total to 103.

The four rescue vessels remained opposite the scene of the dual disaster until dusk Sunday night, and then, realizing that assistance from the sea was out of the question, returned to Norfolk.

The survivors, meanwhile, had been cared for as well as possible by the residents of Nags Head and the keeper of the Lifesaving Station, B. F. Meekins, who had come over from his home on Roanoke Island. The four surviving officers—Ensign Young, Lieutenant Conway, Assistant Engineer R. G. Denig, and Cadet Engineer E. T. Warburton—spent Saturday night at the home of Sheriff Brinkley; the thirty crewmen who had been saved were housed and fed at Station Number Seven.

Sunday morning the small side-wheel steamer *Bonito*, which had been lying abreast of the cut through to Roanoke Island, tied up at the soundside wharf at Nags Head, and Captain Cain volunteered to transport the survivors to Norfolk. The offer was immediately accepted, and Sunday afternoon the shipwrecked sailors crossed over to the wharf from the ocean side.

A reporter for the *Norfolk Landmark* described the scene at Nags Head that Sunday afternoon in vivid terms.

"About 4 o'clock," the reporter wrote, "Sheriff Brinkley and several of his neighbors arrived with banker ponies and three or four steer and mule carts for the purpose of transferring the survivors to the side-wheel steamer *Bonito*, lying at Nags Head wharf. Those who were unable to walk took seats in the carts, and friend Brooke, of the *Virginian*, led the cavalcade, seated upon a pony and wrapped in an army blanket from head to foot.

"Those who were able to walk to the steamer, some two miles distant, straggled along after the vehicles across the immense waste of white sand. A few of the most active ones scaled the barren sand hills, and from their summits stopped a few moments to cast a last look at the noble steamer which had, so short a time before, been their temporary home, but over which, then, the terrible breakers were rolling with relentless fury. The scene, although solemn in the main, had its grotesque phases, and it was well worthy of the artist's pencil. Thirty-four half clad, shoeless and hatless survivors, were toiling over a white and desolate waste, and behind them a long unbroken line of breakers were sounding a harsh and sullen requiem over the watery graves of a hundred or more of their comrades."

And so, Ensign Young and the other survivors of the *Huron* disaster were transported to Norfolk, and in the days that followed a total of ninety bodies was recovered from the surf along the North Carolina and Virginia coast, some washing ashore more than forty miles north of Nags Head.

Ensign Young had lost his locker box, and the lifesaving medal and letter of commendation it contained; but soon after he received, in their stead, a Gold Lifesaving Medal of the first class awarded by his government for gallantry and humanity at the scene of the disaster, and a similar award went also to Seaman Antonio Williams.

As for the *Huron*, to this day she is visible beneath the waters on the beach at Nags Head, a broken, twisted, rusted hulk, frequented by fishermen who claim that the sheepshead and other fish living there are the largest, fightingest, and best tasting on the coast.

IT IS DOUBTFUL THAT
Richard Brooks and Jake Mitteager ever heard of the Cataract
de Inferno and the treacherous falls above it on the River Madeira
in the interior of Brazil. Yet, were it not for the Cataract de Inferno
neither Brooks nor Mitteager would have been cast into the storm-
churned surf off the coast of North Carolina in the cold early
morning of January 31, 1878, in company with some 250 other
innocent persons.

The River Madeira forms in the great watershed of Bolivia in
South America at a point more than a thousand miles closer to the
Pacific than to the Atlantic, but because the Bolivian watershed is
on the east side of the towering Andes the River Madeira flows
toward the Atlantic. Small river boats navigate the Madeira for
several hundred miles eastward to a junction with the Mamoré
River; then for 180 miles the river is dotted with innumerable falls
and rapids, the greatest and easternmost of which is the Cataract de
Inferno. From the town of Bairmo, just below the cataract, larger
boats proceed down the River Madeira to the Amazon and on to
the Atlantic Ocean.

The Cataract de Inferno, consequently, is the bottleneck which
prevents vessels from proceeding some two thousand miles up the

Amazon, Madeira, and Mamoré rivers to the productive Bolivian watershed. And in 1868 the National Bolivian Navigation Company, realizing this, hired a New York engineer to survey the area above the cataract and determine if it was possible to construct a canal or railroad around the falls. Colonel George Earle Church, the engineer hired for the job, announced that the construction of a 180-mile railroad along the river from the town of Bairmo to the intersection with the Mamoré River was feasible, and in early November, 1877, Messrs. P. and T. Collins, contractors of Philadelphia, were awarded a contract for construction of the railroad. That is where Richard Brooks became involved.

Richard W. Brooks, a native Philadelphian, was twenty-three years old when the Messrs. Collins signed their railroad contract with the National Bolivian Navigation Company. He was a bricklayer by trade, and despite his youth had twice before sailed on ocean voyages, had served an apprenticeship with the firm of Weatherstine and Kupp, and had been employed for three years as a journeyman bricklayer by the George Waterhouse Company.

In January, 1878, however, there was little construction work in the Philadelphia area—little work of any kind for that matter—and young Dick Brooks, married and with a child to support, was out of a job. An inducement to signing on with the Collins' was the high wage, the certainty of employment throughout the stay in Brazil, and the fact that all of his expenses would be taken care of and his pay could be sent home. On the debit side was the length of the trip—the Collins' Company was signing workers for a minimum of eighteen months in Brazil—and the fact that he would have to leave his family at home.

In the end Dick Brooks apparently decided that steady work in far off Brazil was better than unemployment at home, and he signed as a bricklayer to work on tunnels and arches.

Dick Brooks signed too late to take the first boat, the *Mercedita*, which left Philadelphia on January 2 with two hundred men, mostly engineers and mechanics, and eight hundred tons of rails, machinery, and engines. But another vessel was due to sail toward the end of January, and a third in early February.

Mr. Thomas Collins, the "T" in P. and T. Collins, had super-

vised the hiring and fitting out of the vessels which were to transport his men and supplies to Brazil. He admitted to being a
superstitious man, and that accounted to some extent for his in-
sistence that he should personally inspect each vessel before departure. He found all in order on the *Mercedita*, and felt that the
firm of Henry L. Gregg, who served as his agents in locating the
ships, had done a good job.

The second vessel they chartered was the former Federal gunboat *Stars and Stripes*, which had seen considerable service in the
New York to Cuba run in recent years; the third was the spacious
Richmond, lately in the passenger service on Chesapeake Bay and
its tributaries. Several British ships had been available, but Thomas
Collins followed a policy of buying and hiring at home when possible. His one trouble, considering his bent toward superstition, was
that he did not check back far enough on the records of the ships
he chartered.

Especially was the above true in the case of the second boat
Collins dispatched from Philadelphia, the former *Stars and Stripes*.
For the war record of the Federal gunboat *Stars and Stripes* in the
War Between the States was distinguished only by her designation
as temporary flagship of the forces under Commander S. C. Rowan
in the attack on Roanoke Island and the subsequent campaign in
the sounds of eastern North Carolina. The *Stars and Stripes* was one
of the first of the Federal vessels to pass through Hatteras Inlet into
Pamlico Sound, and she fired her share of ammunition at the Confederate defenses on Roanoke Island, part of the time discharging
her guns while stranded on a shoal. After that she played a most
inconspicuous part in the Federal campaign, being noted only for
the havoc she had wrought earlier on the coast of North Carolina.

A superstitious man, knowing these facts, might well have been
wary about entrusting his men and cargo to such a ship on the
dangerous passage along that same North Carolina coast, and so it
must be assumed that Thomas Collins knew nothing of the war
record of the vessel he chartered. For that matter, the name of the
Stars and Stripes had long since been changed, she had been re-
fitted completely for the merchant trade, and even her papers had
been altered somehow so that she was listed as having been built
nine years after her participation in the battle of Roanoke Island.

So far as Thomas Collins knew, the vessel he hired for the run to Brazil was the six-year-old steamship *Metropolis*.

Neither, apparently, did Thomas Collins know that the Atlantic Coast Line Railroad had chartered the *Metropolis* (or *Stars and Stripes*) the month previous to transport freight from Norfolk to Wilmington while the railroad's bridge at Weldon was being rebuilt, but because she arrived at Norfolk disabled and in tow of a Navy vessel, had cancelled the charter. More evidence, this, for a superstitious man.

But Thomas Collins seemed not aware of this background, and consequently the *Metropolis*, having been equipped in New York with additional lifeboats for the voyage to Brazil, proceeded to Philadelphia, where her cargo was loaded, and on Monday afternoon, January 28, the railroad workers began coming aboard.

The *Metropolis* was tied up at the Reading Railroad wharf at the foot of Willow Street, and both the wharf and Willow Street behind it were crowded with people—thousands of them, it seemed to reporters who later described the parting scene—and there did not seem to be a dozen among them who were not Irish. It was almost as if every Irishman in Philadelphia, and every Irish woman and child as well, had come to the foot of Willow Street to board the *Metropolis*, or to say goodbye to someone who had, or just to watch the vessel sail.

There were tender scenes aplenty as the *Metropolis* was made ready for departure. There was, for instance, the foreman who, after repeated passionate farewells, could not bring himself to tea his wife's arms from around his neck and finally led her back alon the wharf to where Thomas Collins was standing, surrounded by people, and told him he just could not go; and the big workman who begged fruitlessly to have his motherless son accompany him. And there were those who changed their plans—the engineer, whose baggage had not arrived on time and who consequently waited for the next ship; and Thomas Collins himself, for that matter, who had intended embarking on the *Metropolis* with his wife, but on inspecting the crowded quarters aboard the vessel decided that they would do better to wait for the *Richmond*.

Dick Brooks made it this time, but at the moment when he waved to his wife for the last time and turned to mount the gangway it

would not have taken much for the young bricklayer to change
his mind.

In the end there was such a crowd around the gangway that
some who were trying to get on board were left behind, and others
already on the vessel to see friends off were unable to reach shore,
and so were hired on the spot to take the place of those who had
not made it.

There were 248 people on the *Metropolis* when she moved out
into the stream that evening. Of these 13 were members of the crew,
215 were laborers, and the remaining 20 were saloon passengers,
including three women.

The *Metropolis* was a screw steamer, bark-rigged, listed as being
198 feet in length, 34 feet across the beam, and with a tonnage of
879. Considering the vessel's size, her engines were said to have
been exceptionally small. On the voyage to Brazil she carried, in
addition to the passengers, almost a thousand tons of cargo, including 500 tons of iron rails (enough to lay between seven and
eight miles of track) and 200 tons of stores and 250 tons of coal.
A $42,000 insurance policy on the cargo was not signed until two
days after the *Metropolis* sailed.

She laid at anchor all Monday night, proceeding downstream
the next morning and reaching the Delaware Breakwater shortly
before noon. Soon afterwards the pilot was dropped, and Captain
J. H. Ankers headed his craft toward the open sea. Throughout
that afternoon and night the *Metropolis* encountered calm seas
and fair skies, as the vessel remained out of sight of land. Wednesday morning the sea became choppy, then rough, and by afternoon
most of the laborers had lost both their appetites and most of what
they had eaten since leaving Philadelphia. A peculiar jarring sound
developed in the hold that evening, and on investigation it was
found that the iron rails, improperly stored in close-packed piles,
had begun to shift with the movement of the vessel. At about this
time the frenzied cry of "Fire" was heard, and within brief seconds
men were running in all directions, some dragging heavy hoses,
others with water buckets, and still others searching for the fire or
a means to escape it.

Only in the main cabin, where the passengers were sprawled out
on improvised berths, was there a semblance of order; and this was

not because the Irish laborers there were any more restrained, but simply because many were too seasick to care. Fortunately it was soon discovered that the fire call had been a false alarm, escaping steam from a broken pipe having been mistaken for smoke.

Meanwhile First Engineer Jake Mitteager was having other troubles, for the *Metropolis* was laboring heavily and it was difficult to keep the engines running steadily. Finally leaving the engine room in charge of an assistant, Jake made his way aft and discovered a leak near the rudder post. Soon the water was waist deep in the hold, and Captain Ankers held a quick consultation with Paul J. White, who was in charge of the workmen aboard, and William H. Harrison and J. J. Moore, his assistants. It was decided that the best course was to throw overboard part of the cargo of coal in order to lighten the vessel sufficiently for the circulating pumps to gain on the water still pouring into the hold. Apparently, though they were opposite the mouth of Chesapeake Bay at the time, Ankers did not even consider going into Hampton Roads for repairs.

A general call was sounded for all passengers to assemble in the main cabin, where the seasick ones were dragged forcibly from their berths, and the berths were piled in a corner. Then the hatches were removed, some of the men were lowered into the hold, and a bucket brigade was formed to transfer the coal from the storage bins to the main deck, where it was thrown overboard.

The men were kept at this labor throughout the evening and until well past midnight—Jake Mitteager figured they must have thrown over at least fifty tons—until finally the pumps began to gain on the water and the bucket brigade was discontinued.

This was only a temporary respite for Dick Brooks and the other laborers, however, for the cargo of iron rails shifted more and more with each movement of the vessel, the open seams in her hull widened, and under the added strain the circulating pumps broke down. Again a bucket brigade was formed, this time to bail out the water, but this proved little help and the vessel gradually began to fill.

Jake Mitteager was encountering still more difficulties, for as the water rose in the hold the strain on his engines became greater, and he experienced great difficulty in keeping his fires burning. At the suggestion of Chief Engineer Joseph J. Lovell he finally broke open a barrel of tallow and added this to the fires, and for a while was able to keep up sufficient steam. Then, without warning, a huge wave broke completely over the vessel, taking away the smokestack, seven of the lifeboats, the steam whistle, the engine-room ventilators, skylight, after-mainsail, starboard saloon, and most of the gangway. The galley stove toppled over, crushing the assistant steward beneath it; tables were overturned in the officers' dining saloon, and one of the ladies, Mrs. Harrison, was thrown against a bulkhead and seriously injured.

Even as those on deck were taking stock of the damage Jake Mitteager notified the Captain from the engine room that the water had completely drowned out his fires. And so, just before dawn that Thursday morning in the winter of 1878, the former Union gunboat *Stars and Stripes*, now the *Metropolis*, loaded with almost a thousand tons of coal, iron rails, stores, and human beings, was completely disabled in a turbulent sea, most of her lifeboats washed overboard, her steam whistle out of commission, and only part of her sails still intact.

Through the haze Captain Ankers spotted the beam of a light-house to the west—he said afterwards that he knew all along it was Currituck Beach Light, but others on board thought it was Cape Charles—and realizing that his vessel could not remain afloat for long, ordered all remaining sails set, and headed for the beach.

At Currituck Beach, North Carolina, that morning, as was his custom, N. E. K. Jones left his house on the sound side of the narrow sand spit and walked over to the ocean to see if any ships or stranded property had come ashore during the severe storm of the night before. He was accompanied by Jimmy Capps, a young hunter-trapper who lived near by. Before they reached the ocean front Capps halted, grasping Jones' arm, and peering through the early morning gloom, exclaimed: "Yonder's a vessel ashore."

Jones, the elder of the two, was not able to see anything at that distance, but hurrying forward they discovered through the fog the lone mast and hull of a vessel, close to shore. At first Jones thought it was abandoned, and said to Capps that the crew must have been taken off earlier by a passing ship; but just at that time they heard the sound of many voices raised in what could pass for a cheer, and on closer inspection Capps said he could see people—a lot of them—moving about on board.

Jones and Capps lived in a tiny village forty miles south of Cape Henry and a short distance below the Virginia line. The village (no longer a village, and now known as Poyners Hill) was centered about a hunting club and included only half a dozen houses. Four miles to the north was a larger village (now Corolla), the Currituck Beach Lighthouse, another hunting club, and the newly established lifesaving station designated as Station Number Four. The nearest habitation to the south was Lifesaving Station Number Five, some seven miles distant.

When he learned that there were people aboard the wreck Jones lost no time in dispatching Capps for assistance, sending him back to the village to borrow a horse from a neighbor, Swepson C. Brock. But Capps found the house deserted. He had already caught the horse and was in the process of saddling it when Brock came up from the near-by marsh. On being told of the disaster Brock mounted his horse and rode out to the beach at a gallop, waving his hat as he passed the wreck to let those on board know that assistance was coming, and then proceeding up the beach as fast as he could to pass the word to the lifesavers at Number Four.

On the *Metropolis*, meanwhile, all was confusion. The vessel had struck the outer bar head on and had then drifted over the bar into deeper water, finally coming to rest on the inner bar only a hundred yards from the beach. When the men saw shore they cheered lustily, thinking that they were safe at last, and this was the cheer Jones and Capps heard when they first spotted the vessel from the beach.

The people aboard the vessel were far from safe, however, for they were separated still from the shore by a line of towering breakers. Already several had been washed overboard and drowned, including one of the ladies, and when the vessel struck word was quickly passed for every man to look out for himself. Those who could find them immediately donned life jackets, while others launched the remaining serviceable lifeboat, and six men finally put off in the frail craft. A line was passed on board for them to tow to shore, but in the confusion it was left behind.

At this point Dick Brooks decided the best course left for him was to try to swim ashore, and he jumped overboard, followed by the first mate and a third man. The tide was then low, and as it proved later the great majority could have been saved had they followed Brooks' example at the time. But most preferred to remain aboard, trusting that help would arrive from shore.

Brooks and his two companions reached the beach safely at about the same time that the six men landed in the lifeboat, and the nine of them proceeded up the beach to a line of telegraph poles, which they followed in a northern direction. The only living thing they saw was a cow, which ran away, but they followed her, according to Dick Brooks's account, "running a mile through brush and briar in our bare feet with nothing on but shirt and drawers" and finally reached the Currituck Beach Lighthouse Club. Here they were provided with dry clothes by William Jones, an employee, and on the return of John J. Dunton, owner of the club, word of the wreck was dispatched to the lifesaving station, though the lifesavers had by then been informed of the disaster by Swepson Brock.

Keeper John G. Chappell of Lifesaving Station Number Four was on the beach when Swepson Brock arrived with news of the wreck of the steamship *Metropolis*. When he returned to his station the members of his crew were already loading the mortar, breeches buoy, shot, powder, line and lifesaving suit in the hand cart. Chappell immediately mounted the horse behind Brock, one of his men passed him the station medicine chest, and instructing the crew to follow with the hand cart, he and Brock set off for the wreck.

Long before they had covered the four and a half miles to the scene of the disaster, Brock and Keeper Chappell began to find pieces of wreckage on the beach and an occasional body. Chappell dismounted once and tried to resuscitate a woman (Mrs. Harrison). In this he was unsuccessful, and they proceeded on to a point opposite the *Metropolis*, where a number of people were assembled, including local residents as well as survivors. It was then almost 11:30 and some four hours had passed since the vessel struck the bar; yet most of her passengers and crew, including Jake Mitteager, still clung to mast and spar and anything else that was above water. For the next hour Keeper Chappell's medicine chest was in constant use, and a number of survivors were revived who might otherwise have died.

While their keeper was thus engaged the six remaining lifesavers from Station Number Four were laboriously dragging their heavily laden cart toward the scene. With the mortar and other equipment it weighed in the neighborhood of one thousand pounds—more than 165 pounds per man—and the six-man team found the beach newly covered with storm tides, causing the broad wheels of the cart to sink four or five inches in the sand.

It is doubtful that it was within the capabilities of the six human beings to haul that cart the full distance to the wreck. All of them had been on beach patrol during the night, and had walked from twelve to thirty-two miles along the flooded beach on the lookout for stranded vessels. When less than one third of the way to the wreck, all were nearly exhausted; young William Perry, Jim and John Rogers, Sam Gillett, and Nat Gray had pulled and shoved and lifted the cart each laborious step of the way, while Piggott Gilliken, a fifty-year-old sailor who had just recently joined the service, seemed to do the work of two men. But they had, after a mile and a half of it, just about reached the end of human endurance, and there was hardly one among them who could drag his own weight forward, let alone pull his share of the load.

Fortunately, at this point, John Dunton came up behind the tired lifesavers. He was mounted on his beach pony and was followed by Dick Brooks and the other survivors on foot. Dunton hitched his pony to the cart, thus partly relieving the lifesavers, and in this manner all of them reached the scene of the wreck shortly after noon.

Jake Mitteager had by then been washed overboard and had managed to swim ashore. But a great number of other survivors yet remained on the doomed craft.

Then, as now, the basic means of contacting a disabled craft from shore and removing the survivors was with the breeches buoy. Accordingly, Keeper Chappell set up his mortar there on the beach and attempted to fire a line aboard the wreck.

The *Metropolis* was comparatively close to shore, and though head on to the beach, she nonetheless presented a good target. On the first shot the line passed over the vessel, and before those on board could reach it, had dropped to leeward and into the sea. The line was quickly hauled back on shore by the lifesavers, coiled again beside the mortar, and this time, benefiting from the experience of the first shot, Keeper Chappell aimed lower and succeeded in landing the line across the port fore-topsail yardarm. Immediately, Second Mate Cozens crawled out on the yardarm and secured the line, but not being familiar with the apparatus he passed it down to his companions on deck in such a manner that it still lay over the spar.

Thus, as willing hands bent to the labor of pulling the heavier line and block aboard, the line dragged over the spar, chafing as it did so, and when at last the block was lifted clear of the water and was almost within arms' reach, it broke under the added strain and fell back into the water.

Enough mistakes had been made already to cause luck to take a dim view of the proceedings. For one thing, the *Metropolis* was so old, rotted, and poorly powered that she had been turned down as a coastal freight hauler, and yet had been chartered to transport a human cargo below the equator; for another, when Captain Ankers discovered that his vessel was leaking he chose to press on, instead of taking the safe course of turning back or trying to make Hampton Roads; then, after she had struck the beach, the only serviceable lifeboat had been permitted to leave the vessel without carrying a line ashore; and finally, Second Mate Cozens had not been properly briefed on how to handle the lifeline, with results which had just been seen.

Now it was the lifesavers' turn. For after that second try had proved ineffective, another ball was placed in the mortar, the line was hauled back and spliced to a spare piece, and all was made ready for another attempt. It was then that Keeper Chappell discovered he had brought along only enough powder for two shots. There was ample extra line; there were two spare shots. But there was no more powder. The station, where extra powder was kept, was more than four miles distant, and both beach ponies had disappeared, one on a journey to Kitty Hawk to deliver a message to the telegraph officer there, and the other in the opposite direction to summon additional lifesavers.

Once again Swepson Brock came to the rescue, this time offering to supply powder from a reserve he kept at his home near by. Again

James Capps ran across the sand beach to the Brock home, returning in a short time with the powder, enough for a number of shots.

Maybe the powder was stronger and quicker than the slow-burning type provided the lifesavers; maybe the line was improperly attached to the ball. But in either case (and there was heated discussion on this score for a long time following the disaster) when Keeper Chappell fired the next shot, the ball parted from the line and sailed high above the *Metropolis* to land with a slight splash far to seaward; and when the last ball was attached to the line, this time with special care being taken with the knots, the same thing happened, and the lifesavers were left with an ample supply of Mr. Brock's powerful powder but with no more shots.

When the result of this fourth and final attempt was observed aboard the *Metropolis,* those still remaining on the wrecked vessel, knowing that she was fast going to pieces, realized at last that they would have to reach shore unaided or not at all. Actually, the strongest had already made the attempt, either in the boat or by swimming, and many of those remaining were without life preservers.

Quartermaster James Poland still had not given up. Grasping a line on deck he instructed those standing there to feed it out to him gradually, and placing the end of the line in his mouth he clamped down hard with his teeth, and dropped into the churning surf. The odds were against James Poland all the way. For a short distance he was able to make some progress; then the current began to carry the slack line up the beach, the large waves broke directly on top of him, and his friends back on the wreck ran out of line. So this last effort was thwarted, and Quartermaster James Poland let go of the line and struck out for shore on his own.

At about this same time the mainmast fell, and the remaining section of the cabin was washed overboard, taking many of the survivors with it. The scenes of horror there on the fast disintegrating ship were graphically described by the fortunate ones who managed to reach shore alive.

Second Mate Cozens jumped overboard just as a heavy sea crashed down on the hulk. He was thrown against a lumber raft which had floated loose from the hold, and suddenly found himself entangled in the ropes which held the raft together. "The seas beat

over me mercilessly," he said later, "but with my jack knife I freed
myself from the ropes and managed to swim clear of the lumber
raft."

Chief Engineer Joseph J. Lovell had gained a spot of comparative
safety in the rigging and remained there until the mast fell. Then
he turned to the man nearest him, asked for a chew of tobacco, and
when he had taken a large bite and "jawed" it a couple of times, he
picked up a cabin door and jumped overboard. Three men followed
him, but all three were swallowed up by the sea. Lovell drifted
northward on his door, being constantly buffeted by the huge
waves, and finally gained shore with the help of others waiting there
a half mile above the scene of the wreck.

Alfred Newton, a passenger, was on deck when the mainmast
fell. "Several men got caught in the falling rigging," he said. "A
poor German implored me, for God's sake, to lift the spar off of
him ... it was on his head. Another man had his leg fast. The side
went down and I was washed overboard. I turned to look, and saw
nothing more of the ship but the sea alive with beings struggling
for their lives. I got within about 20 feet of shore when I gave out,
but thanks to the life-saving men and my God I arrived safely."

Dr. G. D. Green, the vessel's surgeon, said: "The scene was
beyond description, the eye alone can tell it truthfully. There were
not enough of the life-buoys, and many poor souls were vainly
seeking for them. The mainmasts went over and every sea surged
over us. Dozens went in the water, struggling for their lives, and I
saw many a good swimmer killed by the rough debris rolling over
them. Those that could swim were so often carried so far out to
sea by the under current that they perished from exhaustion, having
eaten nothing for 24 hours and being chilled through with the cold
water. I am unable to relate how I saved myself, as I was in-
sensible."

Last man to leave the *Metropolis* was J. H. Alcox of Boston, who
remained on the wreck until the last vestige of the hull disappeared
beneath the waves; then, counselling the struggling swimmers
around him "to trust in God and your life-preservers," he abandoned himself to the struggle for life in the breakers.

This was a busy time for those who had gained the shore. Human
beings, many unconscious and not a few dead, were drifting ashore

with every wave. Keeper Chappell, having donned his water-tight lifesaving suit, made an ineffectual effort to swim to the vessel and carry a line, but had to be dragged out of the surf in turn by his cohorts. Soon afterwards Captain Ankers, fully dressed in a life-saving suit identical with that which the keeper wore, was spotted by Swepson Brock, drifting helplessly. He, Piggott Gilliken, and Chappell waded out beyond the first breakers and dragged the Captain ashore, finding his suit improperly fitted and half full of water and the Captain unconscious.

For a mile or more along that wreck-strewn beach brave men, singly and in groups, waded into the deadly surf at risk of their own lives to rescue people they had never seen before. The seven lifesavers led the way; numerous bystanders—Dunton, Brock, T. J. Poyner, Captain Everton, and John Saunders, to name a few—joined in the brave and humane work; and those of the survivors who were well enough did their part also. Dick Brooks helped rescue his share, but in later accounts it was Jake Mitteager who was most frequently mentioned, for the engineer, seemingly everyplace at once, was reported as having saved or helped to save nearly thirty lives.

It was dark when the last of the survivors reached shore, and great fires of driftwood had been built back from the beach. Doctor Green, hampered by a lack of medical supplies, rendered every aid he could to the injured, most of whom were transported on the backs of their fellow survivors or in a horse cart which arrived later to the near-by homes of Brock and Jones, or to Dunton's club and to the lighthouse at Currituck Beach. But some, nearly nude, numbed from the cold, and without food for a day and a half, remained there on the beach by the driftwood fires all night and were still there the following morning when the first outside relief parties arrived.

In Norfolk, Washington, Philadelphia, and elsewhere about the country the first news of the disaster was a telegraph message from the Signal Service operator at Kitty Hawk, sent out at eight o'clock the night of the wreck: "At 6:50 A.M. steamship *Metropolis* struck on Currituck Beach, three miles south of Currituck Light. 248 persons were on board; 50 swam ashore. No assistance from Life-Saving Stations."

The inaccuracies in this first report are attributed to the fact that the message was delivered to Kitty Hawk by a young boy who had left the scene of the wreck at noon. But as this message flashed around the country many official and independent agencies, and not a few individuals, immediately went into action.

The chief Signal Service operator in Washington ordered a man from the Kitty Hawk station to proceed to Currituck Beach at once and open telegraphic communications; the *Times*, of Philadelphia, dispatched a reporter to the scene; the commandant of the Navy Yard in Norfolk sent four vessels to offer assistance, the Coast Wrecking Company and the Baker Wrecking Company sent two other ships, and the mayor of that city called an open meeting of the citizens to lay plans for the reception of the survivors.

It was less than two and a half months since the *Huron* had wrecked on that same coast, and the newspapers of Norfolk were well prepared to offer complete coverage of the disaster to their readers. The *Journal* assigned two reporters to the wreck story, and the *Landmark* put almost its entire staff on the job.

Back at Currituck Beach the last of the survivors had been dragged from the surf, and young Dick Brooks, thinking no doubt of his wife and child back at Germantown, was determined to get home as soon as possible. Shortly after sunset he left the beach and walked over to the sound landing with N. E. K. Jones, who took him across Currituck Sound to the home of N. N. Hampton. He was given a sumptuous meal at Hampton's and provided with a comfortable bed, and the next morning, early, Hampton rowed him up the shore to Currituck Landing, where at 6 A.M. he took the steamboat *Cygnet* to Norfolk. Thus Dick Brooks was the first survivor of the *Metropolis* to reach the outside world, and needless to say his was a royal reception.

When the first message of the disaster had come through the preceding night, two crack reporters of the *Landmark* had immediately begun a search for a steamboat which they could charter for the trip to Currituck Beach. Being unsuccessful in this they had made arrangements to hire a coach, but at departure time the next morning the coach owner failed to show up. Finally they had learned that the Navy tug *Fortune* was to depart at 10 A.M. and

managed to secure passage on that vessel; but the *Fortune* got stuck
in the mud before it cleared Norfolk Harbor and remained there
most of the day, eventually getting clear at about the time that the
Cygnet, with Dick Brooks aboard, tied up at a wharf near by.

Word that Dick Brooks was on the *Cygnet* had been telegraphed
from the locks at Great Bridge, and another *Landmark* reporter
managed to "kidnap" him immediately upon his arrival, with the
result that that newspaper printed the first exclusive account of the
tragedy, and Dick Brooks became the temporary hero of the day.
He managed, however, to get off a telegram to Thomas Collins in
Philadelphia, asking: "What shall I do with the men who are
saved?" to which Collins replied: "Care for them. I will be on
tomorrow."

That same afternoon—Friday, February 1, the day following the
wreck—Dr. Sawtelle of the Marine Hospital Service, Samuel Shipp,
assistant postmaster for Norfolk, and a reporter had reached Currituck Beach on the steam tug *J. W. Haring*.

The following account was received from the scene of the wreck
by the *Landmark* that afternoon: "The beach is strewn with fragments of the wreck, furniture and drygoods. . . . Only the merest
top of the machinery and a boat-davit can be seen. . . . At Van
Stock's and Church Hill's Landing the scene is most piteous; 146
people without hats or shoes, and in many instances almost naked,
several simply wrapped with blankets, despite efforts of the people
to provide clothing. The various statements of the survivors establish the fact that the Life-Saving Station was thoroughly ineffi-
cient, and while the members of the crew at Number 4 did all they
could to rescue the unfortunate castaways, the means provided by
the government were totally inadequate and useless in the emergency.

"Many who happened to save something in their clothing," the
report continued, "were robbed on the beach or when they were
senseless in the surf. In fact, there seems to have been a general
pillage of the bodies whenever found. Clothing was cut from the
bodies with knives, even the body of Mrs. Harrison had a belt cut
from her waist and her underclothing barbarously torn off. Forty-
four bodies were buried and their graves marked by the life crew

on Friday.... Assistant Postmaster Samuel Shipp found the general mails of the *Metropolis* rifled. Ten mail bags reached the shore with special mail for Brazil and all except one were robbed and the letters cut to pieces to secure the contents. The letters were strewn over the beach in every direction."

By this time Captain Ankers, having been saved by Chappell, Gilliken, and Brock and cared for at the latter's home, was re-covered enough to make an official statement. "At 6:45 A.M. we struck the beach," he said. "At 11 A.M. one of the life-saving men appeared upon the beach waving his hat and promising assistance. At 12 noon men of the station made their appearance, but came poorly prepared to save life. All the assistance they could render was to get the wrecked out of the surf as they came ashore. Had they come properly prepared, nearly everyone could have been saved. From my experience here with life-saving, I consider it a farce."

Currituck County and the Lifesaving Service continued to take a beating in the nation's press. The New York *World*, assuming that the lifesaving station "was closed because of bad weather," called for the dismissal of the lifesavers. The Philadelphia *Times*, quoting from a report made earlier by Sumner I. Kimball, super-intendent of the Lifesaving Service, stated that petty politicians had influenced the selection of lifesavers on the North Carolina coast. Only the Norfolk *Landmark* came to the defense of the people of the area, quoting reports concerning atrocities against the dead to the effect that "some of the survivors themselves were engaged in this nefarious work," in addition to local residents, and that the "good people of Currituck County should not be blamed for the work of a few bad ones."

The *Landmark* called for an investigation by the grand jury of Currituck County and the U. S. Post Office Department, decried the false economy of not providing sufficient lifesaving stations and adequate equipment in the area, and suggested that the pay of the lifesavers ($200 yearly for the keeper, and $20 monthly in season for the surfmen) be raised. The next day the paper joined the Baltimore *Bulletin* in editorializing on the "criminal negligence of the owners" (Benjamin P. Lunt, George D. Lunt, and John Hege-man, Jr., all of New York) in sending such an old, rotten and unseaworthy vessel abroad with human beings. "In England," the papers stated, "they hang men for such crimes or send them to the penal colonies."

The Lunts and Hegeman, whose vessel was insured for $100,000, failed to make an appearance at Norfolk to greet the survivors or to provide for them in any way; but Thomas Collins, having wired ahead giving Foreman P. J. White full authority to spend whatever funds were necessary in caring for them, arrived in Norfolk as soon as possible.

Collins found his laborers well taken care of. The survivors had reached Norfolk Saturday morning on the *Cygnet*. A hot meal was waiting for them at Mr. Amos P. Jordan's Market Dining Saloon, and when they had finished eating they proceeded to the Taab Building on Market Square, where mattresses and bedding (loaned by the Navy and other groups) had been arranged for them. The survivors remained in Norfolk as guests of the city and the populace until Monday afternoon. That they were well cared for is attested to by the following sample menu of meals provided them at Mr. Jordan's Dining Saloon.

BREAKFAST: Beefsteak and onions, boiled and fried potatoes, steamed oysters and fried ham, smoked ham and beef hash, egg bread and fresh bread, and coffee.

DINNER: Ham and cabbage, corn beef and turnips, cream potatoes and sweet potatoes, oyster pie, stuffed baked veal, roast beef, corn bread and loaf bread.

SUPPER: Pork steak and beef steak, liver and bacon, cold ham and cold corned beef, coffee, fresh bread and butter.

The official report shows that eighty-five persons lost their lives in the wreck of the *Metropolis*. One hundred and twenty seven of the surviving laborers, being well stuffed with oysters, steak, and the other delicacies listed above, boarded the Bay Line steamer *Florida* Monday afternoon under the personal supervision of Thomas Collins. They were bound for Baltimore, and thence to Philadelphia, where on the tenth of the month they were scheduled to start again for Brazil on the modern steamship *Richmond*.

But Jake Mitteager and Dick Brooks would have no part of it. Jake left Norfolk for New York earlier that morning with the other members of the crew, still an employee of the Lunt brothers and Hegeman. As for Dick Brooks, he had missed out on the oysters and steak, but at that moment he was probably nearing Philadelphia and a reunion with his wife and child, no doubt convinced finally that unemployment at home in Pennsylvania was preferable to a steady job laying bricks beside the Cataract de Inferno in Brazil.

EACH MAN A HERO

1878-1893

THE TRAGIC LOSS of the *Huron* in 1877 and of the *Metropolis* in 1878 occurred at a time when the Federal Government was in the process of organizing lifesaving facilities along the North Carolina coast. Actually, the first North Carolina lifesaving stations were put in commission in the winter of 1874-1875, but the early efficiency was greatly hampered by the interference of what the Lifesaving Service termed "petty local politicians, whose aim was to subordinate the service to their personal ends."

The service charged, specifically, that these politicians attempted to "pack the stations with their own creatures, without the slightest respect to use or competency." Apparently they were partly successful, for though a number of the men first employed as lifesavers went on to distinguish themselves, there were so many misfits at the outset that it took four or five years to finally weed them out.

By 1879 there were twenty stations already built or planned between Currituck Beach and Cape Fear, and for the most they were manned by efficient, brave, and loyal men. That most of the incompetents had been removed from the service was dramatically illustrated in the record for the next fifteen years; for during the period from 1879 through 1893 some of the most daring rescues in the history of lifesaving were accomplished on the North Carolina coast.

M & E HENDERSON

The lifesavers had a comparatively easy time of it at the wreck of the three-masted schooner *M & E Henderson* at New Inlet, November 30, 1879, but the circumstances of the wreck were strange and mysterious from the very outset; so much so, in fact, that the three survivors of the seven-man crew were later imprisoned on suspicion of mutiny and brought to trial in Baltimore.

The 387-ton *Henderson*, an old vessel hailing from Philadelphia, had sailed from Bull River, South Carolina, with a cargo of phosphate rock destined for Baltimore. She had on board in addition to her captain, two mates and a cook (all white men) and three deckhands (all Spanish mulattoes). The evening of November 29 she was seen north of Cape Hatteras, close in to shore but in no danger. There was a stiff breeze and a sizeable surf, but the night was clear, with the entire area illuminated by a bright Carolina moon; no reason there, certainly, for any concern.

At five o'clock the next morning the early morning beach patrolman from Pea Island returned to his station house, started a fire in the galley stove, roused the cook, and mounted the lookout tower for the purpose of inspecting the coast near by. He soon spotted a lone figure on the beach and supposed at first it was a fisherman; but then he noticed that the man was hatless and seemed to be staggering, so he left the tower, awakened the keeper, and took off down the beach to investigate.

His haste was justified, for he soon came upon the man, a haggard and dripping figure, dark-skinned, and able to mutter little more than incoherent sounds. The lifesaver was able to understand that his vessel was aground, the masts already down, and the captain lost.

The castaway was carried back to the station and put under the care of the cook, while the other lifesavers set out in the direction of the wreck. They had gone little more than a mile south of the station when they discovered, near the north bank of New Inlet, great piles of debris in the surf, and offshore, in the breakers, the last solid remnant of the vessel, rising and falling in the eerie false dawn.

Here they met a party of fishermen who said they had discovered one of the survivors and had taken him to their camp on Jack's Shoal, a small island on the sound side of the inlet. The keeper and two lifesavers borrowed a boat from the fishermen and headed for the island, while the remaining Pea Island crewmen began a systematic search of the debris for survivors, a search which proved completely futile.

The keeper had better luck, finding at Jack's Shoal the man the fishermen had saved, now dry, warmed by hot coffee, and swathed in bedclothes. And on his return still a third survivor was discovered, this one crumpled on the sand near the beach. The man was unconscious and hardly breathing, but they hurried with him to the station, stripped him of his wet clothing, rubbed warmth and life into his limbs, administered restoratives, and soon had him sufficiently recovered to be out of danger.

Thus three of the seven aboard the *Henderson* were rescued, but little information could be gained as to the reason for the vessel's loss or the circumstances surrounding the death of the others; for these three were the deckhands, men of foreign birth, unable to speak or understand more than an occasional word of English.

The fact that they were illiterates and of a different race and color seems to have brought suspicion on them in the first place, especially in the eyes of the *Henderson*'s owners. Had they been white men, with sufficient knowledge of our language to state their case, no matter how implausible it might have been, the affair probably would have ended there, with nothing more than unspoken questions as to why the vessel had stranded under such circumstances and how it happened that only deckhands survived. But they were dark-skinned foreigners, and on warrants sworn out by the owners they were arrested, transported to Baltimore, and clapped in jail there, to wait in solitude for many months before their case finally came to trial.

That is all there was to it; for the trial produced nothing new in the way of information, and the three men were set free at last for want of evidence, leaving us with nothing but a sketchy and provoking outline of one more shipwreck mystery on the North Carolina coast.

A. B. GOODMAN

Few of the early lifesavers had worldly belongings worth the mention: a shack back in the woods behind the dunes, a horse or cow and a hand-made cart; a gun of some sort; maybe a little boat and a piece of net; and probably a few acres of sandy beachland, theirs through inheritance or the right of the squatter.

It was an unusual sight, therefore, and one probably never since duplicated along the outer banks, to see seven men gathered around a rough table in the Creeds Hill Lifesaving Station before dawn, April 4, 1881, all engaged in preparing simple wills, bequeathing their meager belongings to their loved ones. Most could not write, and the literate ones did double duty, drawing up the plain documents and indicating for the others the spot where they should make their faltering X marks.

Why this sudden concern over the disposition of worldly goods? Why were seven strong and healthy men, each at the same time— and all for the first time—putting their affairs in final order? The reason was that they were soon to put to sea in their light, flat-bottomed rowboat and head out to the very center of treacherous Diamond Shoals at the height of a raging offshore wind against which, if it continued in force, they could have no hope of ever again returning to the safety of land. For a vessel was aground on the shoals, and human beings clung to her rigging; human beings whose names and homes and nationalities were unknown to the seven men, but whose lives were their responsibility.

B. B. Dailey was keeper of the Creeds Hill Station, and the first to make out his will; his crewmen were Thomas J. Fulcher, Damon M. Gray, Erasmus H. Rolinson, Benjamin F. Whidbee, Christopher B. Farrow, and John B. Whidbee. They pulled on heavy clothes and dragged their boat down to the beach, leaving the wills behind. Snow fell as they made ready to launch, large wet flakes that came at them horizontally from the northwest, plastering their clothes and faces on the side to windward.

The sea there on the south side of Cape Hatteras was calm enough to permit the launching; but once offshore beyond the protection of the land the wind struck them from one direction, the strong current from the other, twisting their boat about in crazy fashion, exposing them again and again to the full force of the sea's awesome uprising.

The surprising thing was that they ever reached the vessel out there on Diamond Shoals, but they did; they got close enough to read the name, *A. B. Goodman*, on her stern and to see four men clinging to her rigging (a fifth had been washed overboard and drowned during the night.) The lifesavers realized the futility of trying to rescue the four men with wind and sea at their angry worst, and so they anchored near by, yet kept their oars in constant readiness. An hour they waited, and then another. Their action in writing wills seemed fully justified, for without a change of wind they could neither rescue the castaways, nor themselves survive.

Then, as their hope and strength waned, and the full realization of their plight came to them, as the *Goodman* began to go to pieces and their own frail boat began to fill, the wind slackened, died out almost completely, then shifted around and blew in from the sea.

They pulled up underneath the tangled rigging then; but as the first of the four seamen climbed down almost within reach, close enough to realize the smallness and inadequacy of the would-be rescue craft, he was overcome with a sudden fear and scrambled back once more to his perch high above. Keeper Dailey pleaded then, convinced another that this was his only hope, inveigled the man into coming close, reached out and grasped him as he too held back and pulled him bodily into the lifeboat. Another ventured close, was seized by the Keeper and torn from the shrouds; and the other two, perceiving this, followed voluntarily.

The rescued captain was seated in the stern sheets of the little boat, the three crewmen on the thwarts. Oars were manned, the anchor hauled aboard, and at last the eleven of them, almost swamping the lifeboat, began the long pull shoreward. The wind was more favorable, but the sea was as rough as before and the current as strong. Hour after hour they rowed, and finally, late that afternoon they passed inside of the shifting shoals, crossed a gully near the shore, and beached their boat at last on the north side of the cape. The rescued men were taken to the near-by lighthouse where food awaited them; but the lifesavers, not waiting for food, hurried back along the beach the six miles to Creeds Hill, where the would-be beneficiaries of their seven wills were waiting.

DULCIMER

Probably there is no connection between the two, but the fact is that the point east of Hatteras Inlet where the sugar-laden bark *Dulcimer* was lost February 12, 1883, has long been considered by surf fishermen one of the finest spots on the Atlantic coast for catching channel bass.

There was $32,000 worth of sugar in the hold of the *Dulcimer* when she came ashore there, and in those days $32,000 would buy a lot of sugar. But though the eleven crewmen of the 290-ton English vessel were saved, the cargo of sugar, picked up in Brazil and scheduled for use on the tables of greater New York, was left there to sweeten the waters now frequented by great schools of the fighting channel bass.

ANGELA

In these days of large ocean-going steamships equipped with every conceivable device for saving life and preventing disaster, of radar and airplanes and blimps and helicopters, of amphibious ducks and jeeps suitable for rapid beach patrol, the mariner in distress has the odds all in his favor. But in times past, when sailing ships dominated ocean traffic and the lifesaver walked his lonely vigil along trackless sand reefs, before ship-to-shore telephone came into usage, or even wireless for that matter, the odds were strictly on the other side.

During the comparatively short period in which the United States Lifesaving Service was in operation on the North Carolina coast—1875 to 1915—hundreds of ships presumed lost off the banks were listed in the annual reports of that agency with the brief notation: "Lost at sea—never heard from." These listings are so numerous, and the information as to time and exact location so sketchy, that they are purposely omitted from this volume. But some idea of the utter helplessness of the crews of these lost vessels, and of the thin threads of chance on which their lives depended, can be gleaned from the accounts of other shipwrecks from which human beings escaped with their lives.

Imagine, for example, the hopeless feeling of the ten Italian crewmen on board the 373-ton barkentine *Angela* when she sprang a leak at sea while en route from Cartagena, Spain, to Baltimore with a cargo of iron ore. The pumps took care of it for a while, then the open seams widened as the vessel wallowed in the sea, until finally it was obvious to all that the *Angela*, heavily laden as she was with the dead weight of the iron ore, could never reach the port for which she had sailed. It was not a situation peculiar to the ten Italians on the *Angela* in the spring of 1883, for the crewmen of many of those "never heard from" ships must have faced the same thing.

Captain Carlo of the *Angela* could have abandoned his craft there, to drift for hours or days or weeks in his frail yawl until it capsized or a passing vessel came in sight, or he and his crewmen died from starvation or thirst or exposure, or the horrible insanity so frequently resulting from any of the three. Instead, he stayed by the ship, headed westward for the coast, hoping that he could beach the *Angela* before she sank completely. Other mariners have chosen the same course and died for it.

At midnight, March 4, with the sky dark and overcast and only the thunderous crashing of the breakers to announce the proximity of land, the *Angela* struck bottom, grated forward momentarily, and then held fast. Still she rolled, as each succeeding breaker struck her, and jagged holes appeared in her hull where only open seams had been before. Having been at sea for weeks without sight of land, and possessing in any event only a limited knowledge of the conformation of this foreign coastline, Captain Carlo was able to do no more than speculate as to the place where they had stranded. It might be the dreaded shoals off Cape Hatteras, or the bar making out from some shallow inlet, or any of a thousand other places on the coast. Land, the dry, hard-packed, above-water kind, might be a hundred yards distant, or fifteen miles. The only thing of which Captain Carlo could be certain was that his vessel was aground, the breakers were fast pounding her to pieces, and now that he had accomplished what he had set out to do the lives of his crewmen were as much in danger as before.

Captain Carlo had his yawl launched there in the dark, hurriedly boarded it with his nine men, shoved off from the *Angela*, and headed seaward. Shortly a light was seen to the west, a brightly burning red light, the international signal that assistance was at hand. Later, shots were heard and at daybreak the Italian captain was able to better understand the situation. The *Angela* had drifted within three hundred yards of shore, and a group of men—lifesavers from Paul Gamiels Hill Station—had set up their beach apparatus there and fired a line aboard the vessel.

Captain Carlo headed for shore, intending to beach his yawl opposite the men. But the lifesavers waved him back, displaying a large red flag as a warning. Soon the Italian tried again, was waved back a second time; he moved up the beach and headed in a third time but was still warned away. What he did not know was that the tide was then at its highest and the beach at that particular spot was so steep that it was impossible to successfully guide a boat through the surf. Not understanding this, the Captain proceeded out to sea, beyond the farthest line of breakers and headed north. Four miles, five, seven, his crew rowed, until a building came into view and another group of men on the beach opposite. This was Caffeys Inlet Station, and the lifesavers there, having sighted the Italian yawl, had hauled their own lifeboat down to the beach, which sloped much more gradually there than at Paul Gamiels Hill. They launched their lifeboat through the still turbulent surf, shipping a barrel of water or more in the process, but reached the yawl, removed five of the Italians, returned them safely to shore, and then went back for the others.

Thus Captain Carlo and his nine crewmen lived; but the *Angela* and her cargo of iron ore were lost there in the surf a quarter of a mile south of Paul Gamiels Hill Station; and had their luck been different, had Captain Carlo taken to his yawl earlier or a strong gale struck them while heading for shore, or if any one of a dozen different circumstances had arisen, the *Angela* and her crew of ten could easily have been listed with hundreds more, simply as: "Lost at sea—never heard from."

EPHRAIM WILLIAMS

During the first thirty years of operation of the Lifesaving Service on the North Carolina coast a total of twelve Gold Lifesaving Medals, highest such award made by our government, were pre-

sented for exceptional bravery in saving life. Of this number, seven
—more than half—were awarded to the lifesavers from Cape Hatteras and Creeds Hill stations who rescued the crew of the barkentine *Ephraim Williams,* December 22, 1884.

The *Ephraim Williams,* a 491-ton vessel loaded with lumber and
bound from Savannah, Georgia, to her home port of Providence,
Rhode Island, with a crew of nine, ran into a storm off Frying Pan
Shoals December 18 and soon became waterlogged and unmanageable.

On December 21 she appeared southwest of Cape Hatteras and
was kept under surveillance throughout that day by lifesavers who
had assembled near the cape point for service if needed. Late the
following morning the vessel, having temporarily disappeared, was
discovered north of Diamond Shoals and almost opposite Big Kinnakeet, to which point the lifesavers then proceeded with their
boats and apparatus. The sea was described by veteran observers
in the area as the roughest they had ever seen, with huge rollers
crashing first on the outer reef a half mile or so from shore, and
then churning all the way in, across the inner reef, to the beach.
Beyond these farthest breakers, wallowing in the huge waves, the
Ephraim Williams seemed on the verge of sinking, for her decks
were awash, and only her masts showed above water.

The lifesavers paused abreast of the vessel, just watching and
waiting, for there was no sign of life on board, and even if there
had been, it was the opinion of most of them—and of their neighbors
who had assembled there with them—that no boat could live in
such a sea.

Then suddenly, as they watched, a flag fluttered out on the mast
of the stricken ship and was slowly hauled upward as a signal of
distress. Someone was yet alive on the derelict vessel!

Keeper Benjamin B. Dailey of Cape Hatteras Station immediately
called on his men to launch their boat. With no more hesitation
than he himself had shown, they carried out his orders, Keeper
Patrick H. Etheridge (who had recently relieved Dailey as Keeper
of Creeds Hill Station) stepping in to take the place of an absent
crewman. Cumbersome clothing was removed, each man donned a
cork belt, and all loose articles in the boat were carefully lashed
down. The boat was hauled to the water's edge. Six men stepped

inside, took their seats, each grasping his oar in readiness. Others helped push the craft into the shallow water, while Keeper Dailey jumped in over the stern, stood there, his feet braced, the long steering oar held against his side.

The very first strokes took them into the inner line of breakers, over one wave crashing down in front of them, then over another and another and another. Each wave tossed the surfboat high in the air, then dumped it into the trough beyond, concealing the boat from shore, flipping it up and down, up and down, while the life-savers pulled with mighty strokes on their heavy oars and Keeper Dailey bent his weight against the sweep.

They passed those first breakers, somehow, moved seaward through the seething, churning turbulent mass of water between the two reefs, paused momentarily as they came to the outer line, waiting for a break in the huge combers before them. At last the break came, Dailey shouted an order, the oars dug in and the little craft fairly leaped forward into the seething foam. The first wave capped over, broke before them, pushing the bow of the boat high in the air, until she stood almost vertical so that the anxious watchers on shore could see every one of her crew, and the decking beneath their feet, and the ropes lashed down beside them. Then, as suddenly as that wave had struck, it rolled beneath them, the boat levelled off, and before the next one could come down on top of them the lifesavers had passed through the outer breakers.

They rescued the crew of the barkentine one by one, for even out there beyond the breakers the sea was too rough to come in close to the sinking vessel. Already the castaways had decided to abandon ship, had lashed together improvised rafts, and one, even, had been pushed off from beside the ship. Had they followed that course, had the lifesavers not come to their aid, they would have faced those breakers with slight hope of making shore alive. But Dailey and his men not only reached them, but managed, somehow, to return through those same breakers to the safety of shore.

"I do not believe that a greater act of heroism is recorded than that of Dailey and his crew on this momentous occasion," reported the officer sent down later to investigate. "These poor, plain men, dwellers upon the lonely sands of Hatteras, took their lives in their hands, and, at the most imminent risk, crossed the most tumultuous sea that any boat within the memory of living men had ever attempted on that bleak coast, and all for what? That others might live to see homes and friends. The names of Benjamin B. Dailey and his comrades in this magnificent feat should never be forgotten."

Benjamin B. Dailey, Patrick H. Etheridge, Isaac L. Jennett, Thomas Gray, John H. Midgett, Jabez B. Jennett, and Charles Fulcher. Those are the names; each the recipient of the nation's highest award for saving life.

ARIO PARDEE

By land it is about ninety miles from Perth Amboy, New Jersey to Chester, Pennsylvania; under normal conditions a sailing vessel can make it down the Jersey coast and then up the Delaware River to Chester in a day or so. But Captain Henry A. Smith of the 198-ton schooner *Ario Pardee*, attempting this trip with his vessel loaded with cement, ran into one gale after another in late December, 1884, and ten days later found himself stranded on the North Carolina outer banks, several hundred miles south of where he wanted to go.

Captain Smith sailed from Perth Amboy at 7 A.M., December 18, with four crewmen. He passed Sandy Hook at 11 A.M., and when off Long Branch early that afternoon ran into a severe snowstorm. By then the wind was blowing strong from the north so Smith decided to ride it out.

That particular northerly gale lasted 56 long hours and was accompanied by continuous high seas which swept everything movable from the *Pardee*'s decks.

The wind then shifted to the south and increased again to gale force. Smith rode that one out, too.

The next day the wind went around to the northwest. Once again it reached gale proportions, and for the third time Smith rode it out.

Finally, the wind calming down a bit, the *Pardee* ran for the land, reaching the Five Fathom Bank Lightship, located off the entrance to Delaware Bay, which is just where Smith wanted to go in the first place. It had been six days since the *Pardee* left Perth Amboy but she was still only halfway to Chester; and to make matters worse another gale blew up, this one from the west, so Smith hove to.

Twelve hours later, the wind abating once again, Smith tried to beat his way into Delaware Bay, but the wind hauled around to the north and his jib blew away. Again he hove to, and since by this time the *Pardee*'s boat had been stove in and the schooner was shipping a lot of water, he hailed a passing steamer and asked to be taken off. The steamer got a line on board and removed one man, but by then night was coming on, the sea was running very high, so the operation was discontinued.

For the next sixty hours the *Pardee*, with four men on board, rode out the northerly gale. Finally it, too, died out, and Smith set what sails remained and steered a west course for land. At midnight, December 28—ten days after leaving Perth Amboy—a light was sighted, and Smith let go his anchors. At dawn the next morning he found the *Pardee* almost in the breakers at Wash Woods, North Carolina, with lifesavers standing by on shore.

After that it was a simple matter for the lifesavers to come out in their surfboat and remove the four men, and soon afterwards the *Pardee* slipped her chains and stranded on the shore, both vessel and cargo eventually being totally lost. Wash Woods was a long way from Chester, but even so Captain Smith seemed happy enough to be on dry land once again.

NELLIE WADSWORTH

The little schooner *Nellie Wadsworth* was anchored in Hatteras Inlet the morning of December 5, 1885, her captain intending to wait there until the strong southwest gale then in progress was sufficiently diminished to permit passage through the shallow cut to Pamlico Sound. But the *Wadsworth* never reached the sound, and her remains are probably still there, buried in the shoals on the north side of the inlet, while somewhere near by the body of one of her crewmen lies interred in an unmarked sand grave.

Lifesavers from Durants Station saw the *Wadsworth* soon after she came to anchor and kept her under close watch throughout the day. In fact, when she dragged in over the shoals they proceeded to the scene with their surfboat, but finding her riding smoothly in calm water just beyond the beach, and seeing no signal of distress from the vessel, they made no effort to reach her at that time.

At 9 o'clock that night the beach patrolman found the vessel still firmly held by her anchor, but when his relief reached the scene at 1 A.M. on December 6 he discovered that the 61-ton schooner had dragged her anchors and was lying in the very midst of the breakers, broadside to the beach about 120 yards off. The surfman, W. R. Austin, signalled to the castaways, and then returned to his station with all possible speed. By 3 A.M. the lifesavers were again on the scene, this time with their beach apparatus, and although the night was dark and the schooner had no lights, the first shot fired at the vessel landed within easy reach of the crew.

It was cold that December night, the temperature well below the freezing point. In the main rigging, where they had been forced to take refuge, the five men on board the *Wadsworth* were so numbed by the cold and so cramped in their precarious perch, that they could hardly budge the line.

The procedure in effecting a rescue by breeches buoy from ship to shore is basically simple. First, a shot is fired over the ship with a strong, light line attached; then a block is tied to the shore end of this, with a heavier line (known as a whip line) threaded through the block. The lifesavers hold on to both ends of the whip line and when at last the block is drawn aboard the vessel and tied high on a mast it is possible for the lifesavers to send something out to the vessel (a hawser, or breeches buoy, or life car, or cork jackets) or by hauling on the other end of the whip, to bring men or equipment to shore.

In the case of the *Nellie Wadsworth* the crew managed to get the block and whip line on board, but had just finished tying the former to the mast when the mast gave way, breaking off just above the block and crashing into the water. The lifesavers quickly tied several cork jackets to one end of the whip line and sent them off to the ship, but when within a few yards of their destination they became entangled in floating rigging. One of the crewmen, a man named George Richardson, jumped into the icy water and swam toward the life belts. He reached them at length but was so overcome by the cold that he finally lapsed into unconsciousness before succeeding in untangling them from the debris.

Meanwhile, unable to see what had happened but realizing that the line was rendered useless, the lifesavers tied their end to the lone beach pony they had employed in hauling the apparatus to the scene, and by driving the pony high on the beach succeeded in releasing the line. In this manner the belts and debris, with the unconscious form of George Richardson entangled in them, were dragged back through the surf to shore.

With the line thus clear the lifesavers were then able to rescue three more members of the crew in rapid succession, though the fifth and last man lost his grip on the line and had to be hauled from the surf bodily.

Both Richardson and the fifth crewmen were revived there on the bleak sand spit and a start was made for the station, three miles away. But Richardson, thinly clad and suffering acutely from his exertions and exposure, begged to be left alone, then closed his eyes, and again lapsed into unconsciousness. He died soon after.

Each of the lifesavers then took one of the castaways in charge, and the long trek toward the station was resumed, but long before it was reached the four survivors became so exhausted that they were unable to walk, and pleaded piteously to be left there on the beach to sleep and rest; a course which almost certainly would have resulted in their death. The lifesavers pressed onward, however, sometimes dragging the limp sailors, sometimes carrying them on their backs along the cold and storm-flooded beach, and finally, at seven o'clock that morning, the station was reached, fires were built, stimulants prepared, and the four men were provided with dry clothing and hot food.

They remained there for several weeks, too feeble and ill at first to rise from the beds on which they had been placed, but in time they recovered sufficiently to return to their homes, leaving their shipmate, Richardson, and the little schooner *Nellie Wadsworth* to rest forever in the sands of Hatteras Island.

ALLIE R. CHESTER

At dawn, January 20, 1889, the lookout on duty at Cape Hatteras Station made out the dim shape of a vessel aground on the outer edge of Diamond Shoals. A close watch was kept throughout that morning, and since no distress signals were seen it was determined that the vessel was a schooner that had been wrecked in the same vicinity earlier.

Twenty-four hours later, however, the lifesavers still were not convinced that the schooner was an old wreck, and so launched their surfboat and rowed to the scene. They approached within one-half mile, still saw no signs of distress or of life on board, and returned to their station. Meanwhile a passing schooner stopped to investigate, as did a wrecking steamer; but both, drawing the same conclusion as had the lifesavers, proceeded on their way.

Late that second afternoon—a day and a half after the vessel was sighted from the station lookout—the schooner *James E. Kelsey*, passing near the wreck, discovered signs of life on board, and on approaching closer, found three men. The survivors said that the vessel was the schooner *Allie R. Chester*, which had stranded on Diamond Shoals while en route from Charleston to New York with a cargo of phosphate. Five other crewmen had been washed overboard soon after the vessel struck, and the three survivors, suffering acutely from exposure, thirst, and hunger, had wrapped themselves in the voluminous canvas gaff topsail where they had remained until rescued, too weak even to signal for help.

HENRY P. SIMMONS

Robert Lee Garnett was a large man, powerfully built; he was a seafaring man, possessing great fortitude, determination, and faith.

In 1889 Robert Lee Garnett was one of eight men comprising the crew of the three-masted schooner *Henry P. Simmons*, a fine, staunch 650-ton Philadelphia vessel engaged in the coastal trade. In mid-October of that year the *Simmons* took on a cargo of phosphate rock at Charleston, and on October 17 put to sea, her destination Baltimore.

The first five days the voyage produced nothing out of the ordinary for seaman Robert Lee Garnett and his shipmates, and by noon of October 23 the *Simmons* was well past Cape Hatteras and nearing the entrance to Chesapeake Bay. With no prior indication that a storm was in the offing, a strong easterly gale suddenly struck the schooner and by eight o'clock that evening was blowing in gusts of hurricane intensity, building up huge seas through which the vessel plunged, shipping great quantities of water in the process.

At this point the captain ordered his men to take in the already close-reefed mainsail, but so strong was the wind and so furious the action of the sea that they were unable to comply, and the captain and his crew were forced to lash the helm and take to the rigging. This left the *Simmons* almost completely at the mercy of the wind and waves, and the two ganged up on her in royal fashion, finally driving the vessel on shore at 10:30 that night on the lower end of Pebble Shoals, right at the boundary line between the states of Virginia and North Carolina.

She bilged and filled with water almost immediately, the top of her cabin was swept away by one of the first breakers which struck her, and the *Simmons* soon settled in the sands until her hull was completely submerged, and nothing but the three masts was left above water.

A torrential rain, which continued throughout most of the night, limited visibility to only a few yards, so that the eight men clinging to the rigging were unable to determine even their general location; all they could do was to hold on there, shielding their bodies as best they could from the wind and the cold, driving rain.

Four and a half hours after they struck the shoal—at 3 A.M., October 24—the steward, numbed, exhausted, and unable to hold on any longer, fell from his perch on the mast and was lost in the churning surf below.

The officer who investigated the disaster later gave this account of the situation confronting the seven men still alive at dawn: "The scene from the rigging of the wreck was a wild and terrifying one. The wind still raged and the waves broke into surf as far offshore as the eye could see through the pelting rain and spoon drift, while to the leeward lay the low sand hills, which ever and anon came into sight and were then hidden by the towering billows that madly chased one another shoreward, and were there scattered with thunderous roar into a smother of foam and spray upon the desolate beach."

The castaways found themselves more than a thousand yards from shore, and when lifesavers appeared on the beach that morning and attempted to fire a line aboard the wreck, the shot covered little more than half the distance. But the fact that the lifesavers were there, and knew of their plight, was at least encouraging.

The seven men, however, were in need of something more tangible than encouragement. Even as the lifesavers were in the process of setting up their gear the second mate was swept from the rigging to certain death, and soon after the unsuccessful shot was fired in their direction a third man met the same fate. This left only five crewmen still alive on what remained of the "fine, staunch" three-master *Henry P. Simmons;* and long before that day was ended yet another fell from the mast, to disappear forever.

That night was the second Robert Lee Garnett spent in the rigging, soaked to the skin, without adequate clothing to protect his body from the winter cold, ravaged by the pangs of hunger, able to gain sustenance only from what rain water he could catch in his free hand and the hollow of his hat.

At dawn the next day—October 25—the lifesavers attempted to launch a surfboat from the beach but were thrown back. As a last resort they dispatched a telegraph message to Norfolk, asking for the assistance of a tug; and a tug did start from Hampton Roads, got as far as Cape Henry, but was thwarted by the terrific sea off-shore and returned to her berth.

At noon that day another of the castaways fell from the rigging of the doomed vessel, leaving only three men alive.

Driftwood fires were lighted on the beach that night, the third the men had spent in the rigging, and at dawn the following day, October 26, the three survivors, including Robert Lee Garnett, were still there, still clinging to what remained of the masts and rigging. Three attempts were made that day to launch a surfboat from the beach, lifesavers from four different stations on the Virginia and North Carolina coast taking part, but each time the would-be rescuers were tossed back on the beach.

That afternoon another of the survivors fell from his perilous perch and was drowned, leaving only two men alive; and still later one of these lost his grip and disappeared in the turbulent sea. Of the eight men who had shipped on board the *Simmons* only Robert Lee Garnett remained alive.

The surfside watch was increased that night; the driftwood fires burned brighter than ever. From shore, in the darkness, it was im-

possible to see the tall thin masts a half mile out there on the shoal
or to tell whether the single man out there was still alive. But he
had been there at dusk, a forlorn and helpless being, still alive; and
for the lifesavers that was reason enough to keep the fires burning
brightly.

Before dawn the next morning the wind died down, shifted to
the westward, breaking the force of the waves which had pounded
across Pebble Shoals for four successive nights. In the early morning darkness a boat was finally launched, lifesavers under command
of veteran Keeper Malachi Corbel rowed the thousand yards to
the sunken ship, waited there until the first light of day appeared
in the sky, then pulled up close beside the wreck.

Miraculously, Garnett was still there, still alive, wrapped in the
tattered remnants of a sail. He climbed down stiffly from the rigging, made his way slowly toward them, dropped into the boat,
and was quickly returned to shore. Eighty hours he had clung to
the rigging, experiencing pain and hunger and thirst and despair
which had proved fatal to his seven companions—eighty hours
through which few other men could have lived. But Robert Lee
Garnett, remember, was a man of powerful physical build—a man
of great fortitude, determination, and faith.

THE OCTOBER STORM OF 1889

The terrible storm of October 23, 1889, in which Robert Lee
Garnett's seven shipmates lost their lives, continued its destructive
work all along the North Carolina coast.

At Nags Head, thirty-five miles to the south, the beach patrol
from Kill Devil Hills Station discovered the upside-down hull of
a vessel in the breakers the next morning. There was no sign of
life, for each wave swept over the upturned hull, but a body was
found on the beach soon after, and a second one was recovered
after the storm had subsided. The vessel was the *Francis E. Waters*,
a 147-ton schooner hailing from Baltimore, which had left Georgetown, South Carolina, a few days previous with a cargo of lumber
destined for Philadelphia and a crew of six men.

At approximately this same time and some twenty-five miles
farther south, the three-masted schooner *Annie E. Blackman* of

Somers Point, New Jersey, bound from Philadelphia to Jacksonville with a cargo of coal, was thrown on her beam ends three miles
off New Inlet. The vessel sank, and the seven crewmen were tossed
into the sea, six of them losing their lives. The seventh, the captain,
had donned a cork life jacket the day before and so floated toward
shore, eventually reaching New Inlet. It was dark when the captain
crawled up on the beach and making his way inland he soon discovered a telegraph pole. Tying himself to the pole with a line
which he happened to have in his pocket he walked round and
round, like a horse tethered to a stake, in order that he might keep
up his circulation. He was still walking when he was found the next
morning by lifesavers.

Hardly had the captain of the *Blackman* been carried back to the
lifesaving station, however, when another vessel was discovered on
the beach in the same vicinity. This was the 437-ton schooner
Lizzie S. Haynes, and even as the lifesavers reached the scene the
three masts broke off near the vessel's deck and, with a crash that
was audible above the roar of the wind, fell into the sea.

There had been seven men aboard the *Haynes* when she stranded.
Now, only fifteen minutes later, only two could be seen from shore.
A line was quickly fired on board and the two men—the captain
and steward—had pulled most of it out to the vessel when it suddenly caught in floating debris and broke in two. Another line was
fired, and yet another, and not until four o'clock that afternoon
was the breeches buoy finally put in operation.

There were delays, even then, for a third man remained alive on
the *Haynes*. This was the mate of the vessel, who had been injured
when the mast fell and by this time was delirious; he had violently
resisted all efforts by the captain and steward to place him in the
breeches buoy and with the approach of darkness was at last left
there while the other two were drawn to safety.

At ebb tide, later that night, a lifesaver went out in the breeches
buoy and found the body of the mate yet warm. The body was
quickly drawn ashore, stimulants were administered, and the lifesavers tried every way they knew to revive him, but to no avail.
And so the mate of the *Haynes* joined four other of his companions
in death, bringing the toll for that disastrous storm to twenty-four
lives lost. Yet the carnage was not ended, for still another vessel

came ashore that afternoon, the 250-ton schooner *Busiris*, of St. John, New Brunswick, which stranded and was lost two hundred yards north of Poyners Hill Station, the fifth craft destroyed by that one storm within an area extending for less than a hundred miles along the Carolina coast.

JOSEPH H. NEFF

One of the few instances on record of the keeper of a lifesaving station on this coast being discharged for negligence resulted, ironically, from the wreck of a tiny schooner of only ten tons burden, carrying a cargo valued at less than three hundred dollars, and with a total crew of but two men.

This was the schooner *Joseph H. Neff* of Wilmington, employed in hauling small cargoes of freight in the vicinity of that city, and en route at the time of her loss from Lockwoods Folly to the Cape Fear River with a load of tar, wood, and turpentine.

She was discovered anchored just beyond the breakers and in distress two and a half miles southwest of the Oak Island Station at 4 A.M., December 17, 1890, by a surfman on patrol who hastened back to his station with the news.

Keeper Savage, who had but recently taken over in that capacity, decided it would be a good idea to brew up a pot of coffee before departing for the wreck, thus occasioning the first of several needless delays. And when finally he and his crew started for the scene they went empty-handed, leaving both their surfboat and beach apparatus behind.

Further, when the scene of the wreck was reached and several barrels were found floating in the surf, the Keeper ordered his men to drag these out of the water and place them above the high water mark before going on to the wrecked vessel.

When the lifesavers finally arrived at the scene of the wreck, two men were hanging to the partly submerged craft. A small skiff belonging to the *Neff* had drifted ashore near by, and the Keeper had this dragged to the scene, but it was then discovered that the skiff had no oars, so one surfman was left on the beach while the remaining members of the Oak Island crew returned the two and a half miles to the station for the surfboat.

Meanwhile the craft went to pieces in the surf, and the lone lifesaver managed to drag both men to the beach, where one was found to be dead. By the time Keeper Savage returned the whole business had come to an end; and so, it developed, had his brief position as keeper.

STRATHAIRLY

One of the most disastrous wrecks in the history of Hatteras Island was that of the 1,236-ton schooner-rigged screw steamer *Strathairly*, which stranded a mile and a quarter south of Chicamacomico Station, March 24, 1891.

The *Strathairly* hailed from Newcastle, England, and was en route from Santiago, Cuba, to Baltimore with a cargo of iron ore and twenty-six in her crew when she encountered a fog north of Hatteras and stranded a little after 4:30 that morning. She immediately sounded distress signals on her steam whistle, and these were soon answered by the red glare from a Coston light, burned by the Chicamacomico beach patrolman, who then hurried back to his station for help.

One hour after the steamer first struck, the crew of Chicamacomico Station had arrived on the scene, and though the wrecked vessel was not visible through the fog an experimental shot was fired in her direction, falling far short of the target. Within two hours of the time she stranded the crews of two other stations and the district superintendent of the Lifesaving Service, as well as a large number of people from the village of Chicamacomico, had assembled on the beach opposite the stranded vessel.

For something like four hours that morning—until shortly after ten o'clock—the people there on the beach were helpless to render aid to the shipwrecked crew. Because of the exceptionally rough sea, boat service was considered out of the question; because of the dense fog the *Strathairly* could not be seen, and only the periodic sounding of her whistle and the sound of human voices were evidence that there really was a vessel aground out there.

The fog finally lifted a little after 10 A.M., and for the first time the lifesavers and Chicamacomico citizens could see the *Strathairly*. Her mainmast had long since fallen; all of her boats had been dashed to pieces in the surf; the vessel itself had broken completely in two; and twenty-three of the twenty-six men who had comprised her crew were huddled together in the bow part, the other three —the captain, first mate and chief engineer—having already drowned when the mast fell.

As soon as the fog lifted the Lyle gun was fired, but the shot fell short, for the *Strathairly* was then a quarter of a mile from shore. The second shot fell short also. The third, with a smaller line attached, landed on the forecastle, where the survivors began to haul it aboard, only to have it break when the gear was within a few feet of the vessel.

Still another shot was fired, this one striking the forward rail. Again the men pulled on it, and again the line broke. The lifesavers tried again, and then again, and again, and again, firing as fast as the lines could be hauled ashore and set up. For five full hours it went on, shot after shot after shot, some falling short of the target, others breaking as the handful of survivors still strong enough attempted to haul them on board. There were, actually, only three of the twenty-three men at this time who were not so overcome with the results of exposure or injuries as to prevent their helping in these activities.

A little after three o'clock that afternoon one of the seamen, Albert Smith, put on a life belt and jumped overboard. Those gathered on the beach finally pulled him from the surf unconscious and nearly dead. He was taken to a near-by residence and revived, the first person saved from the stranded ship. Three others already were dead; the remaining nineteen were still on board the wreck.

Again the lifesavers attempted to fire a line on board; again it broke. Darkness was approaching by then, the tide was once more coming in, and after a full day of steady attempts at rescue they were no nearer than before in accomplishing their purpose.

At twenty minutes before five that afternoon—exactly twelve hours after the vessel first struck—the remaining crewmen, having been provided with life belts, jumped one by one into the boiling, writhing surf, and the current carried them far to the south.

The lifesavers and villagers, aware of the drift to the south, were deployed in that direction for more than a mile. By dark that night sixteen of the crewmen had been dragged from the water. Of this number ten were dead when they reached the shore. Thus, that night, most of the *Strathairly* crewmen were sheltered in the Chicamacomico Station house, seven of them, the living ones, bedded down in the bunks usually occupied by the surfmen, while ten others, all dead, were laid out on the floor. The bodies of the other nine were never recovered.

NOT THE ST. CATHARIS

They say you can still see the bloodstains on the floor of the old Chicamacomico Station (now used as a boathouse) for many of the bodies recovered from the surf following the wreck of the *Strathairly* were badly cut and bruised from striking pieces of wreckage. Some will tell you that the bloodstains are from the ninety crewmen reported lost on a vessel called *St. Catharis*, and there is written evidence in sources usually considered reliable to back up such a statement.

The purpose of this book is to present factual narratives of the more outstanding shipwrecks which have occurred on the coast of North Carolina; certainly a wreck at Chicamacomico in 1891 resulting in ninety deaths would merit inclusion here. Yet the plain facts are: there was no such wreck; and the whole story is the result of a series of coincidences, misrepresentations, and misunderstandings. So that the matter may once and for all be set straight, the facts are published here.

In 1892 the following notation was included in a listing of ship losses for the year 1891: "British ship *St. Catharis* wrecked off Caroline Islands, April 16."

In more recent years the *World Almanac and Book of Facts*, in a listing of "Marine Disasters," included: "April 16 (1891) British ship *St. Catharis* wrecked off Carolina Island." *

* This writer corresponded with the editors of the *World Almanac* in connection with their listing of the *St. Catharis* (as well as their erroneous listing of the *Kensington-Templar* affair in 1871) finally asking the specific question: "Where is the Carolina Island you mention?"

The following answer was received (from A. E. Lenktis, who compiles their listing of Marine Disasters) under date of June 8, 1951:

"As to the Carolina-Caroline controversy, this will be changed to Caroline in the new listing. Not even the Coast Guard would hazard a guess on the location of Carolina Island. Since I found both names, it was not too hard to pick the more tangible location. Thank you for bringing it to my attention."

The deduction here is fairly obvious. Somewhere along the line the letter "e" on the end of "Caroline" seems to have been supplanted by an "a", probably through typographical error. This would not, however, account for the widespread story that the *St. Catharis* was wrecked at the exact point of Chicamacomico and that ninety of the seamen are buried there. Apparently the origin of this is the following published statement: "Close by the station (Chicamacomico) is the burial mound of British seamen drowned in the wreck of the *St. Catharis*, Apr. 16, 1891, in which 90 lives were lost." (*North Carolina, A Guide To The Old North State*, Federal Writers' Project, WPA, Chapel Hill, 1939, page 300.)

This statement has been cited as the authentic basis for more recent reprints of the *St. Catharis* story. But there is no mention of such a wreck in the official reports of the United States Lifesaving Service; neither can any mention of it be found in contemporary newspapers or periodicals. And though there are people living on the outer banks who say they remember their parents telling about the terrible wreck of the *St. Catharis*, two men, both living in the area at the time of the wreck and both still active and respected citizens, say that there was no such wreck there.

Looking over the above facts the probable reason for the unfounded stories of the wreck of the *St. Catharis* at Chicamacomico is easily understood:

Within a month's time two large ships are lost.

Both are British ships.

One (*St. Catharis*) is lost off the Caroline Islands in the Pacific.

The other (*Strathairly*) is lost on one of the islands off the North Carolina coast.

The loss of one (*St. Catharis*) is mentioned in listings of great ship losses at that time.

The listing is reprinted many years later, and the letter "e" on the end of the word "Caroline" is somehow changed to "a".

A WPA writer, coming across this mention of loss "Off Carolina Island" checks with local residents of the islands off the Carolina coast. They remember hearing of a large vessel wrecked in the spring of 1891. Yes, it was a British craft. Yes, a number of people were drowned. Yes, the name was something like *St. Catharis*.

Thus, through a combination of typographical errors, similarity in circumstances and dates, and reliance on stories handed down from deceased ancestors, people begin to accept as fact the published statements that the British ship *St. Catharis* was wrecked at Chicamacomico, April 16, 1891; that ninety lives were lost; that the bodies were laid out on the floor of the old Chicamacomico Lifesaving Station until the floor was covered with blood; and that the unmarked graves of the ninety drowned sailors are still there in the sand. Yet, in reality, the *St. Catharis* was wrecked thousands of miles from Chicamacomico, and the circumstances attributed to the *St. Catharis* were those surrounding the loss of the steamer *Strathairly*, March 24, 1891, as recounted in this chapter from official records.

NATHAN ESTERBROOK, JR.

Frequently delay and loss of life at the scene of a coastal shipwreck are caused by failure to make proper use of the lifesaving apparatus. The wreck of the *Nathan Esterbrook, Jr.* February 20, 1893, is a good example.

The 713-ton three-master was beating her way southward along the North Carolina coast with $33,000 worth of guano in her hold. The night of the nineteenth the wind was from the southwest, strong; the sky was clear, the water rough. At 12:40 A.M. on the twentieth the *Esterbrook* struck the outer bar about two and a half miles north of the Little Kinnakeet Station and was discovered twenty minutes later by Surfman L. B. Gray. Patrolling on horseback, Gray dismounted when he first spotted the craft about 1,000 feet offshore and immediately tried to light a red Coston signal to let the people aboard the wreck know that help was at hand. But the signal, and the two spares he carried with him, failed to burn, so he mounted hurriedly, whipped his horse to a gallop, and in the eerie darkness pounded along the hard-packed beach to the station.

Picture the confusion at Little Kinnakeet Station at 1:30 in the morning of February 20, 1893. Even as the sleepy-eyed men pulled on their heavy waterproof jackets and trousers and hip boots, the voice of Keeper E. O. Hooper could be heard shouting orders:

two men were to hitch Gray's horse to a cart; a third, to load the cart with medical supplies, blankets, life belts, extra shot, and powder; the others, to wheel out the heavy beach apparatus.

Meanwhile Hooper telephoned the nearest stations—Gull Shoal to the north and Big Kinnakeet to the south—for assistance, then he mounted the lookout tower and burned a red Coston flare in the hope that those aboard the wreck would know that help was on the way.

Hooper then started off in the cart, while the six members of his crew—one was at home, ill—hitched on to the beach apparatus wagon like a six-mule team and set off behind him. Long before they reached the wreck, however, the Big Kinnakeet crew, with a pair of government horses, overtook the six men. They all arrived at the scene at about 3 A.M., and the Lyle gun was immediately brought into requisition. It was carefully sighted by the lights of the schooner, which were still burning, and a moment later a friendly shot went whizzing through the air toward its mark.

Despite the distance and the wind, Hooper had aimed true. But the shot, striking the heavy forestay, glanced off, carrying the attached line into the water and out of reach of those aboard the ship.

The line was hauled in and a second shot attempted, this one falling short. But the third shot, with a lighter line attached and a heavier charge of powder in the gun, landed in an excellent position across the ship, midway between the foremast and mainmast.

Captain George L. Kelsey of the *Esterbrook* and his eight crew members eagerly grasped the line, hauling it aboard until they could reach the block sent out by the men on the beach. This they attached to the mast and signalled by means of a lantern to send out the breeches buoy.

Everything seemed to be proceeding in shipshape fashion up to this point. But Kelsey, no doubt handling lifesaving apparatus of this kind for the first time, had caused the block to be tied too low on the mast, with results which later proved fatal.

When the breeches buoy reached the ship, the second mate, Charles Clafford, was assisted into the contraption, slipped his legs into the two open holes provided for them, and his mates gave the signal to haul away. It was Clafford's last ocean voyage.

Just as the lifesaving crew began pulling on the line to haul Clafford ashore, the wreck shifted, the low hanging line slackened, and for the next five minutes Second Mate Charles Clafford, instead of travelling high above the water in a comfortable perch in the breeches buoy, was dragged through the rough surf. Somewhere between ship and shore he swallowed a lot of water; somewhere else he was struck by floating debris and injured internally. And when his unconscious form was finally dragged out on the beach there was not a man among the lifesavers assembled there who gave him a chance of living.

Nonetheless, an effort was made to resuscitate him, and surprisingly enough he was soon breathing normally and was able to provide information as to the number of men remaining aboard the wreck, the condition of the ship, and the manner in which the hawser was tied.

Hooper was convinced, when he heard Clafford's story, that it would be disastrous to attempt to land others in the breeches buoy, so, despite the rough surf, he ordered the surfboat launched, took the steering oar himself, and attempted to reach the ship. But the high wind, furious surf, and exceptionally strong longshore current proved too much for the small boat, and Hooper eventually turned about and landed on the beach again.

It was daylight when Hooper and his men again assembled opposite the wreck. The crew of the stricken vessel could be seen clearly by this time, and the lifesavers signalled them to change the block and lines to the lee bow, where there could be sufficient clearance. Meanwhile, Clafford was returned to the station, and the crew members were sent back for the life car, a fat, cigar-shaped contraption, made of metal, watertight, and large enough to hold four men. When this piece of apparatus eventually arrived at the scene it was slung on the hawser in place of the breeches buoy and sent out to the *Esterbrook*.

Two men came ashore in the life car on the first trip, two more on the second, and so on until four trips had been made and the eight men remaining had been removed to safety. It sounds easy, written that way, but actually so many perplexities were encountered in the operation that it was well into the afternoon before the last man had arrived safely on the beach.

At 3 P.M.—fourteen hours after the ship came ashore, and twelve hours after lifesaving operations were begun—the three crews of surfmen left the scene, taking the rescued men from the *Esterbrook* to the Little Kinnakeet Station. Later that night Second Mate Clafford, turning weaker as each hour passed, finally succumbed and was buried near the station the following day.

In the annals of the Lifesaving Service—and in the record of the Graveyard of the Atlantic—the wreck of the *Nathan Esterbrook, Jr.* was routine. But it points up the value of the lifesaving stations along the coast at that time and demonstrates the versatility of the men and their equipment. Telephonic communications were used to assemble additional men at the scene; the breeches buoy, once the only means of rescue, was found inadequate, and the newer life car was successfully substituted in its place. You can find the record of the *Esterbrook* today in the lifesaving report for 1893: eight lives saved; one life lost; $33,000 worth of guano given up to the sea; a $20,000 schooner totally wrecked; and twenty-three tired lifesavers and three government horses on double rations for one meal to compensate for energy expended.

THE LONG DAY OF DUNBAR DAVIS

1893

IT WAS ALMOST like a vacation with pay for Dunbar Davis and his family during those summer months of 1893. They had free run of the big house the government had built four years earlier on the wide sandy beach near old Fort Caswell. They could bathe in the surf if they chose, or swim in the still waters at the mouth of the river just back of the house, or visit the old fort and look for Civil War souvenirs, or fish, or crab, or sail, or just loll in the sun and take it easy.

The cool summer breezes coming in off the ocean made it more pleasant there than at Southport, two miles to the north, or at Wilmington, twenty miles up the Cape Fear River. If they got lonesome, Dunbar and his wife and five children could visit with the keeper of the near-by lighthouse and his family, or have friends over from the mainland, or even get around to see some folks in Southport on Saturday evenings when they went for supplies.

The only thing was, sometimes they wished they could take off for longer—the way they used to when Dunbar was sailing his charter sloop along the coast—but now he had to stay on the island for the full four months and keep a watch out for ships in distress; for Dunbar Davis was keeper of the Oak Island Lifesaving Station,

133

and his seven-man crew was relieved of duty from the end of April until September first.

Some folks had said that it was a waste of money putting a life-saving station there on the west side of the entrance to the river when there was one already at Smiths Island on the other side. Dunbar did not think so, for he had served earlier as keeper of that other station, and he knew that Keeper Watts, who had relieved him there, had all he could do patrolling the long open beach to the north and east of Cape Fear and keeping a lookout for trouble on Frying Pan Shoals. Watts had no time to do anything about ship-wrecks to the west—at Lockwoods Folly, or Shallotte Inlet, or Tubbs Inlet, or down along the South Carolina border. And there were times, too, when more than one crew was needed to assist the wrecked vessels and their crews, for Cape Fear and Frying Pan Shoals had taken a huge toll of shipping in times past and there was no prospect of a let-up.

Had Dunbar Davis been a student of history he could have borne out this argument with a quotation from the diary of the colonizing expedition sent out by Sir Walter Raleigh in 1585, the group which went on north to Roanoke Island and established there the first English settlement in America. The first mention of the North Carolina coast in that diary was a portent of things to come: "The 23rd (of June)," the account stated, "we were in great danger of a wreck on a breach called the Cape of Fear."

Three hundred and eight years had passed, and in 1893 there was still that same danger for any mariner sailing past Cape Fear. But visitors that summer would have wondered about all the talk of danger, for there had been no shipwrecks there in 1893, no lives lost, not even so much as a skiff overturned in the river so far as the official record showed. And late in August, as Dunbar Davis and his family prepared for the return of the full station crew to Oak Island, it still had the appearance of a vacation spot—un-crowded, cool, and quiet.

In retrospect, that most certainly would have seemed an ominous quiet. For disaster, full-fledged, unpredictable, wanton disaster, struck the Carolina coast that last week in August, 1893.

In the Cape Verde Islands, two thousand miles east of the Caribbean, a storm blew up on August 17. It gained in intensity as it headed westward, became a lusty, full-grown hurricane on August 18, picked up speed and force August 19, 20, 21, and 22, pushed north of Haiti on August 23 and 24, and passed between Cuba and Bermuda on August 25 and 26. It followed a gentle arc as it sped westward, moving faster than do most hurricanes, and apparently knowing all along, so gently did it curve, just where it was headed.

Its destination was the city of Charleston, South Carolina, and it struck there in the heat of the late summer at a time when vacationists had flocked to the near-by beaches, inflicting property damage estimated at ten million dollars and taking hundreds of lives.

So sudden and unexpected was the hurricane's appearance that most ships in the vicinity had no warning of its presence until the terrific winds actually struck.

The 335-ton schooner *Roger Moore* had passed by Oak Island shortly before, en route from Wilmington to Ponce, Puerto Rico, with a cargo of lumber. She was caught on the fringe of the storm, and before it was over lost part of her sails and deck cargo, and one of her eight crewmen was washed overboard. But the *Roger Moore* was lucky.

The schooner *Mary J. Cook*, 436 tons, was bound from Port Royal, South Carolina, to Boston with a cargo of lumber and carried one passenger in addition to her crew of seven; the schooner *L. A. Burnham*, 389 tons, bound from Savannah to Portland, Maine, carried lumber and a crew of seven; the schooner *A. R. Weeks*, 445 tons, from Satilla Bluffs, Georgia, to Elizabethport, New Jersey, carried lumber and a crew of eight; the schooner *George W. Fenimore*, 673 tons, from Brunswick, Georgia, to Philadelphia, had lumber and a crew of eight; the schooner *Oliver H. Booth*, 247 tons, from Brunswick to Washington, D. C., had lumber and a crew of six; the schooner *Gertie M. Rickerson*, 219 tons, from New York to Caibarién, Cuba, had a general cargo and a crew of seven; the schooner *John S. Case*, 198 tons, from Jonesport, Maine, to Puerto Plata, Santo Domingo, had lumber and a crew of six; and the schooner *Lizzie May*, 201 tons, was en route from New York to Fernandina, Florida, in ballast with a crew of six.

None of these eight ships was ever seen again; no trace of them or their crews was ever found. They just disappeared, swallowed up in the center of the hurricane, battered to pieces, turned over, sunk in the middle of nowhere. Fifty-five crewmen, one passenger, and 2,808 tons of shipping lost, before the hurricane even reached the coast. *Mary J. Cook—L. A. Burnham—A. R. Weeks—George W. Fenimore—Oliver H. Booth—Gertie M. Rickerson—John S. Case—Lizzie May*. Eight names, eight ships; no details; just dull, lifeless statistics, typical of countless similar losses in other hurricanes which have struck the Carolina coast.

The Cape Fear area, though escaping the direct fury of that August hurricane of 1893, got its share of winds, tides, and trouble, and the summer vacation ended a week early for Dunbar Davis and his family at the Oak Island Lifesaving Station.

At midnight on August 27 the three-masted schooner *Three Sisters*, of Philadelphia, fully loaded with pine lumber she had picked up in Savannah, was off Frying Pan Shoals Lightship. By 1 A.M. of August 28 the wind had reached hurricane force, and within an hour the sails and mizzenmast had been lost, and both master and mate washed overboard and drowned. This left the cook in charge of the five-man crew, and though the cook may have been a good man with a skillet of eggs and a pot of coffee, he was strictly out of his element when it came to handling a 286-ton schooner, especially one without mizzenmast or sails.

Throughout that day the vessel drifted, wallowing in the rough seas, shipping large quantities of water, and slowly being driven toward the Carolina coast. She was spotted at two o'clock that afternoon from the watchtower of Cape Fear Station by Keeper J. L. Watts and shortly afterwards by Dunbar Davis at Oak Island. The apparent intention of the cook was to run her ashore, but Watts and Davis knew that such action in the tremendous seas then breaking northeast of the cape would be fatal to both vessel and crew, and Watts managed to signal the schooner to anchor there and await assistance.

That was the easiest part for the lifesavers. The real job would be in providing the assistance that had been promised.

The schooner, by then, was so close to shore opposite Smiths Island that Davis could see only her masts above the beach; so he

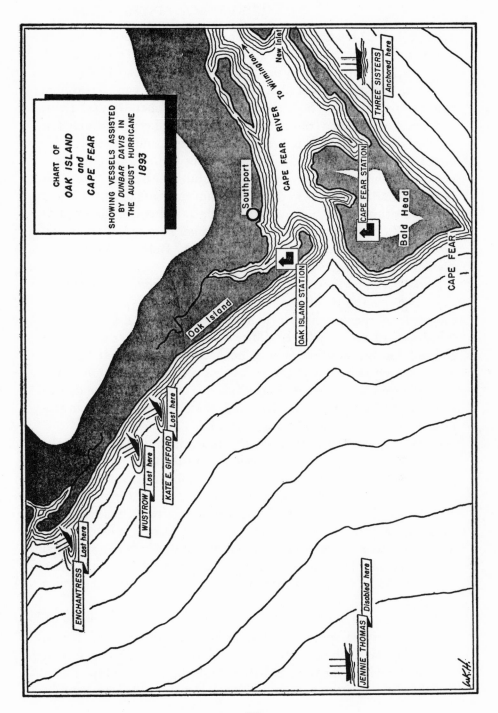

CHART OF
OAK ISLAND
and
CAPE FEAR

SHOWING VESSELS ASSISTED
BY DUNBAR DAVIS IN
THE AUGUST HURRICANE
1893

New Inlet

CAPE FEAR RIVER TO Wilmington

Southport

THREE SISTERS Anchored here

CAPE FEAR STATION

Bald Head

OAK ISLAND STATION

Oak Island

CAPE FEAR

WUSTROW Lost here

KATE E. GIFFORD Lost here

ENCHANTRESS Lost here

JENNIE THOMAS Disabled here

got out a small boat, kissed his wife goodbye, and poled out into the mouth of the river in an attempt to cross over to the island. Meanwhile, Watts had returned to the Cape Fear Lighthouse, where he had borrowed a boat and hired a young man to help him row the five miles to Southport. En route he met Dunbar Davis and quickly outlined the situation. The two keepers decided it would be best for Davis to return to his station and make his surfboat ready for sea duty, while Watts went on to Southport for a crew of volunteers. Both were successful in carrying out their respective tasks and at 8:30 that night Dunbar Davis left Oak Island again, this time in his surfboat with Keeper Watts and nine volunteers: J. E. Price, Samuel Brinkman, Samuel Newton, Tommy St. George, Wesley Smith, Crawford Watts, Robert Weeks, Joe Newton, and Moses Stepney.

It took them better than an hour to cross the narrow river mouth, so strong was the wind and tide, and two more to proceed along the back of the beach to a point opposite the place where the schooner had been anchored. They found her there, riding easily and holding her position. The wind had died down, but the surf was as strong as ever, and the vessel was too far from shore to use the Lyle gun and breeches buoy. So, the two keepers decided to leave Davis' boat and walk back along the beach to Cape Fear Station, where Watts' surfboat was anchored.

They reached the station about 1 A.M., eleven hours after the schooner was first sighted and waited until daylight to attempt to take the surfboat out through the channel into the open sea.

Before dawn the eleven men shoved off, rounded the cape without accident, and reached the schooner soon after sunrise. Despite the heavy seas, it was a comparatively simple matter to take off the five crewmen and return with them to Southport where medical attention could be had. As for the *Three Sisters*, she was left there at anchor, to be towed into the harbor for repairs when the storm subsided.

So far, except for loss of sleep, tired muscles, and a thorough soaking from the spray, Dunbar Davis had not fared so badly, though he was anxious to get back to Oak Island, dig into one of his wife's midday dinners, and then catch up on his sleep. But it would be many an hour before Dunbar Davis could sleep again.

"After landing the crew of the schooner *Three Sisters* at South-port," he reported later, "I saw a signal on the pole at the station indicating that there was a vessel in distress." The crew of volunteers had departed, and Keeper Watts was occupied with tending to the wounded men they had taken off the schooner. So Davis scouted around the village, rounding up the two Newtons, Watts, Smith, and Weeks of the original group of volunteers, and D. W. Manson, J. L. Daniels, and T. B. Carr to take the place of those he could not locate.

When they reached the station Davis learned that his wife had hoisted the signal. The German brig *Wustrow* had stranded about nine miles west of Oak Island Station, near Lockwoods Folly, and gone to pieces. Subsequently, however, word had been brought to the station that the crew of the brig had reached the beach with the aid of some fishermen in the vicinity. Davis was on the verge of dismissing the volunteer crew, but before doing so he climbed to his watchtower on the off chance that he might be able to see the *Wustrow*. Almost immediately he spotted a vessel, closer to the station than had been reported, and obviously still intact. For a moment, a very brief moment, the tired, fifty-year-old lifesaver felt a surge of relief; but as he focused more clearly on the vessel he suddenly realized that the situation was worse rather than better, for this was not a brig, but a three-masted schooner. Two ships were aground west of his station!

The schooner seemed to be anchored and was beyond the line of breakers, so Dunbar called on his volunteers and once again they put off in the Cape Fear surfboat. This time, however, they got only as far as Cape Fear Bar; the wind and tide and breakers combined to hold them in an almost stationary position no matter how hard they rowed, so finally they gave up and started back inside again.

Another hope appeared, for a pilot boat and a tug, larger vessels built for rough weather, had come down the river on learning of the vessel in distress. But though Davis pleaded with the captains of both craft to tow his tiny surfboat across the bar and into the open water beyond, he was twice refused, and was left with only one other course—to return to his station and proceed down the beach on foot with his lifesaving apparatus.

It was midafternoon when the ten men—they had been joined
by Tommy St. George, one of Davis' winter crew—began the long
trek along the coast, pulling the apparatus cart behind them.

"The beach was so cut through in many places," Davis said, "that
we made very slow time, and I saw that we could not reach the
wreck (the schooner, which later proved to be the 419-ton *Kate
E. Gifford*, of Somers Point, New Jersey) before night; and further
saw that she was not aground. I unloaded a part of the gear and
pushed on, thinking to be of some service to the crew of the brig.
On coming within about two miles of the schooner I met a man
with a mule and cart who stated that the crew of the brig had gone
to a farmhouse and a party of fishermen was taking everything as
it came ashore."

Davis immediately hired the man with the cart to take him to the
spot where the *Wustrow* had come to grief, and arriving there
they found the beach littered with boxes and crates and wreckage,
but of it all there was only one chest which had not been broken
open.

"In the meantime," Davis' report continued, "the schooner had
tried to get underway and had grounded. It was now sunset, so I
signalled to the schooner that I would assist her as soon as possible.
I left a man to keep a fire opposite the schooner, and engaged the
man with the mule to return for the balance of the gear. Even
with the mule's help we could make but little headway, for the
sand was boggy and every half mile or so we would come to deep
gullies. On one of our stops a man came up with a yoke of oxen.
I engaged them, and while hitching them up Keeper Watts came
up with F. W. Fulcher, D. W. Fulcher, H. E. Mints, L. A. Gal-
loway and Ramon Williams. This was about 10 P.M., and still a
hard job was before us, but I made no other stops and reached the
vessel at 2 A.M."

There in the darkness, with the waning winds of the hurricane
striking them from across the open sea, with the spray and spindrift
rolling across the flat beach like tumbleweed on an open prairie,
with the debris from one wreck washing at their feet, and the lights
of a second dimly visible in the treacherous breakers before them,
Dunbar Davis and his volunteer crewmen methodically set up their

Lyle gun, sank a sand anchor, hooked on the line and ball, loaded the gun with powder, and with careful aim sent the shot straight and true toward the stricken vessel.

The line landed on the schooner; they knew this, even though they could not see clearly at that distance, for the line was held aloft and in place, not drifting in the surf as it would if it had missed the mark. But the seven men aboard the nineteen-year-old *Kate E. Gifford*—which already was going to pieces—did not see the line in the darkness, so it just dangled there, the ball swinging back and forth in the wind.

Forced to wait until daylight to resume their rescue attempt, the lifesavers built great driftwood fires on the beach, affording some assurance to the shipwrecked sailors that they had not been left to their own meager devices. And when dawn came at last the line was soon spotted and made secure at a point high on the mast, and heavier lines and the breeches buoy were hauled aboard.

The breeches buoy looks like a pair of English hiking shorts with a sort of round toilet seat at the top where the belt should go. It is designed so that a shipwreck survivor can put his legs through the two openings, hold on to the line to which it is fastened, and be drawn to shore in safety, if not in comfort. The round rim at the top keeps the breeches buoy spread open and in the event the thing dips into the water—as frequently happens—this buoyant rim helps keep it afloat.

One of the *Gifford* crewmen climbed into this contraption as soon as it reached the vessel, raised his arm and waved to the life-savers, and was quickly drawn ashore. Back again went the breeches buoy, and a second survivor climbed in and was hauled out on the beach; then a third, a fourth, until finally all seven of the crewmen had reached the beach safely. Dunbar Davis immediately loaded six of them in the ox cart and sent them to the station; the seventh, the mate of the *Gifford*, remained at the scene with Dunbar Davis to watch over the gear that had come ashore and the shingles from the schooner's deck cargo, already littering the beach.

It was afternoon by then, August 30. The record to that time contained three vessels: schooner *Three Sisters*, grounded, captain and mate washed overboard, crew of five saved; brig *Wustrow*, beaten to pieces in the breakers, crew of nine safely ashore and cared for by near-by farmers; schooner *Kate E. Gifford*, grounded and breaking up, crew of seven rescued in breeches buoy.

Dunbar Davis thought again of his wife's cooking, and of sleep, but the job was not yet done. He and the *Gifford's* mate built up the driftwood fire and had about decided to take turns sleeping, when they spotted a small boat coming in from the sea. The boat, a ship's yawl, came up opposite them and then headed into the surf, landing safely with the assistance of the two men on shore.

There were seven men in the yawl—cold, wet, hungry, and exhausted. The boat, they told Davis, was from the three-masted schooner *Jennie E. Thomas*, which had become waterlogged about thirty-five miles southwest of Cape Fear. All food and water on board the schooner had been exhausted, so the mate and three men left her and boarded a near-by vessel in hopes of getting supplies. But the other vessel, the 371-ton schooner *Enchantress*, carrying a cargo of railroad ties from Port Royal, South Carolina, to New York, was in as bad a condition as theirs; worse, even, for one member of the crew, the mate, had been washed overboard already, the captain was injured, and the *Enchantress*, waterlogged and unmanageable, was drifting toward shore. So the captain and two of her crew had joined those in the yawl from the *Jennie Thomas* and the seven had headed for the beach, eventually spotting the fire which Davis had built. (Later, the *Enchantress* stranded near Lockwoods Folly and became a total loss, and the *Thomas* was towed into Southport and repaired, the remaining crew members of both being saved.)

"These men had been without food for four days," Davis said of the seven who had come ashore in the yawl, "so we hauled their boat up and I sent them to the station for food and clothing. The team did not return until sunset, and the oxen were so badly used up that they had to rest for the night. By this time I was getting pretty fagged. I had gone without food for two days and without water for 12 hours, and had been wet all the time. So I engaged a man to watch the gear and the mate and myself started to the station."

When Dunbar Davis finally returned to Oak Island Station at nine o'clock that night he found the place crowded with shipwrecked sailors. There were six from the *Kate E. Gifford*, plus the mate; seven from the *Jennie Thomas* and *Enchantress*, and four from the brig *Wustrow*, who had come to the station in his absence, badly bruised and nearly naked. All of the food in the station had long since been used up, and the clothing too. But the keeper of the lighthouse and his wife had come over to assist Mrs. Davis in tending to wounds and cooking, and they had provided considerable additional food from their own larder.

Dunbar Davis found that the beds were all taken as well, but he did not care; the way he felt that night he could sleep anywhere and any way.

Also, he had to catch up on his sleep that night, for the next day was the last of August, and the winter crew was due back on duty September 1. Dunbar Davis' summer vacation was over.

HE SEA HAS long provided a livelihood for the residents of eastern North Carolina. Today, hundreds of thousands of inland folk come down to the shores to look at, bathe in, or fish from the sea, and so the tourist business is now the main source of income. Earlier, before modern roads and bridges made the seashore accessible to the tourists, it was commercial fishing that brought in most of the needed dollars; earlier still, shipwrecks provided the bulk of the income.

It is hard today to think of shipwrecks in terms of employment and profit. Yet, before the turn of the century, hundreds of our coastal men had steady jobs as lifesavers, lighthouse tenders, and crewmen on wrecking schooners. In addition, almost every community had a wreck commissioner or underwriter's agent. And for those left out when the steady work was passed around, there was ample opportunity for a man with business sense to make a good profit buying and selling salvaged material, and frequent jobs were available removing cargo of vessels lost on the beach.

The magnitude of this over-all wrecking operation can best be seen by referring to the statistics for a given period of time. In the six years from August, 1893, to August, 1899, for example, an average of almost one ship per week was stranded on the North Carolina coast. The majority were gotten off, yet there were enough totally lost to leave nine full shiploads of lumber and eight of phosphate on the coast, as well as five shiploads of coal, two of shingles, and one each of iron ore, coffee, sugar, salt, grain, lime, molasses, cotton, marble, and crushed stone, not to mention a number that carried general cargoes or were in ballast. Shipwrecks, in those days, were big business; and business was rushing.

EMMA J. WARRINGTON

It was quiet on the Carolina coast for a month after the August hurricane of 1893; then, on October 4, things began to pick up for the lifesavers stationed at their lonely outposts along the banks.

At Paul Gamiels Hill Station, opposite the village of Duck, the lookout spotted a two-masted schooner heading for shore about half a mile south of the station. By the time Keeper A. J. Austin and his crew reached the scene, the schooner was high up on the beach and her four crewmen were safely ashore.

The vessel was the *Emma J. Warrington*, the survivors said, a 59-ton schooner en route from New Bern to her home port of Somers Point, New Jersey, with $500 worth of pine boards. No, none of the survivors was injured, said owner-captain R. E. Young when the lifesavers came up. Yes, they'd appreciate a change of clothes and some warm food and coffee back at the station. No, the lifesavers needn't bother going aboard the vessel just then, for they could come back later when the rough surf subsided and see about salvaging the rigging and the pine boards that hadn't been washed overboard. On second thought, though, they might take a look in the cabin and see if the two passengers were still alive.

Passengers! Keeper Austin and his crew lost no time in rigging up a ladder and boarding the vessel, and in short order they were back on shore again with two tame bears—the passengers—who had been locked up in the cabin.

CHARLES C. DAME

The eight men aboard the 598-ton three-masted schooner *Charles C. Dame*, of Newburyport, Massachusetts, had a tougher time of it than those who had stepped ashore from the *Warrington*. The *Dame*, disabled at sea, grounded about eight miles from shore on Frying Pan Shoals and was seen at dawn, October 14, 1893, by the lookout from Cape Fear Station.

At 7 A.M. that morning, having lined up an additional hand to help with the surfboat, Keeper J. L. Watts put to sea. There were eight men in the tiny craft: Keeper Watts, six regular surfmen, and the additional man he had hired for the job. They rowed steadily for eight full hours in a sea that constantly threatened to swamp or overturn the small craft. Soaked to the skin from the moment they first put to sea, they were uncertain time and again whether they could reach the vessel or return safely to shore. There was no certainty, even, that any living persons remained aboard the ship, but they pushed on anyway, hour after hour, against odds that prevented the Oak Island crew from getting across the bar to help them and kept the Southport tugboats anchored at their berths inside.

"We did not reach the vessel until three o'clock P.M.," Watts said in his report. "The schooner had sunk on the shoal, her decks were under water, and every sea was washing over her. The crew members were huddled together on the jib boom, the only place they could get clear of the sea."

Once he had arrived at the scene, however, it took Watts only ten minutes to remove the crew of eight, and with his boat jammed with people, he immediately turned about and began the long and dangerous trip home. They shipped water with every sea on that return trip, and more than once the surfboat seemed on the verge of capsizing, but their destination was finally reached just before dark that night.

Following this experience Samuel S. Grove, master of the *Dame*, sent a letter of thanks and appreciation to Keeper Watts, which read as follows:

> Baltimore, Maryland
> October 19, 1893

> Dear Sir: Allow me to extend the thanks of myself and crew of the schooner *Charles C. Dame* to you and the heroic men who manned the lifeboat from your station to my vessel on October 14, when she was breaking to pieces on Frying Pan Shoals. Without your assistance it is more than probable that myself and crew would have been lost in the terrible seas that swept our decks.

> Your heroic fight of twelve hours to reach the vessel was a superhuman effort that deserves a record in the annals of the Life Saving Service, which I, as a mariner,

always regard as a sailor's hope when shipwreck stares him in the face in storm-ridden seasons along our coast. Your rescue of every man, and the safe landing of your own and my crews, was a piece of work that it delights me to pay tribute to, and the kind treatment of us while under your care requires me to double my thanks, and extend the same from my officers and crew. This but feebly expresses the feeling of gratitude that animates my writing this; but believe, dear Captain, that in my heart there is a warm affection and admiration for the keeper and crew of the Southport Life Saving Station. I hope we may meet again when you will be in my care, but under different circumstances.

I remain, sincerely,
Samuel S. Grove,
Late Master of Schooner *Charles C. Dame*

Captain J. L. Watts,
Keeper of Southport Life Saving Station, Southport, North Carolina.

Such letters were not uncommon, just as the daring rescues were not uncommon, and the annual reports of the Lifesaving Service, and later records of the Coast Guard, contain hundreds of such attestations to the bravery of the lifesavers on the outer banks.

CLYTHIA

News reached Virginia Beach, January 22, 1894, that a large Norwegian bark, the *Clythia*, had stranded early that morning near Wash Woods, just south of the Virginia-Carolina line. The local people, as always, were anxious to get more details; especially to learn whether any cargo had come ashore. Their interest was shared by a guest at the hotel, Mr. Evans, of Baltimore, who had stopped off in Virginia Beach en route to that same section of the coast for a few days of duck shooting at the Ragged Island Gun Club.

Mr. Evans figured if he could start early enough he might have time to get a first-hand look at the stranded ship and still not miss any hunting that day. But even as he was arranging transportation to the scene further details of the wreck reached Virginia Beach, and Mr. Evans was forced to change his plans.

The *Clythia*, it was learned, carried a crew of seventeen and was en route from Genoa, Italy, to Baltimore with $29,000 worth of statue marble when she struck Pebble Shoals in a thick fog early the same morning. She was sighted soon after by the north patrol from Wash Woods Station, and by eight o'clock Keeper Malachi Corbel and his crew had reached the scene. By then, however, the tide had risen sufficiently for the *Clythia* to clear the shoals, and she had drifted in to the outer bar and stranded there less than five hundred yards from shore.

The same rising tide had completely flooded the sandy coast— "running over the beach half-boot deep," according to Keeper Corbel—so the lifesavers were compelled to throw up a bank of logs and sand before they could get a firm footing for their Lyle gun. While thus engaged the *Clythia* drifted still closer to shore, so that by the time the gun was mounted she presented a good target, three hundred yards away, her bow pointed toward the beach, and her glistening white marble figurehead clearly visible to the lifesavers.

Keeper Corbel landed a shot on the forward deck of the bark soon after 9 A.M., and the tedious business of hauling the sailors ashore was commenced, an operation which continued until mid-afternoon. A total of thirty-four trips were made with the breeches buoy, rescuing all seventeen crew members and bringing ashore a load of personal belongings for each.

The iron-hulled *Clythia* carried more than 1,100 tons of the marble, and even before the last of her crewmen reached shore she was firmly imbedded in the sands with no hope of ever being floated. Salvaging the marble was another story, and repeated attempts were made in future years to save it, the last about 1925 when a diver went down inside what remained of her hull and found that much of the marble was worm-eaten. It is still there, or was the last time anybody investigated.

But what did all this have to do with Mr. Evans of Baltimore? Why was he forced to change his plans as soon as he learned the details of the wreck? It developed that the cargo of marble aboard the *Clythia* was consigned to the Evans Marble Company of Baltimore, thus making it necessary for Mr. Evans to forego his hunting trip and return to his office at once to place an order for another shipment to take its place.

FLORENCE C. MAGEE

Frustration and hard luck were the rules of the day at the wreck of the new four-masted schooner *Florence C. Magee*, which stranded six hundred yards from shore off Bodie Island at midnight, February 26, 1894.

Keeper J. T. Etheridge of Bodie Island Station, who reached the scene with his crew soon after the wreck was sighted, had hard luck from the very start. His first shot struck the wreck, but by then she was completely under water with only her masts showing, and the survivors could not reach the line. It was hauled back and a second shot fired, this one falling short; a third broke off at the shank; a fourth struck a mast and glanced off; a fifth finally hit the rigging and stayed there, but in the darkness the men on board the vessel could not find it. They located it at daybreak, however, and attempted to haul it off through the surf, but by that time the whole thing was so tangled up in rigging and wreckage that they could hardly budge it.

Etheridge gave up, so far as that means of rescue was concerned, and with a picked crew—the Nags Head lifesavers had reached the scene also—he tried next to launch his surfboat. The wind was from the east, the tide low. The waves, huge ocean-bred rollers, were breaking out as far as the eye could see. But the surfmen succeeded in passing through the surf, picking their time and spot, and so large were the waves they encountered that the surfboat was obscured from the sight of those on shore more often than not. A line had been tied to the stern of the rescue craft, and the other life-savers played this out as the breakers were passed, remembering no doubt other crews who had failed to return on just such expeditions as this.

A fishing smack now appeared offshore and, approaching as close to the wreck as possible, lowered a dory. Thus two rescue craft reached the ten crewmen clinging to the shrouds of the *Magee* at about the same time, the fishing dory removing four of them, and Etheridge taking off the remaining six.

The four in the dory were soon transferred to the surfboat, and the trip back through the breakers was begun. "It was blowing so hard the oars would not hold the boat back," Keeper Etheridge reported, and without the assistance of the men left holding the line on shore—now pulling the line taut, relaxing their hold each time Etheridge signalled, then pulling it in again—it is doubtful they could have kept the boat on an even keel between the great rollers. It was a slow, tortuous, deathly game, but the lifesavers won out. Another mission accomplished. Ten more lives saved. Another cargo of fertilizer good only for fish food. And if you know where to look and catch it when the tide is right, you can still see part of the hull of the 1,081-ton *Florence C. Magee* about a mile up the beach from the Bodie Island Lighthouse.

OGIR

Many a mariner has been lost through an inability to interpret signals, and especially has this been true with vessels sailing in foreign waters.

The loss of the Norwegian bark *Ogir* illustrates the point.

The *Ogir*, 547 tons, was in ballast from Hull, England, to Wilmington. She arrived off Cape Fear, October 10, 1894, and anchored just beyond the bar to await daylight and a pilot. During the course of the night the vessel and the lifesavers on shore exchanged signals, leading the latter to believe that the craft was in no danger. Yet the following morning the *Ogir* was discovered aground on the outer bar, with two of her masts already cut away, breakers completely surrounding her, and the eleven men aboard in imminent peril of their lives.

Keeper Dunbar Davis of Oak Island—with a full crew at his disposal this time—launched his surfboat and arrived in the vicinity of the wreck three miles offshore a little after six o'clock that morning. The vessel was right in the middle of the largest breakers, surrounded by masts, spars, rigging, and other wreckage. Every wave threw this floating debris high in the air, then dropped it down again with tremendous force, tossing huge masts around like noodles in a pot of boiling water, up and down and sideways, a surging, seething mass of wreckage in which no frail surfboat could ever live.

Davis surveyed this hopeless task. He saw the huge breakers blocking his way to windward, the wreckage on the lee side, and the eleven men, helpless and nearly hopeless, grouped forlornly on the stricken ship. Unless the sea calmed down before the vessel went to pieces there was only one hope; just one slim chance—and without hesitation Davis decided to try it. The spanker boom had fallen overboard with the other debris but was off by itself on the port side, one end still lying on the deck. Davis signalled for one of the men to crawl out on this, then, waiting for a comparatively smooth spot to show up between breakers, he dashed forward; a lifesaver reached over and grabbed the sailor, Davis shouted orders, the oarsmen dug in, and they were out in the clear again before the next wave reached them.

Even without the floating wreckage to hinder them it was a touchy game there on the tumultuous bar, as time after time the operation was repeated; two men saved, then three, four, five, and finally nine of them aboard the surfboat. The remaining two refused to chance it and signalled to the others to head for shore. They waved goodbye as their comrades slowly moved out of sight and they were left alone there on the doomed ship.

But Dunbar Davis had not given up. As soon as the nine survivors were safely ashore he turned about again, headed back for the ship, and tried to get the two remaining crewmen to climb down on the spanker boom as the others had done. But they were seamen, remember; and seamen supposedly are blessed with a special intuition when it comes to what the weather is going to do. Dunbar Davis felt it too, by then, a lessening in the force of the wind, a different formation in the cloudy sky, the prospect of clear, calm weather.

And so the two crewmen remained on the *Ogir* throughout that night, and the next morning Davis and his crew made a third trip across the bar. The waves had lost much of their force, the wind had died down, and this time the surfboat reached the side of the hulk that had but recently been a proud sailing craft. The two survivors slid down lines they had hung over the side, and the *Ogir* was left on the bar to die alone.

RICHARD S. SPOFFORD

Captain Roger Hawes of the three-masted centerboard schooner *Richard S. Spofford* was a trusting man. His main trouble seemed to be that he trusted the wrong things at the wrong time.

Captain Hawes was en route from his home port of Boston to Darien, Georgia, in late December, 1894, with stone ballast in the hold of his 488-ton vessel. The day after Christmas, having passed Cape Hatteras, he ran into a squally southeast wind, and anticipating a shift to the westward, decided to sail in closer to shore so that he would not be driven into the Gulf Stream.

The wind did shift to the west as he predicted, a strong gale-force wind, blowing with such intensity that Captain Hawes was unable to go about on the offshore tack for fear of losing his mainsail. So he held the *Spofford* the way she was, confident that he could reach the comparatively sheltered area in the lee of Cape Lookout and anchor there until the storm passed by. And having made up his mind as to what he wanted to do, Captain Hawes seemed to forget about it, trusting implicitly that the thing was as good as done.

With her centerboard down the *Spofford* drew twenty feet of water, yet throughout that afternoon and evening Captain Hawes took no soundings; and so complete was his trust, that he went to his bunk as usual that night and slept until 3 A.M., at which time he awoke, possibly because of a premonition of danger and decided that maybe after all it would not be a bad idea to check on the depth of the water.

Captain Hawes might just as well have remained asleep, for his decision came too late. The *Spofford*, instead of being a few miles east of Lookout, was in reality a few miles west of Hatteras; and there was no lee there, no deep water for safe anchoring, only shoals and reefs and breakers, tossed up at the entrance to Ocracoke Inlet.

The *Richard S. Spofford* struck these shoals in the darkness, bumping along from one to another with a terrific jarring impact, until at last the centerboard became wedged in the sand, a sort of pivot on which the vessel swung back and forth. But the waves soon drove her around, broadside to, wrenching the centerboard from the hull, and the *Spofford* drifted over the outer bar into comparatively calm water. She rested there long enough for Captain Hawes and his seven crewmen to put out anchors, and then dragged still closer to shore, coming to rest finally on the inner bar about three hundred yards from the beach and almost directly opposite the village of Ocracoke.

Now, Ocracokers are fine people, as any visitor to that quaint and interesting village can attest, but on this occasion, if we are to accept the findings of the government inspector sent down to investigate the circumstances of the loss of the *Spofford*, they did not react in true Ocracoke fashion. For when the *Spofford* was discovered ashore the next morning and a number of people of the village had gathered on the beach near by, it was soon obvious that no rescue attempt could be successful without proper lifesaving equipment. And though there was a fully-manned lifesaving station fourteen miles away on the east end of the same island and a second one across the inlet at Portsmouth (though this station was new and not completely equipped), no effort seems to have been made to notify either.

The result was that the men aboard the *Spofford* were left to shift for themselves as their vessel, half submerged, continued to take a terrible beating from the storm-driven breakers. Shortly before noon, convinced at last that no help was coming from shore, five of the crew launched the schooner's yawl and headed for the beach, leaving Captain Hawes, the steward, and a third crewman on board. The yawl overturned almost as soon as she cleared the ship, each of the five men grabbing whatever he could find to hang on to, and in this manner they eventually reached the inner breakers where they were rescued by the citizens of the island.

So great were the hazards these five men faced in their successful attempt to reach shore that Captain Bragg, an experienced Ocracoke pilot, later said: "I don't believe that one of them would be saved again under similar circumstances."

Fortunately for those still aboard the wreck, Keeper F. G. Terrell of the Portsmouth Station had observed the *Spofford*, and though he was not certain she was in danger, had mustered a volunteer crew and started across the inlet in an old rowboat, no other equipment being at hand. His first act on reaching the scene was to dispatch word to the other lifesaving station at the far end of the island; his second was to attempt to raise a crew to row out to the wreck in the yawl, but in this he was not successful. When the Ocracoke lifesavers arrived at eight o'clock that night the three remaining members of the schooner's crew were huddled on the bowsprit, the only part of the wreck on which they could be clear of the breakers.

Because of the darkness and the uncertain target the lifesavers were forced to wait until dawn to attempt a rescue. In short order, thereafter, Captain Hawes was drawn ashore in the breeches buoy, and the other crewman soon followed him ashore, but the steward, having suffered injuries previously, was dead, his body lashed in the rigging.

On returning the fourteen miles to their station the Ocracoke lifesavers found their feet so badly swollen that they could not get their boots back on for two days, so the people of the village recovered the body of the steward. As for Captain Hawes, having sold what was left of the rigging and furniture, he took his departure from Ocracoke, a tired, despondent man, no doubt considerably less trusting than before.

J. W. DRESSER

The 602-ton barkentine *J. W. Dresser* of Castine, Maine, was bound from Guantanamo Bay, Cuba, to New York with a cargo of sugar in late July, 1895. On July 22, with a heavy sea running and a strong wind from the southwest, Captain R. O. Parker sighted a lighthouse on his starboard beam. Figuring it was Bodie Island he decided to head in closer to shore to escape the effect of the wind and strong sea, but shortly after noon, while still ten miles offshore, the vessel grounded.

Captain Parker got out his charts and did some quick figuring, but the more he figured the more certain he was that he could not run aground ten miles off Bodie Island Lighthouse; there just were not any shoals out there. In that part of his figuring the Captain was absolutely correct, but the plain facts were that the lighthouse he took to be Bodie Island was in reality the one at the point on Cape Hatteras, and the *J. W Dresser* was hard aground in a heavy sea on the most dreaded spot along the Atlantic Coast. The *Dresser* had struck on outer Diamond Shoals.

Captain Parker could not have picked a worse time for it, since at that time of year the lifesaving crews along the coast were on vacation except for the keepers, and at Cape Hatteras Station the keeper was sound asleep, confident that nobody was fool enough to run a ship ashore just because of a little breeze from the southwest.

Consequently, the vessel was not discovered until late that afternoon, too late for a volunteer crew to be mustered before dark. Meanwhile, the *Dresser* broke in two during the night, and Captain Parker and his nine crewmen made a fruitless attempt to launch the ship's boat. They had about given up hope of rescue when, at 5:30 the next morning, a pair of tiny specks appeared on the western horizon. Soon two surfboats, one each from Cape Hatteras and Creeds Hill stations, came up alongside and the ten men were quickly transferred to the boats, though Captain Parker was knocked overboard in the process. By ten o'clock that morning the survivors were bedded down ashore—almost within the shadow of the tall, spiralling tower which the Captain had mistaken for Bodie Island Lighthouse.

E. S. NEWMAN

The wreck of the three-masted schooner *E. S. Newman* of Stonington, Connecticut, south of the Pea Island Station on October 11, 1896, though involving no great financial loss, did provide considerable excitement. The *Newman*, a 393-ton schooner en route from Providence, Rhode Island, to Norfolk in ballast, tangled with a severe storm shortly before reaching her destination. Before it was over her sails had been blown away and the vessel, unmanageable, had drifted almost a hundred miles southward along the coast.

The *Newman* struck the beach at 7 P.M. when the storm-driven tide was so high that the entire island was inundated—water extending from sea to sound—and the vessel drifted within thirty yards of the normal high water mark before her keel struck bottom.

It was a harrowing prospect which Captain S. A. Gardiner faced that October evening; doubly so, because his wife and three-year-

old child were on board the vessel with him. Gardiner did what
any mariner in similar circumstances would have done; he sent up
a distress signal, spoke reassuring words to his wife, comforted his
child, and waited.

At Pea Island Station, two miles to the north, Keeper Richard
Etheridge had been forced to discontinue beach patrols during the
height of the storm, but he kept a man on watch in the lookout
tower, constantly scanning the raging seas in both directions.

Surfman Theodore Meekins, on watch from dusk until 9 P.M.,
was having difficulty seeing even the outlying buildings of the station, for sea spray covered the glass windows of the tower, and
blowing sand cut through the dark night to further obscure his
vision. Then, suddenly, to the south, he thought he saw a rocket,
a red flare against the blackness of the night. But then, just as
quickly, it was gone; had he really seen a flare, or were his already
bloodshot eyes playing tricks? Surfman Meekins took no chances.
He immediately lighted a red Coston signal, held it aloft until the
flame died out, then shouted for Keeper Etheridge. A second signal
was burned, and now two pairs of eyes peered through the darkness
to the south. They saw it then, both of them. No mistaking it this
time; a red torch-light was burning on the storm-tossed beach to
the south. A vessel was in distress.

"It seemed impossible under such circumstances to render any
assistance," Keeper Etheridge reported later, but he mustered his
crew anyway, hitched a pair of mules to the apparatus cart, and
headed down the beach. "The storm was raging fearfully, the storm
tide was sweeping across the beach, and the team was often brought
to a standstill by the sweeping current," he reported, but the lifesavers pushed on.

Dick Etheridge had spent most of his life on the beach at Pea
Island. A Negro, he had fished there during his early years, and
before the Lifesaving Service began operations on the coast, he led
so many successful rescue expeditions that he was given command
of the station at Pea Island when the government first put it there.
Now, almost twenty years later, he was one of the most experienced, able, and daring lifesavers in the entire service.

But the wreck of the *E. S. Newman* proved something new for
Dick Etheridge. Never before had he come so close to a wrecked

vessel with full lifesaving apparatus at hand, only to be thwarted in every attempt to fire a line aboard. For the water was so thick it was impossible to sink a sand anchor or build a platform on which to mount a gun; the only chance was to forget the modern life-saving gear and see what human strength, perseverance, and luck could do. Dick Etheridge had a plan.

Two of the strongest surfmen were called to his side, and the idea explained to them. Foolhardy, some might have said—hopeless, or sure death. But not these two. They had served under Dick Etheridge long enough to understand that nothing was proved impossible until it was tried; and they volunteered for the job.

A heavy line was then tied around their bodies, firmly, so that they were lashed together. They grasped another line in their hands, and with their fellow surfmen holding the other end of the line on the bank they moved slowly into the breakers, past the high water mark, into the deeper waters beyond. They bent low against the wind yet were forced to rise up high each time one of the pounding waves rolled in past the stranded vessel before them. It was tortuous work, slow and dangerous, with not one chance in a hundred of success.

Captain Gardiner and the eight others clinging to what remained of the *Newman*'s deck structure had seen the arrival of the lifesavers and cheered them, and now as this final effort was made Dick Etheridge heard "the voice of gladdened hearts" from on board the vessel. Captain Gardiner did his part, lowering a ladder over the schooner's side, the side nearest the two struggling surfmen. Finally they reached the stricken ship, grasped the ladder, held it steady as a crewman climbed gingerly down into the riotous mass of water in which the lifesavers stood. The extra line they carried was wrapped around the sailor, tied securely, and together the two lifesavers carried him back up to the bank, their buddies pulling and dragging them through the water and boggy sand.

There were eight more people on the *E. S. Newman*, the crewman said; eight more, including a woman and a child. The lifesavers had proven that their keeper's idea was sound; others replaced the two who had gone out first; again and again and again the surfmen went back through that raging sea, back to the side of the wrecked vessel, back to the ladder hanging down its side. The child was taken ashore, the woman, the other crewmen, and finally the Captain. Nine of them, altogether, literally carried from their waiting graves to safety on the flooded beach.

Dick Etheridge, and the brave men under his command, had accomplished the near impossible once again.

GEORGE L. FESSENDEN

There had not been a life lost because of shipwreck on the North Carolina coast for three and a half years when the three-masted schooner *George L. Fessenden* came to anchor four miles off New Inlet, April 26, 1898.

The *Fessenden,* a 394-ton schooner hailing from Bridgeton, New Jersey, was twenty-four years old, and as one crewman later said, "as rotten as a pear." She had sailed from Philadelphia, March 30, 1898, loaded to capacity with 521 tons of stone destined for Southport. Four weeks later, still loaded with stone, still heading for Southport, the *Fessenden* anchored off New Inlet.

Her interim activities were somewhat obscure. It was known that she had put into Hampton Roads shortly after leaving Philadelphia, though she had not been scheduled to stop there; it was also known that she had managed to get as close to her destination as Cape Lookout. But a furious southeast gale had struck her there, compelling Captain C. B. Norton to put about and head for the comparative safety of the area north of Cape Hatteras; an area comparatively safe, that is, because Norton apparently figured that the *Fessenden* would then be protected from the southeast winds.

That was about like jumping out of the way of a runaway horse into the path of an oncoming locomotive, for by the time the *Fessenden* had rounded Cape Hatteras and proceeded northward a bit to the comparative safety Captain Norton sought, the wind had swung around and a strong northeaster was tearing into the coast.

The two storms were too much for the old *Fessenden,* and by the morning of April 26 her foremast was broken off about one-third of its length below the crosstrees, her main-topmast was gone, and she had lost most of her sails. That is when Captain Norton headed in close to the mouth of New Inlet and anchored.

Surfman E. S. Midgett of the Chicamacomico Station saw the *Fessenden* bearing in toward the coast in a partially disabled condition and hastened back to his station with the news. By that time the schooner had anchored without any show of distress signals, so Keeper L. B. Midgett set his code flags to inquire whether she wanted any aid. The flags were ignored by the schooner.

The weather was clear; the northeaster had died down and there was only a moderate wind. But Keeper Midgett realized that the vessel was in a dangerous position should the winds increase again, so he ordered a constant watch maintained and had the lifesaving gear brought out in readiness for immediate use if needed.

At dusk the *Fessenden* was still anchored there, riding easily at her moorings. No distress signals were seen during the night, and although the wind had freshened, she was in approximately the same position at dawn of April 27. Shortly afterwards, however, it became evident that her cables had parted and she was heading for the beach.

Midgett had already alerted the stations on either side of Chicamacomico. He now ordered his crew out with the gear, telephoned Gull Shoal and New Inlet stations for immediate assistance, and proceeded up the beach to a spot one mile north of his station, where it seemed likely the vessel would strike the beach.

Captain Norton's reasons for not answering the lifesavers' signals, and for refusing to show any sort of a signal of distress after the *Fessenden* had anchored, were never explained; for Captain Norton was washed overboard just as the vessel struck the bar, the first human casualty aboard the unlucky schooner.

The remaining six members of the crew were gathered on the forecastle deck at this time, but as soon as she grounded the heavy load of stone secured the *Fessenden* there on the shoal as firmly as if she had been part of a man-made jetty, the breakers began to sweep across her deck, and the crewmen were forced out on the jib-boom.

Keeper Midgett fired only one shot with his Lyle gun, placing the line almost in the hands of the sailors hanging on to the boom. Because of their precarious position and the strong current sweeping down the coast they had difficulty hauling the line aboard, and they were still engaged in this work twenty minutes later when the vessel suddenly went to pieces, disintegrating like a piece of fragile pottery dropped on a stone wall.

Two crewmen were said to have been killed by the debris before they had a chance to strike out for shore; another was swept down the beach and drowned before crossing into shallow water. But the lifesavers, each with a heaving line, immediately scattered along the beach and succeeded in dragging the three remaining crewmen from the surf. One of these was unconscious, apparently dead, but artificial respiration was applied and in time he recovered his senses.

Thus, of seven men aboard the *George L. Fessenden,* four, including Captain Norton, lost their lives; and so completely was the vessel wrecked that there was no visible sign of her on the bar when the northeaster subsided; only her rotten timbers cluttered the surf, grim reminders that the area north of Cape Hatteras offers only false security to the seafarer seeking safe anchorage.

ALFRED BRABROOK

Ice, twelve hundred dollars worth of it, was the cargo of the three-masted schooner *Alfred Brabrook* of Fall River, Massachusetts, when she sailed from Boothbay, Maine, in early March, 1899. The 563-ton *Brabrook,* with eight men in her crew, was en route to Charleston, South Carolina.

It was a cold trip all the way, with or without the ice; for when she approached Cape Hatteras in the predawn hours of March 7, the *Brabrook* ran into a severe snow storm, and before the captain could get his bearings the vessel stranded two miles north of Gull Shoal Station.

The lifesavers were on the scene by daybreak, but though the first shot fired by Keeper D. M. Pugh was successful, it took most of the morning to set up the breeches buoy in the freezing cold and rescue the crew.

Shortly afterwards the vessel disintegrated, spreading icebergs, shipwreck style, along the beach for miles.

THERE ARE PEOPLE still living along the Carolina coast who had intimate knowledge of San Ciriaco, whose most poignant memories are of San Ciriaco, whose friends were killed by San Ciriaco, whose homes were destroyed by it and whose lives were changed by it, but who have never before heard the name and will not recognize it now.

The people of Puerto Rico knew San Ciriaco. They knew it and remembered it and have made a place for it in the history of their island home, for it was the Puerto Ricans who gave San Ciriaco * its name.

San Ciriaco was the hurricane of 1899. There were others that year, but San Ciriaco was *the* hurricane of 1899. It was spawned in the southern oceans near the equator, was bred on the islands of the Caribbean, spent much of its mature life off our own coast, and

* San Ciriaco was the name of the saint on whose day the hurricane struck Puerto Rico.

died a slow death in the Azores. It lived for almost a month, took thousands of lives, destroyed innumerable buildings, and sank ships wherever it went.

The impending arrival of San Ciriaco was heralded along the outer banks in the early morning of August 16, 1899. A high and troubled surf pounded the shore at Cape Hatteras, the sky became overcast, and the wind, normally light and from the southwest at that time of year, went around to the east and got down to the serious business of blowing. By noon it had reached fifty miles per hour.

At about that time the three-masted schooner *Aaron Reppard*, having left Philadelphia on August 12 with a cargo of coal for Savannah, was anchored off the coast somewhere between Cape Henry and Cape Hatteras. Captain Osker Wessel, apparently not aware of the approach of San Ciriaco, had decided to ride out the storm. But San Ciriaco was not the kind of storm you could ride out, as Captain Wessel soon discovered; for his craft drifted closer and closer to shore, and in the early afternoon breakers were seen astern. Even at that late hour, had he chosen, Captain Wessel could have let go his anchors and stood a good chance of drifting high on the beach. But Captain Wessel took the other course, held fast to his anchors, even hoisted sails, and the *Reppard* slowly dragged into the pounding surf.

There were eight men aboard the 459-ton *Reppard:* Captain Wessel, six crewmen, and a passenger named Cummings. When the vessel struck, all hands immediately climbed into the shrouds, Cummings taking to the mizzen-rigging, a sailor named Tony Nilsen to the main-rigging, and the others to the fore-rigging. From those vantage points they could see the beach, a long sand bank almost completely covered with storm tides and behind it the shallow waters of the sound, the whole of it barren, submerged, and un-inviting. Their situation seemed hopeless. But even as their gaze swept the beach, figures appeared there, fifteen or twenty of them, waving their arms and signalling.

The people they saw were lifesavers, guardians of the coast, who had been aware of the proximity and plight of the schooner for some time and had now assembled from the Chicamacomico, Gull Shoal, and Little Kinnakeet stations to render aid

The survivors clinging to the rigging of the *Reppard* saw these men make preparations for their rescue, watched as the first shot burned loose from its line and sailed overhead, saw the second fall short, and were almost struck by the third as it lodged squarely across the head stays, almost within their grasp. Yet they could not reach the line, let alone attempt to pull it aboard, for every bit of their time and strength was required in hanging on as the *Reppard*, heavily laden with some seven hundred tons of cargo, pounded against the bottom with a terrible jarring impact as each breaker swept in across the reef.

Cummings, the passenger, was the first to lose his balance and fall from his perch high on the mizzenmast. For a moment it looked as if he could be saved, for his leg caught in a rope as he fell; but immediately the wind began slamming his limp body against the mast with such force that life soon left him. And even as Cummings body swung there, his face bruised almost beyond recognition, the vessel began to disintegrate. The mainmast went first, throwing Nilsen to the deck, from whence he was washed overboard; then Captain Wessel jumped into the sea, swam toward the beach, changed his mind, started back for his ship, and sank from sight just before reaching it.

The foremast fell next, carrying the five survivors into the churning breakers, killing one as he struck the water. The others struck out for shore, while the lifesavers waded into the surf to meet them. Only three came in close enough for the lifesavers to drag them through the breakers; three saved, of the eight aboard the *Aaron Reppard* when she left Philadelphia two days earlier. San Ciriaco had taken its first toll of shipping and life on the Carolina coast.

The nine men and one woman aboard the 741-ton three-masted schooner *Florence Randall*, next to encounter the wrath of San Ciriaco, were more fortunate. They struck two miles south of Big Kinnakeet Station—and about fifteen miles south of where the *Reppard* had gone ashore—at about the same time that the three surviving members of the *Reppard*'s crew were being dragged from the surf. Again, the lifesavers were on the scene when the vessel struck, but this time their first shot landed on board the vessel, the breeches buoy was soon set up, and by dark Captain C. A. Cavillier, his wife, and the eight crewmen were safe on shore. But the

Randall, and the four thousand dollars worth of fish scrap which she was carrying from Promised Land, New York, to Charleston, were lost to San Ciriaco.

The next day—August 17—San Ciriaco loosed its full fury against the narrow string of sandy reefs and islands which constitute the North Carolina outer banks. At 4 A.M. the wind at Cape Hatteras was blowing at 70 miles per hour; at noon it was between 84 and 93 miles; at 1 P.M. it was recorded at 120 miles per hour, and throughout that afternoon and night winds of more than 100 miles per hour prevailed. "There were not more than four houses on Hatteras Island into which the tide did not rise to a depth ranging from one to four feet," the government reported; and Hatteras Island, even then, included more than half a dozen separate communities. So intense were the winds and so high the tides accompanying San Ciriaco that it was impossible for lifesavers to maintain their patrols, with the result that most of the vessels wrecked on the coast were not reached—were not even discovered—until the morning of the eighteenth, when the winds had begun to subside.

At Portsmouth Station, Surfman William T. Willis saw a vessel with a distress signal flying in Pamlico Sound two miles northeast of the station when daylight came that morning. Keeper F. G. Terrell immediately put out in his surfboat and rowed to the vessel. En route, another craft, a small two-masted schooner, the *Lydia Willis,* was seen sunk near the mouth of Ocracoke Inlet, but there was no sign of life aboard, so the lifesavers proceeded on to the vessel in distress. This proved to be the *Fred Walton,* a 441-ton hulk which the Norfolk and Southern Railroad was using as a lay boat for the company's steamers. She had broken loose from her moorings, drifted on Hog Shoal, and broken in two. The master, Captain Bill Gaskill, and his wife, "Miss Annie," survived the disaster and were taken ashore by the lifesavers.

On the way back to Portsmouth the next day a signal was seen flying from the mast of the sunken *Lydia Willis,* and on pulling up beside the vessel Terrell learned that there had been six men aboard, that two had been washed overboard, and that the remaining four had spent almost two days in the rigging before the seas quieted down enough for them to climb down to the deck. Exhausted from their forty-eight hours aloft, they had fallen asleep almost immediately, which accounted for the absence of a signal and signs of life when Terrell passed by the first time.

Meanwhile, at Little Kinnakeet Station, midway between the wrecks of the *Aaron Reppard* and *Florence Randall*, the three-masted schooner *Robert W. Dasey* was discovered ashore. She had been en route from Philadelphia to Jacksonville with coal and had stranded there at the height of the hurricane. The beach was so badly flooded still that the mules, attempting to haul the apparatus cart to the scene, mired down in the muck at every step, and it was more than two hours before the three-quarters of a mile from the station to the wreck could be covered. Even then the beach apparatus was not needed, for the *Dasey* was bow on to the beach, with the outer jib stay hanging over the side, enabling the lifesavers to walk into the surf and hold the jib stay fast while the seven survivors came down it to safety. But though the rescue of the crewmen was a comparatively simple matter, the *Dasey* was so high on the beach that there was no chance of floating her. Like the hulk *Fred Walton* and the schooner *Lydia Willis*, she too was a total loss.

Across Pamlico Sound, meanwhile, the 66-ton schooner *General E. L. F. Hardcastle*, from Wilkins Point to Baltimore with a load of lumber, had foundered in the storm, and part of her cargo and all five of her crew were lost.

And at Creeds Hill, to the west of Cape Hatteras, lookout F. J. Rollinson discovered a vessel ashore about a mile southwest of the station. When the lifesavers arrived they read, in huge block letters along the side of the vessel, the words *Diamond Shoals;* this was no ordinary vessel—it was Lightship No. 69, which had dragged loose from its permanent berth on the outer point of Diamond Shoals at the height of San Ciriaco's fury and drifted ashore. The nine crewmen were rescued in the breeches buoy—and subsequently were rescued in like manner three more times while salvage operations were in progress—but in time the lightship was floated and returned once more to Diamond Shoals, a lonely sentinel warning mariners away from the dreaded shifting sand bars.

They tell the story of the wreck of the barkentine *Priscilla* with pride along the outer banks; the Midgetts do, especially, for the hero of the story was one of the family, Rasmus S. Midgett, surf-man at Gull Shoal Station.

You can get the outline of the story from the official report of the keeper of Gull Shoal Station: "R. S. Midgett, surfman No. 1, on south patrol from 3 A.M. to sunrise. He found a wreck broken to pieces 3 miles south of station and on stern was ten men. He managed to save them all without coming to station to report."

That is the extent of the keeper's report concerning the exploits of Rasmus Midgett that stormy morning; but there is more to the story if you care to look for it.

Before dawn on August 18 Rasmus Midgett mounted his beach pony and went out on his beat to the south. His course took him past the remains of the *Aaron Reppard*, past the spars and timbers of countless other ships wrecked in days gone by, across gullies, through newly-cut inlets, along a stretch of barren beachland still buffeted by the waning winds of San Ciriaco. He had been one of the lifesavers on the scene when the *Reppard* came ashore two days earlier, and chances are he paused there, remembering the cries of anguish from the dying; yet within half a mile he was to hear such cries again and see through the gloom the hazy, ghost-like shape of still another ship committed to the Graveyard of the Atlantic.

The voyage of the 643-ton barkentine *Priscilla* had started out as a sort of family affair. When she left Baltimore the preceding Saturday, August 12, en route to Rio de Janeiro with a general cargo valued at more than $34,000, she carried a crew of twelve, including Captain Benjamin E. Springsteen and Mate William Springsteen, the Captain's son. Mrs. Virginia Springsteen, the Captain's wife, and twelve-year-old Elmer Springsteen, their other son, were also on board. The *Priscilla* encountered San Ciriaco just north of Cape Hatteras and managed to buck the winds until the hurricane had passed. But she was so badly damaged that Captain Springsteen could not prevent her from driving ashore, and she struck early in the morning of August 18 three miles south of Gull Shoal Station.

Because she was pounding so hard the Captain ordered the port-rigging cut away, and as soon as this was accomplished the three masts fell. Still no lives had been lost, but the waves were now breaking across the vessel with tremendous force. The Captain clutched his younger son in his arms, and the Mate attempted to comfort and shelter his mother and the young cabin boy, Fitzhugh Goldsborough. The efforts of both were futile, for a towering wave struck the *Priscilla*, tearing young Elmer Springsteen from his father's arms and washing the cabin boy, Mrs. Springsteen, and Mate Springsteen overboard. In just that instant Captain Springsteen's family was taken from him.

It must have been at about this same time that Rasmus Midgett heard the cries of distress and saw the stranded vessel, already beginning to go to pieces. There was not time to return to the station for help, but what could one man do under such circumstances? Rasmus Midgett thought he knew.

Dismounting from his pony he ran down to the bank, waited there for a huge breaker to roll in to shore, then raced into the water toward the ship as the giant wave receded. He shouted hurried instructions to the ten men crouched there on the forward part of the barkentine, then ran for shore again as the next wave came in.

They probably thought he was insane; but Rasmus Midgett was their only hope of rescue, and the men aboard the *Priscilla* obeyed his instructions. When next he ran toward the ship in the wake of one of the crushing breakers, a crewman climbed down the ropes hanging over her side to meet him. Rasmus Midgett grabbed the man, dragged him bodily from the path of the next onrushing breaker, and deposited him safely on the beach. Then he returned again for a second rescue attempt. He made seven trips that way, rescued seven men, accomplishing the near impossible in the face of the greatest adversity, yet the job was not yet done. For three men yet remained aboard the *Priscilla;* three exhausted, bruised, and feeble men, unable to climb down the side of the vessel and be saved in the same manner as their seven cohorts.

To Rasmus Midgett, standing there on the beach with the seven castaways he had pulled from the very arms of death, there was only one course open. He dashed into the surf again, fought his way through the turbulent waters to the side of the vessel, grasped the ropes, pulled himself hand over hand to the deck. He lay there for a moment, breathing hard, his muscles aching, his strong body taxed almost beyond human endurance. But he rose again, stumbled across the deck to the side of one of the three men lying crumpled there. Lifting him to his shoulders, he returned to the ropes, slid down into the sea, and staggered toward the shore with his heavy burden. Again he dashed into the angry surf, climbed to the deck of the ship, lifted the second man, and carried him, somehow, to the place of sanctuary on the shore. The whole grueling, painful, harrowing operation was repeated a third time and was again successful.

Rasmus Midgett gave his coat to Captain Springsteen, the most badly injured of the survivors, and attempted to rouse his tired pony but without success. Instructing the ten men to follow, he hurried back along the beach to his station, reporting the *Priscilla* wrecked. What of the crew, he was asked? All saved. All safe on shore.

For that feat, unparalleled in the annals of lifesaving, Rasmus S. Midgett was awarded the Gold Lifesaving Medal of Honor, the highest honor which can be bestowed for the saving of life in peacetime.

Rasmus Midgett's work was done for the time, but the effects of San Ciriaco were yet to be revealed. A mile and a half northeast of Chicamacomico Station that same morning the three-masted schooner *Minnie Bergen* of Philadelphia, a 387-ton vessel en route from Philadelphia to Nuevitas, Cuba, with a cargo of railroad iron, coal, and oil, was discovered by the lifesavers. A Lyle gun was set up and fired, the breeches buoy run out, and the seven crewmen safely hauled ashore. And at Core Bank, the next day, the little schooner *George Taulane* of Beaufort, bound from its home port to New Bern with a cargo of fish scrap, ran ashore, and the five men aboard were rescued by the lifesavers.

Meanwhile six other vessels—the schooner *John C. Haynes*, 1,346 tons, from Port Tampa, Florida, to Baltimore, with a cargo of phosphate rock and nine crewmen; the schooner *M. B. Millen*, 336 tons, from New London, Connecticut, to Brunswick, Georgia, in ballast with seven crewmen; the barkentine *Albert Schultz*, 498 tons, from Baltimore to Savannah with coal and a crew of eight; the schooner *Elwood H. Smith*, 439 tons, from New York to Jacksonville in ballast with seven crewmen; the brig *Henry B. Cleaves*, 389 tons, from Haiti to Stamford, Connecticut, with logwood and eight crewmen, and the schooner *Chas. M. Patterson*, 834 tons, from

Philadelphia to Savannah with coal and eight crewmen—encountered the wrath of San Ciriaco and disappeared forever.

Seven vessels lost on the beach—*Aaron Reppard, Florence Randall, Lydia Willis, Fred Walton, Robert W. Dasey, Priscilla, Minnie Bergen,* and the lightship driven ashore from Diamond Shoals; six others disappeared at sea without a trace—*John C. Haynes, M. B. Millen, Albert Schultz, Elwood H. Smith, Henry B. Cleaves* and *Chas. M. Patterson.* More than fifty lives lost; hundreds of homes inundated; fishing nets, small boats, livestock, gardens, even furniture ruined. All of it caused by San Ciriaco. Remember the name this time. San Ciriaco, *the* hurricane of 1899.

TEAMSHIPS first appeared along the North Carolina coast early in the nineteenth century, but it was more than a hundred years before they were able to wrest away from sailing craft the bulk of the coastal trade, and it took a world-wide war to accomplish it even then.

During the years immediately preceding World War I, there were more sailing vessels than ever plying the coastal routes, and their main nemesis, as in days gone by, was that series of broad shifting sand bars jutting out from Cape Hatteras in a vague diamond shape. The prevailing wind there is from the southwest, and at times the southwesters blow for weeks on end. At such times the sailing vessels, unable to beat their way around Diamond Shoals because of the combined force of the wind and the waters of the Gulf Stream flowing up from the south, were forced to remain there on the north side of Cape Hatteras for weeks at a time.

As a result, according to the older bankers, there were sometimes as many as seventy-five or eighty sails in view off Kinnakeet, just north of the cape; and when a shift finally did come, it was not uncommon for the newly arrived northerly winds to reach gale force before the first of these sailing ships could make their way around the cape. The result, frequently, was shipwreck.

In the eighteen-year period from the fall of 1899 to the spring of 1918 a total of 108 vessels were totally lost on the North Carolina coast. All but fifteen of these were sailing craft, and a large percentage were wrecked on Hatteras Island. It was an auspicious and deadly climax for the reign of sailing craft.

ARIOSTO

In compiling a set of "Instructions to Mariners in Case of Ship-wreck" soon after its formation, the United States Lifesaving Service emphasized the following statement: "Masters are particularly cautioned, if they should be driven ashore anywhere in the neighborhood of the stations, especially on any of the sandy coasts, where there is not much danger of vessels breaking up immediately, to remain on board until assistance arrives, and under no circumstances should they attempt to land through the surf in their own boats until the last hope of assistance from the shore has vanished."

Hundreds of mariners have failed to heed that advice and have died for it, though probably the most noteworthy case on the Carolina coast was the wreck of the steamship *Ariosto* in 1899.

The *Ariosto* was due to arrive in Norfolk, Virginia, December 25, and the thirty crewmen were no doubt looking forward to partaking of a fine Christmas dinner in that port. But as it developed, nine of them ate Christmas dinner instead on the island of Ocracoke, and then assisted, even before the meal was digested, in burying the lifeless bodies of twenty-one of their former shipmates.

The schooner-rigged steel steamer, a 2,265-ton vessel bound for Hamburg, Germany, via Norfolk, had on board a cargo of wheat, cotton, lumber, and cottonseed valued at more than one and a half million dollars when she cleared from Galveston, Texas, earlier in the month. The *Ariosto* bucked a smart wind and rough sea after passing Cape Lookout the night of December 23, and at 3:45 the next morning she suddenly struck breakers, careened over on her starboard side, and held fast.

Captain R. R. Baines, roused from his berth, assumed the craft had stranded on Diamond Shoals, and after a hurried consultation with his officers made plans to abandon ship. Meanwhile, he ordered distress signals fired, and almost immediately there was a responding red flare from off in the north. Though such a flare was the universal signal that assistance was on the way, and despite the fact that there is no land to the north of Diamond Shoals from which a signal of that kind could come, the Captain persisted in his belief that his vessel was on the dreaded shoals, and the order to abandon ship was carried out.

Even as other flares were seen in the north two boats were lowered away, men crowded into them, and both were cast loose before all of the crewmen had reached them. Thus four men, including Captain Baines, were left on the stranded steamer, while the two boats pulled off a short distance and stood by, waiting for daylight. Long before light came, however, the two boats capsized in the rough sea, and of the twenty-six persons occupying them only two managed to swim back to the *Ariosto*. In the darkness of night, in the midst of tumultuous breakers, the twenty-four others were forced to fend for themselves.

They were not, however, on the outer end of Diamond Shoals as Captain Baines had supposed, for the flares they had seen were lighted by a surfman patrolling the beach and the lookout at Ocracoke Station (located, then, just west of Hatteras Inlet). The *Ariosto* was aground approximately three miles southwest of the inlet and half a mile from shore.

When the Ocracoke lifesavers, plagued by cart break-downs and a mucky beach, arrived on the beach opposite the stranded vessel an hour and a half after her distress signals were first seen, they discovered a lone figure staggering toward them. This was Seaman Karl Elsing, a former occupant of one of the capsized boats and the only one of the twenty-four who had succeeded in swimming ashore.

The lifesavers soon set up their beach equipment, and in the darkness an experimental shot was fired in the direction of the steamer. It fell far short, and all hands bent on the line in an attempt to pull it back to shore, but it pulled hard as if it had caught on something out there in the darkness. It had!

Boatswain Aleck Anderson, one of those thrown into the breakers when the lifeboats capsized, was a poor swimmer. At first he tried to find something to hold to, but he was unsuccessful and could only tread water in a frantic effort to stay afloat. It was a hopeless task for a man hardly able to swim. With both ship and shore beyond his reach, and buffeted constantly by the chaotic breakers, he was at last in the process of resigning himself to certain death when something struck him across the shoulders.

He reached up, found a firm line resting there, and with his last strength wrapped it around his arm. Then he lost consciousness. Out there a quarter of a mile from shore or better, the lifesavers' line had reached the lone figure. When they pulled in their line, Boatswain Aleck Anderson was the dead weight they felt; half-drowned when he was dragged ashore, he soon was revived sufficiently by the trained surfmen to recount his harrowing and miraculous experience.

The rest of it was routine. A third man was dragged from the surf, worked over, and resuscitated. More shots were fired toward the steamer, until one landed fairly, and by mid-afternoon the rescue of Captain Baines and the five others aboard the *Ariosto* was effected. Nine of thirty were rescued; twenty-one others were buried there at Ocracoke because heed was not taken of the advice that "under no circumstances should they attempt to land through the surf in their own boats until the last hope of assistance from the shore has vanished."

HETTIE J. DORMAN

A steamship is an impersonal thing, heavy and sluggish and unfriendly in appearance. For, in the final analysis, a steamship is only a machine, and like any other machine is completely useless without fuel to run it and men to guide it.

But a sailing craft is something else again. A sailing craft is a living thing; a lovely woman, lithe and feminine and temperamental, possessing a heart and soul and will of her own; a sweetheart, to be loved and coddled and referred to always in endearing terms. You question that? Then try calling a sailing craft "he" sometime and watch the reaction of seafaring men.

Take *Hettie Dorman*, for instance. *Hettie J. Dorman* was her full name, but most people called her *Hettie*, or just *Dorman*. In 1900 she was only thirteen years old, but already she possessed knowledge and experience, especially experience, that few men gain in a lifetime. She weighed 124 tons, somewhat overweight by human standards, yet she was as pert and saucy as you would ever want to see. Her home town was Drawbridge, Delaware, a sleepy little port, so small you would not even find it on the road maps.

But she spent little time there, returning only occasionally for a
new outfit or to visit awhile with the folks she had been brought
up with.

Hettie was a wanderer. She liked going home, but always after
a brief stay she was ready to leave again, to run toward the open
sea, pushing her head into the winds and spreading her sails to catch
the breeze, like a little girl on iceskates. She moved gracefully across
the water, bound for distant places—romantic, yet fearful, places
that most people only heard of and never saw.

What kind of a woman is that, you say; traipsing all over the
world, alone and unescorted? But *Hettie* was not alone, nor was
she unescorted, for her constant companion on those trips was a
man, a neighbor from Drawbridge, even more widely travelled than
Hettie; a rough, hard working, seafaring man, yet tender and loving
in his treatment of young *Hettie Dorman*. His name was Sabiston—
Captain J. W. Sabiston.

They left Drawbridge together that spring of 1900. They sailed
together along the coast, past the entrance of Chesapeake Bay, past
Cape Henry, past the awesome shoals off Hatteras and Lookout,
and arrived, finally, at Bogue Inlet, North Carolina.

They had work to do there, loading newly cut pine boards, two
thousand dollars worth of them, with the aid of the four crewmen
who were with them always. When the job was done they set sail
again, passed Lookout a second time, headed east beyond Cape
Hatteras, then turned north. Their destination was Patchogue,
Long Island.

They were nervy, those two, *Hettie Dorman* and her Captain; for
they sailed in close to Diamond Shoals, actually crossed the outer-
most point, not worried about it the way most seafarers are, for
they had crossed shoal water before and done it without mishap. But
they had overlooked one thing that day; they had forgotten the
many other ships, large lumbering steamers and sailing vessels which
had grounded there and sunk; and, with a sudden, horrible, grind-
ing, grating, ripping sound they struck one of those wrecks, tore
loose the under planking, and shipped water at a fearful rate.

Men do strange things under stress, strange and mean and thought-
less things, just as Captain Sabiston did there on the outer fringes

of Diamond Shoals. For, without a backward glance, without bothering to take in *Hettie*'s sails or even say goodbye, Captain Sabiston lowered a yawl, ordered the four crewmen over the side, and climbed in himself, leaving *Hettie Dorman* alone there on the shoal.

Lifesavers from Cape Hatteras came out that afternoon and rescued Captain Sabiston and his crew. They, too, ignored *Hettie*. But *Hettie*, like any woman, resented being left alone, and when they headed shoreward she took out after them. Injured internally, able to drag along at only a fraction of her usual speed, she made a slow trip of it.

Before dark that night Captain Sabiston and his crew reached shore and were bedded down in the lifesaving station; and in the darkness, trailing her loved one as best she could, *Hettie Dorman* navigated the full length of Diamond Shoals (a seemingly impossible feat, even for the most experienced of sailors) and then headed for the open beach to the north of the cape where last she had seen her Captain.

At four o'clock the next morning Surfman O. J. Gray of Big Kinnakeet Station sighted *Hettie* a mile or so offshore in the dim false dawn. He burned a Coston signal as a warning that she was dangerously near the shore, but *Hettie* ignored him. He burned another, and finally a third, but *Hettie* kept on, and before the surfman could return to his station for assistance she struck the beach, only four miles north of the station where Captain Sabiston was even then being roused by the lifesavers.

Surfman Gray and his cohorts went out to *Hettie* that morning, looked her over, asked questions, tried to find out what she was doing there; but all they learned from *Hettie* was her name. A woman has her pride, you know; there are some things none of them will let on to strangers.

That is all there was to the story of *Hettie Dorman*, except that Captain Sabiston came to her later in the day, realized the error of his ways, and tried to help her get clear of the sand bank on which she rested. The lifesavers, inspecting her injuries, thought maybe she could make it. But they just did not know *Hettie Dorman*; they did not know about her soul and heart and will. *Hettie*'s injuries were not the kind you could see; they were deep within her, and fatal. *Hettie J. Dorman* died there on the beach, as Captain Sabiston looked on.

EA

For a full dose of suspense take a close look at the repeated attempts to save the twenty-seven Spaniards aboard the steamship *Ea*, stranded on Lookout Shoals in March, 1902.

The *Ea* (full name) was a 2,632-ton steamer bound from Fernandina, Florida, to Hamburg, Germany, via New York with a cargo of phosphate rock and rosin, when she struck the outer tip of the shoals, twelve miles from Cape Lookout Lighthouse, in mid-afternoon of March 15, 1902.

Lifesavers from Cape Lookout Station, under command of Keeper William H. Gaskill, spotted the steamer at 3:30 that afternoon and immediately put off in their surfboat to render assistance. The wind was blowing moderately from the southeast, but the sea was very rough and the sky overcast, and by the time they reached the vicinity of the wreck it was dark. Despite the huge seas breaking all around them, and the mist and darkness in which they were enveloped, the lifesavers rowed about for several hours in a futile attempt to find the vessel.

Returning to shore at 1:30 the next morning Keeper Gaskill contacted the revenue cutter *Algonquin* at Morehead City, and shortly after dawn the lifesavers again headed for the wreck, this time in tow of the cutter. The *Ea* was clearly visible in the daylight, but when Gaskill cast loose from the cutter and tried to row in closer he found that the steamer was completely surrounded by huge, frothing breakers, blocking his way in all directions.

By this time the twenty-seven Spaniards must certainly have been aware that every effort was being made to rescue them, for in addition to the cutter and the Lookout surfboat, the tug *Alexander Jones* had also come up to offer assistance. But the tug could do no more than the others, and late that afternoon the three craft headed back to the cape.

Early the next morning, the seventeenth, the fleet of rescue vessels, joined now by the large wrecking tug *I. J. Merritt*, returned again to the wreck; the lifesavers made another attempt to row in close but were thwarted; and after another day of waiting and watching and hoping, they returned again to Cape Lookout for the night.

March 18 was the day of decision and final action. For, when the rescue vessels reached the outer tip of the shoals that morning they discovered that the steamer had broken completely in two, with both her bow and stern ends below water, and the crew was gathered on the bridge. The wind had shifted and the breakers, though still pounding with tremendous force against the *Ea* and the shoals surrounding her, seemed to have abated slightly.

Once more Keeper Gaskill cast off, headed in toward the wreck from the leeward side, but the force of the waves was so great that he could make no progress, and yet again it was necessary for the little surfboat to be taken in tow. She was hauled around to the windward side this time and turned loose there. The lifesavers took up their oars and dug into the churning sea with full strength, following the shouted commands of Keeper Gaskill who stood in the stern, the steering oar pressed hard against his body, his eyes constantly searching the breakers behind and in front and on the sides. The frail craft pounded down and across the shoal, lifted to the top of one breaker, and was thrown down into the trough between that and the next, flipped around like a falling leaf caught by autumn winds, always moving forward toward the wrecked steamer *Ea*. But it was all in vain, for they passed the wreck, unable to slacken their speed sufficiently to slip into the comparatively calm spot to leeward, and rode out the breakers, far beyond the stricken ship.

A lifeboat, with seventeen men aboard, put out from the *Ea* then, navigated the breakers, and was picked up by the tug. But ten men remained on board, and it was up to the lifesavers to try again. Once more they were towed to windward, were cast loose just beyond that riotous line of breakers, drifted into them, darted forward toward the *Ea*. Keeper Gaskill steered closer this time, almost struck the vessel as he went by, dug in with his steering oar, shouted for his oarsmen to exert their every effort, and succeeded somehow in making the lee, coming up beside the ship.

It was easy going from then on. The ten survivors climbed down from the bridge and crowded into the boat with room for each to hang on and nothing more. The line that held them to the wreck was cut, and Keeper Gaskill steered them through the leeward breakers to safety beyond. The ten men were pulled aboard the tug, once more the surfboat was taken in tow, and the entire flotilla headed in toward Lookout Bight. It had taken three full days but the rescue was complete.

OLIVE THURLOW

No record is available, unfortunately, of the conversation between the master of the little tug *Atlantic* and Captain Jerry O. Hayes of the barkentine *Olive Thurlow*, while the latter vessel lay at anchor in Lookout Bight on the morning of December 4, 1902, nine months after the survivors of the *Ea* were landed there. Even more important, there is no information as to the amount of money the master of the *Atlantic* wanted to charge Hayes for towing his vessel to a safe harbor. It is a reasonably certain guess, however, that the amount was only a fraction of $14,000, which was the value of the *Thurlow*, or even of $6,000, the cost of the more than 200,000 feet of pine lumber she carried in her hold and on her deck.

It is known, definitely, that the *Thurlow*, a 660-ton vessel of New York, bound home from Charleston, had struck bad weather off Bodie Island three days previously, and that Captain Hayes had turned about, sailed past Cape Hatteras, and sought a safe anchorage in Lookout Bight. In the process, taking the wheel himself, the Captain got caught between the tiller and the quadrant, breaking a bone in his leg.

Also, if you want to look at the thing from the Captain's point of view, a man with a broken leg, who has been without medical assistance for three days, is not likely to have the patience required for successful haggling over towage fees, or even for correctly sizing up the coming weather conditions. Which might account for the fact that Captain Hayes refused the terms offered by the master of the tug *Atlantic* and refused also to take the advice of Keeper William H. Gaskill of Cape Lookout Station, who smelt a storm in the offing and suggested that he be allowed to move the *Thurlow* to a safer anchorage.

So Captain Hayes was taken to Beaufort where a doctor set his leg, and the *Thurlow* remained at anchor in Lookout Bight, to the north of the cape, throughout that night. First Mate Florian, in charge of the barkentine, put over one anchor, and this with only about thirty fathoms of chain attached. Later he let out that much again, but by then the wind was blowing between seventy and eighty miles per hour, the sea was so rough that Keeper Gaskill said he had never seen anything like it in his fifteen years' experience on the cape, and the *Olive Thurlow* was doomed.

Mate Florian burned two blue Coston signals as soon as he saw that the vessel would pile up on the beach, and an immediate answer came from the lifesavers ashore who had kept a constant watch in anticipation of just such a situation. It was then about 4 A.M., December 5.

By six o'clock the lifesavers had set up their apparatus and fired a line aboard the wreck, within reach of the six sailors who had been forced to take to the mizzen shrouds. But even as the sailors reached for the line the mast broke, throwing the men, mizzenmast, and rigging to the deck in a tangled mass, crushing the skull of Steward John Chalkly beneath the mast, and seriously injuring two others. Chalkly's body washed overboard and was never seen again, while the five men remaining attempted to extricate themselves from the mass of wreckage surrounding them.

Observing this calamity from shore, Keeper Gaskill again fired a line across the wreck, and the sailors had reached it and were in the process of making it fast to the stump of the mast when the whole ship went to pieces. The five sailors managed to cling to the top of the deckhouse.

"They lay down with their arms through the skylight holes," Keeper Gaskill reported later, "those unhurt holding those injured as best they could. At times all must have been ten feet under water. One man was washed off but managed to hold out 'till in reach of assistance, when he was taken out of the sea. By this time those on the top of the house had reached the beach and were being taken out of the surf more dead than alive."

The sea was filled with floating wreckage and pieces of lumber, tossed end over end by the huge breakers and constantly endangering the lives of both the shipwrecked sailors and of the surfmen, fishermen, and two lighthouse keepers who were pulling them from the surf. But the rescue was completed without further serious injury, the five survivors were carried back to the station, and a doctor was summoned from Beaufort to attend to their wounds.

Meanwhile, the tug *Atlantic* was in safe harbor, her master poorer by one small towing fee than he might have been, but better off, by far, than Captain Hayes and the owners of the late barkentine *Olive Thurlow*.

VERA CRUZ VII

Keeper F. G. Terrell and his crew of the Portsmouth Lifesaving Station had their hands full on May 8 and 9, 1903, for in that time they rescued a total of 421 shipwrecked persons. Not only that, but 416 of them were cared for on Portsmouth Island (fewer than 10 residents there now) and a total of 1,248 meals were provided. To give an idea of the size of this undertaking, four and a half barrels of flour were required just to make bread for the survivors.

It all began when the 605-ton brig *Vera Cruz VII*, a twenty-nine-year-old vessel hailing from the Cape Verde Islands, stranded on Dry Shoal Point while trying to enter Ocracoke Inlet at 2 P.M., May 8. To this day there is confusion as to why the *Vera Cruz* was headed for Ocracoke Inlet, for she had sailed from the Cape Verde Islands and was en route to New Bedford, Massachusetts, and Ocracoke Inlet is considerably off course. The explanation of Captain Julius M. Fernandez was that his supply of fresh water was exhausted and he was attempting to get through to Ocracoke and replenish the supply. On the other hand, it has been generally accepted on Ocracoke ever since that he was, in reality, attempting to smuggle some 399 Cape Verde Islanders into the United States by way of the eastern North Carolina sounds.

Those who tell this story add details to the effect that Captain Fernandez escaped the authorities at the time of the shipwreck and later smuggled his own way aboard a New Bedford whaler in a sperm oil barrel.

But smuggler or not, Captain Fernandez provided ample excitement for Terrell's lifesavers and the people of Portsmouth. To begin with, one of the passengers died of dysentery and had to be buried there on the island. After that a first class, man-sized fight

broke out on the *Vera Cruz*, and the lifesavers had to go aboard
to quell the riot. And finally, it was no small task to transport 421
persons, including 23 women and three children, from the wrecked
vessel to safety on Portsmouth Island in the midst of a strong
northeaster, with the sea tide so high it flooded most of the beach.

Terrell accomplished the task of transportation by hiring every
available man and every available boat and skiff on the island. The
women of Portsmouth pitched in and did the cooking, bedding was
spread on the floor of just about every house in the community,
and somehow the 421 persons were taken care of and made comfortable, though not a handful of them could speak English.

From first to last it was a trying time, though in the final analysis
a very successful operation; for in addition to rescuing 399 passengers and 22 crewmen, the lifesavers also managed to salvage the
entire cargo of sperm oil, 214 barrels of it, valued at six thousand
dollars. But the *Vera Cruz VII*, at least the remnants of her, are
there yet on Dry Shoal Point.

JOSEPH W. BROOKS

A shipwreck close to shore is bad enough, but when it occurs ten
or twelve miles at sea the task of effecting a rescue is just that much
harder. Two of the veteran lifesavers on this coast seem to have had
more than their share of these long-distance rescues, and almost
invariably they came at a time when the wind was blowing a gale
and the sea was exceptionally rough. Keeper J. L. Watts of Cape
Fear was one—he guided his lifesavers on more than a score such
rescues—and close behind him in the number of similar relief expeditions was Keeper William H. Gaskill of Cape Lookout.

Keeper Gaskill's report on the wreck of the 728-ton schooner
Joseph W. Brooks, of Philadelphia, on the outer point of Lookout
Shoals, January 17, 1904, is fairly typical of these rescues. Gaskill
was a seaman, his life dedicated to saving others; but his official
report, written in longhand and submitted in duplicate to Lifesaving
Service headquarters when the rescue mission was completed, is
surprisingly concise, well-written, and interesting. It follows:

"At 9:45 A.M. the day watch dimly discovered with the telescope
through the mist and smoke which hovered over the shoals the

mast of a schooner ashore on the end of Lookout Shoals. The life-boat was gotten out and a start for the wreck made. Having a strong fair wind was soon within hailing distance of what proved to be the schooner *Joseph W. Brooks*, lumber laden, from Savannah, Geo., bound to Baltimore, Md., which was laying in a bed of heavy breakers, with a bad list to port, full of water, boat gone, and the sea going over her from end to end. Getting a favorable chance I got hold of a line from the end of the jibboom to the boat, and the bight of another line down from the same place, which the wrecked crew was instructed to come down on. And when the heaviest breakers would pass, I would haul up under the end of the jibboom, a man come down and be taken in the boat, and pull out again when compelled to do so by the sea. In this means the entire crew of seven was taken on board the lifeboat. When all was taken off we pulled out clear of the breakers and made a start for the shore, arriving at the station at 7 o'clock P.M. The wrecked crew was wet, cold and hungry, having eaten nothing since supper the day before and had been wet since early morning. All were provided with a warm supper, and an entire suit of clothing (Captain excepted, who needed none) from the supply furnished by the Women's National Relief Association, and all made as comfortable as possible for the night. The 18th, a boat came from Beaufort and took captain and crew of wrecked schooner *Brooks* to Beaufort, N.C."

SARAH D. J. RAWSON

If you check carefully through the voluminous reports of the Secretary of the Treasury and the Lifesaving Service you will find the following brief announcement: "In recognition of heroic conduct exhibited on the 9th and 10th of February, 1905, in the rescue of 6 men from the wreck of the schooner *Sarah D. J. Rawson*, gold lifesaving medals were bestowed upon the following members of the Life-Saving Service: keeper William H. Gaskill, surfmen Kilby Guthrie, Walter M. Yeomans, Tyre Moore, John A. Guthrie, James W. Fulcher, John E. Kirkman, Calupt T. Jarvis, and former surfman Joseph L. Lewis, all of the Cape Lookout Station."

There is more to the story than that, considerably more, for the rescue of the captain and crew of the three-masted schooner *Sarah*

D. J. Rawson, a 292-ton vessel hailing from Camden, Maine, was one
of the most daring ever recorded on our coast, and the fact that the
vessel went to pieces soon after the rescue was accomplished, makes
it almost certain that the entire crew would have been lost but for
the work of the lifesavers.

An epidemic of influenza had practically incapacitated the crew
of Cape Lookout Station in early February, 1905, and on the ninth
of the month Keeper Gaskill and every one of his surfmen still
suffered the weakening effects of the disease.

The ninth was a cold day, cold and foggy at Cape Lookout, with
tremendous breakers pounding across the shoals offshore. A constant
watch was maintained in the tower, though visibility was limited
to not more than a mile or so and the entire outer area of Lookout
Shoals was shrouded in the fog. At twelve noon, when the watch
changed, Keeper Gaskill went himself to the tower, took up the
glass, trained it on the fog-enveloped shoals. There was nothing
there, just the grayish smoke-like fog, the white-capped breakers
underneath, an occasional patch of blue water. Then, suddenly, a
break appeared, a rift in the fog, a long open channel of visibility
and on the far side of it an alien object, the mast of a sailing vessel.

That was all, for the fog closed in again, the open path was there
no more—just the smoky grayness, the whitecaps, and the seething
surf in close to shore. A man of lesser experience, a cautious man,
an ordinary man, might have let it go at that; for his eyes could have
been playing tricks on him, or it might have been the mast of an
old wreck, or even if it was a ship out there it might not be in
danger. But Keeper Gaskill knew what he had seen, knew there
were no old wrecks there, and when he checked the course and
estimated the distance on the chart before him, the answer was
clear; a sailing ship was aground far out on Lookout Shoals.

Nine sick men left their station, then, hauled their lifeboat down
to the surf, pulled their oilskins tight around them, and shoved off
into the troublous surf for what could only be a long and harrowing
journey. It took them almost four hours to reach the *Sarah Rawson*,
but that was just the beginning, for she was surrounded by breakers,
her boat had been smashed to pieces, her bowsprit, foremast, main-
topmast, deckhouses, and rigging were gone, and the lumber from

her deck load literally filled the surf around her. Already one of her crew had been washed overboard; the six remaining were huddled together on the canted deck of the wreck, or what was left of the deck.

Keeper Gaskill attempted to guide his boat through the mass of wreckage, came within two hundred yards, but was beaten back. Again he tried, and again and again and again—"I expected to see the lifeboat pitched end over end in the turbulent sea," said the captain of the *Sarah Rawson* when questioned later—but at last, with the approach of darkness, the lifeboat was forced to pull away.

The Cape Lookout surfmen anchored there that cold and damp and stormy night, anchored as close to the wreck as prudence allowed, to be at hand if she went to pieces. There was no sleeping for the lifesavers, no rest of any sort; for they were in constant danger of being swamped by the waves or sunk by drifting wreckage. They had anchored downwind, in the very path of the spars and lumber floating away from the *Rawson;* they wanted to be near at hand if survivors were washed overboard.

The fifteen of them survived the night somehow—nine lifesavers in their little boat, six shipwrecked sailors on the remnants of the schooner—and at dawn, with neither food nor water to nourish them, soaking wet and cold, coughing and sneezing, cramped and sore of muscle and limb, the lifesavers tried again to reach the wreck; they rowed in time after time but were thrown back as before.

Early that morning the wind shifted; later the tide changed too. For a time the sea calmed down a little, and the surfboat came in closer. Still it could not reach the wreck, though it was close enough this time for a surfman to heave a line aboard. One of the sailors tied it around his waist, jumped into the cold and angry sea, and was pulled safely on board the rescue craft. Back went the line, another sailor tied it around him, and like the first was pulled to safety. Six times that operation was performed; six men rescued, six lives saved. And as each sailor came aboard, soaked and nearly frozen, a lifesaver would remove his precious oilskin, wrap it around the man whose life he had helped save, still coughing, still sneezing, cold and wet himself. But the lifesavers could keep warm, would have to keep warm. For there was still before them the trip to shore;

nine miles of pulling the heavy oars in a sea too rough for safe passage of larger boats.

They made it back, those nine brave men, and landed their surfboat at the cape once more after twenty-eight hours at sea. Fires were built in the station stoves, food prepared for themselves and the six survivors, dry clothing provided for the men they had saved. And then, their work done, the nine of them sought their beds; for there was still an epidemic of influenza at Cape Lookout Station.

HILDA

Here is the log of attempts to rescue the crew of the three-masted schooner *Hilda* at Cape Hatteras, February 6, 1907:

2:15 A.M.—Surfmen B. F. Etheridge and U. B. Williams of Cape Hatteras Station discover vessel in the direction of Diamond Shoals. Burned three Coston signals.

2:30 A.M.—Keeper P. H. Etheridge, in the lookout tower of his station, could see the vessel in the moonlight. Was slowly moving southward.

4 A.M.—Vessel stopped, presumably anchored. Made no signal of distress. Lifesavers fired rocket to let her know they had her under surveillance.

6 A.M.—Lookouts at both Cape Hatteras and Creeds Hill stations reported distress signals from vessel. Rockets fired in response.

6:30 A.M.—Cape Hatteras surfboat launched.

7:20 A.M.—Creeds Hill surfboat launched.

8:00 A.M.—Two surfboats met near inner Diamond Shoals. Northwest wind blowing at gale force. Sea very rough. Temperature below freezing and still falling. Vessel a three-masted schooner hard aground on inner shoals five miles from Cape Point, and surrounded by huge breakers for half a mile in all directions.

8:15 A.M.—Surfboats attempted to go through breakers to stricken vessel, but thrown back by raging sea. Vessel now sunk, waves sweeping over her fore and aft. One man seen clinging to remnants of cabin.

9:00-12:00 A.M.—Repeated attempts made to reach vessel. All unsuccessful. Surfboats frequently almost submerged by tremendous breakers.

12:00 Noon—Having exhausted every means of rescue and in constant danger of capsizing, surfboats head for shore.

12:30 P.M.—Mast of Creeds Hill surfboat breaks off. Boat wallowing in waves. Impossible to use oars because of size of waves and force of wind. Mast finally hauled aboard and patched up.

1:30 P.M.—Cape Hatteras surfboat reached shore safely.

4:00 P.M.—Damaged Creeds Hill surfboat finally beached near Cape Point.

February 7, 1907:

6:00 A.M.—Crews from both stations again assemble on beach to attempt rescue. Weather murky.

7:00 A.M.—Sky clears. Wind still blowing strong. Surf high. Schooner has completely disappeared, presumably broken up with loss of all hands.

That is the final entry. It was learned later, however, that the vessel was the 647-ton schooner *Hilda* of Philadelphia, which had been en route from Philadelphia to Savannah with a cargo of coal and crew of seven—all presumed lost. Just another routine entry in the lifesavers' log.

FLORA ROGERS

The cypress-laden three-masted schooner *Flora Rogers* was driven ashore a mile north of Bodie Island Station, October 23, 1908, and became a total loss, though the crew of seven and the captain's wife were rescued in the breeches buoy. Because the vessel was rolling violently in the breakers the actual rescue was a slow and dangerous operation, and all of those brought ashore were thoroughly dunked in the surf en route. The picture eyewitnesses remember, however, is of the crewman who left the ship with a fine derby hat on his head and was still wearing it at a jaunty angle when he climbed out of the breeches buoy on the beach.

BREWSTER

Because of the treacherous nature of the ever shifting sand bars off Cape Hatteras the area has long been provided with a number of aids to the mariner, both signals to warn him away from Diamond Shoals and facilities for saving life if the warnings failed.

In 1909, for instance, two warning beacons were in constant operation. One was on top of Cape Hatteras Lighthouse near the point of the cape itself, and the other was on Diamond Shoals Lightship, fourteen miles southeast and just beyond the extreme outer edge of the shoals. In addition, the coast in both directions was dotted with lifesaving stations, the average distance between them being less than seven miles. Cape Hatteras Station was located adjacent to the lighthouse; Big Kinnakeet, first station to the north, was five miles distant near the village of Kinnakeet (now Avon); Creeds Hill, first station to the southwest, was also five miles distant, near the village of Frisco. Each of these was equipped with special boats, sail and oar powered, designed for quick launchings from the beach through heavy surf. And at Hatteras Inlet Station, on the eastern end of Ocracoke Island fourteen miles away, a larger, thirty-four-foot power lifeboat was kept in constant readiness to proceed through the inlet and join in rescue attempts.

All of the above played a part in the wreck and rescue of the crew of the German steamship *Brewster*, bound from Port Antonio, Jamaica, to New York, November 29, 1909, with seven thousand dollars worth of bananas, pineapples, and coconuts in her hold. Yet, strangely, the reason the *Brewster* wrecked in the first place was too much assistance, rather than too little; for Captain F. Hinz of the *Brewster* took his bearings from the Cape Hatteras Lighthouse thinking it was the Diamond Shoals Lightship and set a course that would take him up the coast some five miles east of the light.

Now, a course five miles east of Diamond Shoals Lightship would have put him in deep water on the fringe of the Gulf Stream; but five miles east of the Cape Hatteras Lighthouse landed the German right in the middle of the most rugged part of Diamond Shoals.

Captain Hinz was not the first mariner to make this mistake, nor the last; for the log books of ships lost in the Graveyard of the Atlantic and the official reports of the lifesavers show wreck after wreck caused by the same error. The big difference in the case of the *Brewster* was that she was a larger ship than most which have stranded there, and she carried, all told, a crew of thirty-three men.

Lifesavers from all four of the stations mentioned above went into action when the vessel was first spotted from Cape Hatteras

at 6:30 that morning. Acting Keeper Baxter B. Miller of Cape
Hatteras and Keeper E. H. Peel of Creeds Hill launched their self-
bailing surfboats from the beach; Keeper A. T. Gray of Big Kinnakeet mustered his crew and hurried to the cape to render assistance
if needed; Keeper D. W. Barnett of Hatteras Inlet boarded his
thirty-four-foot power lifeboat at the dock in Pamlico Sound and
proceeded out through the inlet. Even H. L. Gaskill, fishing offshore in his larger power boat, and the crew of Diamond Shoals
Lightship got into the act.

It was too rough to be fooling around out there in a little surfboat
in the first place, as Peel discovered when his craft sprang a leak
and sank even before reaching the shoals. The Cape Hatteras boat
rescued Peel and his crew, some of whom were transferred to Gaskill's fishing boat, and then Gaskill towed the surfboat as near as
possible to the wreck, where the boat was cast loose and attempted
to reach the *Brewster*.

By this time Peel had taken charge of the rescue operation. "Ow-
ing to the high seas which were breaking over the ship fore and
aft," he said, "it was impossible to board her. We rowed up as near
as we could, and I advised the captain to abandon his ship, which
he refused to do."

The wind, by this time, had increased greatly in force, with the
breakers making up higher and higher as time passed. Already five
crewmen from the *Brewster* had taken off in a yawl and were proceeding toward the lightship. But the remaining twenty-eight just
stayed there, refusing again and again to leave the vessel, while the
tired, soaked, and nearly frozen lifesavers remained in the breakers
alongside, bobbing up and down like a cowboy on a bucking horse,
pleading with the stubborn Captain Hinz, between soakings, to
get out of there.

It took an hour for Hinz to see the wisdom of this advice, and
by then the only way the rescue could be effected was by floating
a life preserver down toward the surfboat while each crewman,
individually, clung to the line and was drawn on board the small
rescue craft. But the boat was filled when only about a third of the
survivors had been taken off, so the lifesavers were forced to leave
the *Brewster*, return through the breakers to the comparative calm
where Keeper Barnett's power lifeboat was anchored, transfer the

sailors to the larger boat, and then return again through the raging breakers to continue the work.

Three times the surfboat was filled with the castaways, but at last all twenty-eight were safely transferred to the lifeboat, and the two craft started back for shore, the power boat towing the other. The rest was simple, for the survivors were landed through the surf while the lifeboat went back and towed in the sunken Creeds Hill boat. And just to round it off in fine fashion, the five crewmen in the yawl reached the lightship and were cared for there until the sea subsided and a cutter could remove them safely ashore.

Keeper Peel of Creeds Hill and acting Keeper Miller of Cape Hatteras received Gold Lifesaving Medals for directing the rescue of the twenty-eight crewmen from the *Brewster*, and Silver Life-saving Medals were awarded the following surfmen: O. O. Midgett, I. L. Jennett, Y. O. Gaskins, E. J. Midgett, U. B. Williams, W. L. Barnett, W. H. Austin, H. S. Miller, and D. W. Fulcher.

The bananas and pineapples and coconuts littered the beach in the days that followed, but the *Brewster* remained right where she was on the shoal, a grim reminder to other mariners that there are two warning lights at Cape Hatteras, and it is best to locate both of them before setting a course.

GEORGE W. WELLS

The largest sailing ship ever wrecked on the North Carolina coast (and one of the largest wooden sailing ships ever built) was the six-masted schooner *George W. Wells*, of Boston, which was lost at Ocracoke, September 3, 1913.

While en route from Boston to Fernandina, Florida, the 2,970-ton *Wells*, a fast but comparatively unwieldly vessel, was struck by hurricane winds off Hatteras, lost her sails (she had twenty-eight in all), became partly filled with water, and drifted into the breakers midway between the Ocracoke and Hatteras Inlet stations.

Because of the exceptionally strong winds seven shots had to be fired before the lifesavers succeeded in landing a line on the huge sailing craft. As it turned out, however, the seventh attempt was no more successful than the others, for the line broke as it was being hauled out to the vessel, and communication was not definitely established until Captain Joseph H. York of the *Wells* attached a line to a floating object, enabling the lifesavers to pull this out of the surf and then set up their breeches buoy.

After that the fifteen crewmen, three women, and two children on board were safely landed in the buoy. The $80,000 vessel was too far gone to be refloated, and her hull was later set afire and burned, reputedly because of a disagreement as to who was to salvage her.

SYLVIA C. HALL

The United States Lifesaving Service, originally set up on a nation-wide basis in 1871 and expanded to include part of the North Carolina coast in 1876, was amalgamated with the older United States Revenue Cutter Service on January 28, 1915. The name given to the new federal agency thus formed was United States Coast Guard, but the change actually made little difference along the coast, for the same stations, the same equipment, and the same crews were still employed.

At the time of the formation of the Coast Guard there were twenty-nine stations on the coast of North Carolina. These were, from north to south: Wash Woods, Pennys Hill, Whales Head, Poyners Hill, Caffeys Inlet, Paul Gamiels Hill, Kitty Hawk, Kill Devil Hills, Nags Head, Bodie Island, Oregon Inlet, Pea Island, New Inlet (abandoned the following year), Chicamacomico, Gull Shoal, Little Kinnakeet, Big Kinnakeet, Cape Hatteras, Creeds Hill, Durants, Hatteras Inlet, Ocracoke, Portsmouth, Core Bank, Cape Lookout, Fort Macon, Bogue Inlet, Cape Fear, and Oak Island.

The first instance of a ship loss in North Carolina within the domain of the new Coast Guard was the wreck of the 384-ton schooner *Sylvia C. Hall* on Lookout Shoals, March 17, 1915. It was an auspicious beginning for the new service.

The three-master *Hall*, loaded with lumber, was bound from Jacksonville to New York with a crew of five. Buffeted by a strong gale during the night she struck the shoals just before dawn and was sighted from Cape Lookout Coast Guard Station soon thereafter.

Keeper F. G. Gillikin launched his powerboat at 6:45 A.M., ran into exceptionally rough seas en route, and on arriving at the vessel could not approach close enough to effect a rescue. While waiting for the tide to change and the wind to moderate the powerboat was struck by a huge wave, completely burying the small craft and seriously injuring one of the crew. That is when Gillikin decided to return to shore for his self-bailing surfboat, in which he could stand a better chance of getting alongside.

They did not reach shore until late that afternoon, however, and delayed their second start until early the next morning. Then they towed the surfboat to the scene with their powerboat, maneuvered the surfboat in close enough to reach the survivors on the jib boom, and effected the rescue. Thus the Coast Guard took up where the Lifesaving Service had left off.

PRINZ MAURITS

What was described as "the worst storm in the history of central and eastern North Carolina," hit the state Saturday, April 3, 1915, with northeast winds reaching a velocity of seventy miles an hour as far inland as Raleigh.

The winds were accompanied by heavy snow—nearly two feet in the capital city—and exceptionally high tides which inundated most of the seacoast. A number of sailing craft—the schooners *Hugh Kelly*, *Alice Murphy*, *M. E. Cresser*, *Rob Roy*, *Clintonia*, *John B. Manning* and *Robert Graham Dunn*, and the bark *Edna M. Smith*—were disabled off Hatteras, and the Diamond Shoals Lightship was torn from its moorings and drifted four miles off station.

The schooner-barge *William H. Macy* stranded and became a total loss at Wash Woods after breaking loose from the tug *Edward Luckenbach* (which subsequently went to pieces in the surf just north of the Virginia-North Carolina line with the loss of fifteen lives).

At Kill Devil Hills the schooner *The Josephine* came ashore one and three-quarters miles south of the station and broke in two, with four crewmen reaching safety on pieces of wreckage and three others drowning. And at Gull Shoal the coastguardsmen rescued all seven crewmen from the schooner *Loring C. Ballard*, which was lost one-half mile south of the station.

But the big news in that spring storm was the loss of the Royal Dutch West Indies Line steamer *Prinz Maurits*, which last reported from a point approximately ninety miles east of Kitty Hawk that she was "sinking fast." A number of vessels, including two British warships which were blockading Hampton Roads to keep the German sea raider *Prinz Eitel Friedrich* from escaping, went to the assistance of the Dutch steamer, but when they reached the scene the following morning, April 4, there was no sign of her.

The *Prinz Maurits*, 285 feet in length, was registered at 1,328 net tons, and at the time of her loss carried a crew of forty-five and four passengers, all forty-nine of whom were presumed lost, making the sinking of the *Prinz Maurits* one of the half dozen most disastrous ship losses off the North Carolina coast up to that time.

THE UNITED STATES de-
clared war on Germany, April 6, 1917, and by May of the following
year had shipped an estimated two million fighting men overseas.
In order to transport an army of this size to France, every available
warship was pressed into service for patrol and convoy duty, with
the result that our own shores were left unguarded.

The Germans had demonstrated already that their submarines
were capable of making extended cruises of distances up to 12,000
miles, and shortly before the war the *Deutschland*, Germany's first
large "merchant" submarine, had visited our east coast.

To guard against attack by submarines of the *Deutschland* type
the United States Navy commandeered innumerable small vessels—
yachts, coastal freighters, fishing boats, and powerboats—and armed
them as sub chasers and mine sweepers. In addition, huge steel nets
were spread across the entrances to the larger and more important
harbors, and in certain sections aircraft units were assigned to
antisubmarine patrol.

The night of May 21, 1918, the government radio station at
Arlington terminated its regular news report with the same announcement it had been giving for months: "No submarine. No
war warning!"

At the entrance to Chesapeake Bay this report was picked up by a number of ships, for traffic was heavy in and out of the great port of Hampton Roads. Undoubtedly many a radio operator and master and crewman slept more soundly that night as a result of the reassuring message; but none received it with more relief than the seventy-seven men aboard the German submarine *U-151*, which at that moment was cruising nonchalantly on the surface at the very mouth of the bay, midway between Cape Henry and Cape Charles!

The *U-151* was the first enemy fighting ship to invade our waters since the war of 1812, more than 105 years earlier. She was commanded by Korvettenkapitän Von Nostitz und Janckendorf, a veteran sub man, and had left Germany just thirty-two days before, well supplied with mines, ammunition for her two deck guns, torpedoes, and a cable cutting device.

Her immediate assignment was to lay mines across the entrance to Chesapeake Bay, and this she accomplished without detection, though before she left the area a cruiser almost ran her down without knowing of her presence, and she was momentarily caught in the glare of searchlights from a small patrol boat. Still the Arlington radio continued to report "No submarine. No war warning," and the *U-151* moved up the east coast, laying the remainder of her mines in Delaware Bay (where she was caught in a dense fog and had to run on the surface for several hours blowing her compressed air whistle at regular intervals). She finally proceeded to New York harbor where for several days she was engaged in cutting cables, surfacing at night within view of the lights of Broadway.

Her mines deposited and her cable cutting assignment completed, the *U-151* headed south to inflict what damage she could on coastal shipping. In this department, too, she was eminently successful, and by the time she reached the Carolina coast early in the morning of June 5 she had already taken a sizeable toll of property and lives.

At nine o'clock that morning Von Nostitz sighted the 4,588-ton British steamer *Harpathian* at a point approximately ninety miles southeast of Cape Henry and almost directly opposite Knotts Island, North Carolina. The *Harpathian*, bound from Plymouth, England, to Newport News in ballast, had a crew of forty men. She was a formidable looking vessel, of the type which frequently carried armament and trained gun crews, and the U-boat skipper decided to take no chances with her. He submerged before the steamer sighted him, and manuevered for half an hour before reaching just the right position for a torpedo attack.

The explosion, as the torpedo struck the *Harpathian*, was the first notice the crew had that a sub was near by. The vessel settled rapidly, and Captain Owens ordered his lifeboats launched. In short order the boats had pulled clear of the sinking ship and the sub surfaced near by. One of the twenty-six Chinese in the crew, a fireman, had been injured at the time of the explosion, and the Germans took him aboard the sub, where he was treated by Dr. Frederick Korner, the boarding officer and surgeon. While the injured crewman was being cared for, bully beef, tobacco, and fresh water were passed to each of the lifeboats. Finally the wounded fireman was placed on board one of the boats also, Von Nostitz gave Captain Owens the course toward land, and the sub resumed its hunt. Later the *Harpathian's* lifeboats were sighted by the British steamship *Potomac*, which transported the survivors to Norfolk, and even as late as 1944 the sunken vessel was located by a Coast Guard patrol boat, in deep water sixty miles off the Carolina coast.

That was just the beginning of the *U-151's* activities for June 5, 1918. In midafternoon she sighted two New Bedford whalers, the *Ellen Swift* and the *A. M. Nicholson*. The former was too far away for a successful attack, but the latter was directly in the U-boat's path, and at 4 P.M. Von Nostitz ordered her to heave to.

Captain J. T. Gonsalves of the ancient *Nicholson* was either a very sincere man or a top-notch liar, for when his boat had pulled over to the sub he offered such a convincing story of hard luck—of the *Nicholson* being owned by several very poor Mississippi families, whose entire livelihood was dependent on the meagre income from the whaler's expeditions—that the Germans let him go, and he reached New Bedford safely four days later.

The Norwegian steamer *Vinland*, sighted by the *U-151* an hour later, was not so fortunate. She was en route from Guantanamo Bay, Cuba, to New York with a full cargo of sugar, a commodity which was already in short supply on the Atlantic seaboard. When Captain Bratland of the *Vinland* first sighted the sub, he mistook her for a tramp steamer and continued on his northward course, and only when Von Nostitz fired a warning shot over the vessel was he aware that he was under attack. Dr. Korner and a picked crew lost no time in boarding the steamer, and while they placed small bombs in strategic positions about the vessel Captain Bratland and his crew gathered their personal belongings, loaded them in lifeboats and rowed clear. At 6:30 the bombs exploded and the 1,143-ton *Vinland* and her valuable cargo of sugar disappeared below the surface, approximately fifty miles east of the spot where the *Harpathian* was sunk.

For two days the *U-151* cruised off the North Carolina coast from the Virginia line to Cape Hatteras. The only vessel sighted during this period was the *Mantilla*, a British ship which escaped in a rough sea and warned other vessels of the U-boat's location. But shortly after dawn June 8, the 3,179-ton Norwegian steamship *Vindeggen* was sighted by the *U-151*, and at 5:30 A.M. Captain Ballestead halted his vessel and despite the rough sea ordered his crew to abandon ship. The starboard boat, first to go overboard, capsized as she struck the water, and one of the crewmen—the deckhands were all Chinese—was drowned. By that time the Germans had come close enough to establish contact, and on learning that the *Vindeggen* carried two thousand tons of copper bars in addition to six thousand bales of wool and hides, Von Nostitz decided to try to transfer part of the cargo to his own vessel.

The sea was too turbulent to attempt such a transfer at that time, however, so the German ordered Captain Ballestead to get his own vessel underway again, and with the U-boat following close behind, the *Vindeggen* headed toward the open sea.

Shortly afterwards another steamer appeared, and using the *Vindeggen* as a sort of decoy the U-boat was able to approach almost within hailing distance before being seen. This was another sugar ship, the *Pinar Del Río*, 2,504 tons, from Cuba to Boston. In short order her crew of thirty-four launched two lifeboats and when they were clear of the vessel the sub began shelling her at short range. She sank, with 25,000 bags of sugar, approximately eighty miles northeast of Nags Head. Eighteen of her crew, including Captain John MacKenzie, were picked up shortly afterwards by a fruit steamer en route to New York, and the remaining sixteen were discovered by a second steamer, this one bound overseas. The captain steamed in close to shore abreast of the Nags Head Coast Guard Station, however, and signalled for the surfmen to come off and pick up survivors, an operation which was accomplished in the rough sea in two trips of the Coast Guard surfboat. The story which came out of Manteo the following day was that the submarine which had sunk the *Pinar Del Río* was accompanied by a large "mother" steamer which presumably was serving both as a supply ship and as a decoy.

Meanwhile, the *U-151* and her so-called "mother" ship, the *Vindeggen*, proceeded further offshore, and when the sea calmed down a woman and child—the wife and young daughter of Mate Ugland—were moved to the underseas craft, where the officers' quarters were turned over to them, while the crews of the two vessels transferred some eighty tons of the copper bars to the sub, replacing pig iron ballast which was thrown overboard. Then, on June 10, bombs were placed inside the ship, the crew of the *Vindeggen* took to lifeboats, and with the sub crew standing at attention and the Norwegian flag flying at her masthead, the *Vindeggen* exploded and sank.

Throughout that day Mrs. Ugland and her small daughter remained aboard the sub while the *Vindeggen*'s lifeboats were towed along behind. Still another ship was sunk during the afternoon, the 4,322-ton Norwegian steamship *Heinrich Lund*, and her lifeboats were added to the small flotilla of open boats being towed by the U-boat. That evening the sub sighted the steamer *Brosund*, which was given a choice of taking aboard the survivors of the *Vindeggen* and *Heinrich Lund* or being sunk; and fifteen minutes later the *Brosund*, with Mrs. Ugland, her daughter, and sixty-six crewmen from the two sunken vessels, left the scene with dispatch.

Korvettenkapitän Von Nostitz, having disposed of his mines and most of his torpedoes, ammunition, and fuel, turned eastward and began the long trek back to his home base at Kiel, probably well pleased with the results of the first invasion of American waters by an enemy craft in more than a century.

In all, seven German submarines were dispatched to the east coast of the United States during the war. Two of these, the *U-156*, which was already in mid-Atlantic when Von Nostitz started back to Germany, and the *U-155*, formerly the *Deutschland*, operated off the coast of New England, concentrating for the most on sinking the small vessels of the fishing fleets. Two more, the *U-152* and

the *U-139* departed too late to reach our shores before the end of
the war. The other two not only crossed the Atlantic without
mishap but made substantial additions to the toll taken by Von
Nostitz in the *U-151*.

Fregattenkapitän Waldemar Kophamel had served as lieutenant
on the maiden voyage of Germany's first submarine and as the
commander of her second one. At the outbreak of the war he was
the most experienced of Germany's submarine officers, and in the
underseas campaign against Britain and France had sunk sixty ships,
and set a long distance record for submersibles with a twelve-thou-
sand-mile voyage down the west coast of Africa and back.

It was a fitting reward for Kophamel, therefore, that he should
be placed in command of Germany's newest, largest, and most
modern submarine, the 380-foot *U-140*, on her maiden voyage to
the coast of the United States.

The *U-140* carried thirty-five torpedoes for her eight torpedo
tubes, as well as four thousand rounds of ammunition for her two
deck guns—a six-incher on the foredeck and a four-incher just aft
of the conning tower. She departed from Germany, June 22, 1918,
shortly after being commissioned at the Krupp works at Kiel and
proceeded leisurely across the North Atlantic, reaching the vicinity
of the Virginia Capes in early August.

The *U-140* encountered her first major victim, the 10,000-ton
tanker *O. B. Jennings*, approximately sixty miles southeast of Cape
Henry on August 4, and Kophamel immediately fired a torpedo
at the tanker's port bow. The *Jennings*, a Standard Oil Company
tanker, carried a full gun crew and was returning empty from
Plymouth, England, to Newport News. Her captain, George Nordstrom, personally spotted the torpedo shortly after it was fired and
managed to swing his vessel in time to elude it. He then ordered
full speed ahead, the single four-inch gun on the after deck was
manned, and for the next hour the tanker and the submarine engaged in a running gun battle.

Fregattenkapitän Kophamel had the advantage all the way. His
was the faster vessel—a twenty-six-knot top speed on the surface, as
against ten knots for the tanker—and he was able to stay out of
range of the *Jennings'* four-inch gun while his six-incher found the
range. Even so, Captain Nordstrom gave him a good chase of it,

zig-zagging time and again to confuse the U-boat's gunners, and even dropping smoke boxes overboard to screen his vessel. The *U-140* fired forty shells—one-tenth of her total supply—before finally making a hit; but at 11:30 her gunners began making contact at almost every shot, and ten minutes later a shell struck the engine room, and a second one hit the tanker's magazine, causing a tremendous explosion.

Her ammunition expended or destroyed, and her engines out of commission, the *Jennings* was licked. One of her crewmen, Second Steward James H. Scott, had been killed, and several others were wounded. She sent a frantic wireless message for assistance, and as the crew lowered the boats Captain Nordstrom exchanged clothes with the dead steward and joined the others in the lifeboats, leaving the doomed vessel at 12:20 P.M.

Three lifeboats were launched, one in command of Captain Nordstrom (now dressed as a steward), the second under Chief Engineer Albert Lacey, and the third under First Officer William J. Manning. The U-boat came up alongside the three boats to inquire for the Captain but was informed that he had been killed. They then took on board as a prisoner Second Officer Rene Bastin, fired several more rounds at the *Jennings,* and as she rolled over and sank the sub left the scene, with Second Officer Bastin still aboard.

During the night the three boats became separated. The destroyer U.S.S. *Hull,* which had intercepted the *Jennings'* final wireless message, arrived in the vicinity shortly after dark and located the lifeboats commanded by the engineer and First Officer, picking up the thirty-three men in the two boats. The third boat, with Captain Nordstrom in charge, was located the following morning by the Italian steamer *Umbria,* which took the fifteen remaining men in close to Currituck Beach, where the lifeboat was again launched and Captain Nordstrom and his men rowed to safety.

This was the beginning of some concentrated warfare for the *U-140.* That same afternoon, approximately 110 miles off Cape Hatteras, she spotted the four-masted schooner *Stanley M. Seaman* and sent a shot through her rigging. Captain William McAloney of the *Seaman,* en route to Puerto Plata, Santo Domingo, from Newport News with his 1,060-ton sailing craft loaded with coal, lost no time in taking the U-boat's hint. In fact, he abandoned ship in such a hurry with his eight-man crew that he took off in a small yawl instead of spending the extra time to lower a motor launch which the *Seaman* also carried. Further, in their haste the nine men failed to take with them water or provisions of any kind.

When the sub came up alongside and Kophamel learned of this he suggested that they return and exchange boats; the *U-140* waited while ample provisions were stored in the motor boat and the nine men had again pulled clear. He then sent the *Seaman* to the bottom with bombs, and for the next three days the crew of the schooner wandered about off Cape Hatteras, finally being picked up by a British steamer which landed them right back at Newport News where they had started.

The following day the *U-140* surfaced within sight of the Diamond Shoals Lightship. It is entirely possible that at that time Kophamel had no intention of attacking the light vessel, for his immediate target was the 3,024-ton coal-laden American steamship *Merak* en route to Chile from Newport News. The day was calm, with a moderate southwest breeze and a hazy sky. As soon as the *U-140* surfaced she began firing on the *Merak*, but the steamer zig-zagged down the coast at full speed, and more than thirty shots were fired at her without a hit. But the shifting sands of Diamond Shoals, a first-class menace to shipping in peacetime, proved even a more fatal wartime foe to the *Merak*, for suddenly she grounded on the fringe of the shoals and stuck fast. Two lifeboats were launched quickly, with twenty-three of her crew boarding one and the remaining twenty shoving off in the other.

Seeing that the *Merak* was aground on the shoals and that her crew was abandoning her, Kophamel now turned his attention to the lightship.

First Mate Walter L. Barnett of Diamond Shoals Lightship No. 71 had been born and brought up in Buxton, the tiny fishing village nestled in the lush, wooded dunes just back of Cape Hatteras. He had joined the United States Lighthouse Service in 1901 at the age of thirty, and in the ensuing seventeen years had served at various posts along the Atlantic coast. Just recently he had been transferred to No. 71, and on the day that the German submarine attacked her, Captain Charles Swanburg was on liberty and First Mate Barnett was in command of the light vessel.

Shortly after noon Barnett heard the sound of shellfire north of the lightship and climbed the mast to the wide gallery which surrounded the vessel's huge flashing light, visible on a clear night more than sixteen miles away. For some time he remained there, attempting through binoculars to locate the source of the firing. Suddenly, he spotted a puff of smoke, then another, and as the haze lifted slightly he could make out the low-slung outline of the submarine less than half a mile away, and in the distance the merchant vessel which she was shelling.

He hurried back to the wireless shack (which in this case was, literally, a shack that had been built on the lightship's deck some time after the vessel was launched) and sent the following message: "Enemy submarine shelling unknown ship E.N.E. ¼ mile off lightship."

This message may have spelled doom for the lightship, for not until then did the *U-140* turn her guns on the anchored vessel. "Her first shot took away our wireless," Barnett says, "but the next five were aimed wide and missed us. We had been painting our yawl-boat that morning, and she was hauled up on the davits with nothing inside but a small canvas sail. I called for her oars, and had the yawl lowered to the water."

No. 71 was a sitting duck; a tub-like 124-foot vessel, held in place by 185 fathoms of heavy chains (the links were eight inches in diameter) firmly attached to a 5,000-pound mushroom anchor imbedded in the sandy shoal. She was a coal burner, and her fires were always banked, but with the necessity of getting up steam and at the same time hauling in the huge anchor and chain, it normally took her something like five hours to get underway. Even if it had taken only five minutes Barnett would have stood practically no chance of eluding the U-boat in his lumbering light vessel that August afternoon.

As it was, the prudent thing was to get out of there in a hurry before the sub's gunners found the range again.

"Within ten minutes we had the whaleboat overboard, and the twelve of us had shoved off from No. 71," Barnett said. "We had seven oars, six fourteen-footers for rowing, and a sixteen-foot sweep oar. I put the large oar over the stern and six of the crew grabbed the others, and we headed to the west'ard as fast as they could row.

Roberts, the chief engineer, had left his false teeth behind, and none of us had saved anything but the clothes we had on our backs, but nobody seemed bothered too much about that.

"We rowed for maybe five miles (local rumor has it that Guy Quidley, another Buxton native in the crew, rowed so hard that he broke two of the fourteen-foot oars before they reached shore, but Barnett would not confirm the story) and all the time the sub kept firing at No. 71. Finally, we could just see her go down in the distance. By then the sub was way out of sight, so I told the boys to pull in the oars, and I mounted the sail, using the sweep oar for a mast."

In the village of Buxton, meanwhile, Mrs. Walter Barnett and her neighbors had heard the firing offshore throughout the afternoon. A lot of people walked down to the sea on the chance that they could get a look at what was happening, but Mrs. Barnett remained home and tried her best to go about the usual housekeeping chores. Her husband had said more than once that if enemy subs showed up they would need the lightship as much as our own ships did, so he was not in any danger. But she had a feeling that day maybe he had been wrong.

Barnett's whaleboat had left the lightship at 2:35 P.M., fourteen miles from the point of Cape Hatteras, but land was not sighted by the twelve survivors (she normally carried a crew of fifteen, but two seamen were on liberty in addition to the master) until just before dark. They finally came up close to shore about a mile north of the Cape Hatteras wireless station, so Barnett hauled down his improvised sail, the crew manned the oars again, and they rowed down the coast to a point opposite the wireless station, where at 9:30 P.M. they landed through the surf.

Barnett reported via wireless to Navy headquarters (during the war the Lighthouse Service was under Navy control) and got word back that he and his crew should not discuss the sinking until a full official report could be made. He then made his way along the familiar sandy, dune-fringed road to his house, where he was met at the door by his wife, who had known all along, somehow, that he would be home that night.

While all this was going on, one of the boats from the stranded *Merak* had reached shore and the other had been picked up at sea by a patrol boat. Meanwhile, Fregattenkapitän Kophamel's *U-140*, having sunk the lightship, returned to pick up the *Merak's* papers and finish off the vessel with bombs. And at about the time that Barnett and the crew of Lightship No. 71 were sighting the familiar coastline of Cape Hatteras, the lookout on board the *U-140* spotted two other ships running for safety. One, the steamship *Mariner's Harbor*, had witnessed the attack on the *Merak*; the other, the British steamship *Bencleuch*, had been warned by Barnett's wireless message. Of the two the *Bencleuch* had the narrowest escape, for at one time she was within gun range of the *U-140*. But under cover of darkness both vessels, and a third which was also in the vicinity —the American passenger steamer *Cretan*—hugged the shore with all lights out and proceeded in safety along the coast.

In addition to these three vessels, twenty-eight more, in convoy off Cape Lookout and due to round Cape Hatteras that night, were warned of the U-boat's presence and put into a safe harbor at Beaufort. And though, for a time, mariners rounding the dreaded Diamond Shoals did so without the friendly warning beacon of the lightship, a relief vessel, Lightship No. 72, was returned to the same station less than six months later. Her first mate? Why, Walter L. Barnett, of course. For Diamond Shoals, remember, was only four-teen miles from home.

Off Kill Devil Hills, two days later, the *U-140* attacked the Brazilian passenger steamer *Uberaba*. This time, however, a United States destroyer, the U.S.S. *Stringham*, was near by and picked up the *Uberaba's* distress signal. For a time it looked to the 250 passengers on board the *Uberaba* as if they were doomed, for the U-boat gained steadily on the slower steamship. But the *Stringham* appeared on the horizon and, screened by the steamer, darted out and attacked the sub with gunfire and depth bombs.

Shortly afterwards the destroyer sent the following report of the engagement: "Enemy submarine sighted. . . . Dropped fifteen depth charges. . . . Escaped undamaged."

The message from the destroyer may have meant that she and the steamer escaped undamaged, but if it referred to the submarine it was badly mistaken. For the *U-140*, in a crash dive to three hundred feet, was rocked by a depth charge; her lights went out, seams opened and water gushed in, and for a time the undersea raider, by then four hundred feet under water, was unmanageable. All this time Second Mate Rene Bastin, of the sunken tanker *O. B. Jennings*, was a prisoner aboard the U-boat. He reported later that for a time he was certain the vessel was lost; then fuses were replaced, the lights came on, water-tight compartments were closed and seams were patched up. Finally, under control once again, the *U-140* moved toward the open sea, surfacing next morning with no sign of the destroyer and then proceeding as rapidly as possible back to her home base in Germany.

While the *U-140* was sinking the *Jennings, Seaman, Merak* and *Diamond Shoals Lightship*, a sister ship, the *U-117*, was attacking small fishing boats off Georges Bank and laying her mines along the New England and middle Atlantic coasts. On August 14, with nine mines still remaining, she arrived off the Carolina coast and laid the mines near Wimble Shoals, stringing them out in a two and a half mile line across the shipping lane.

Two days later the *U-117*'s mines took their first toll, resulting in one of the most dramatic rescue operations in the annals of the Coast Guard.

The British tanker *Mirlo*, 6,679 tons, with a crew of fifty-two, picked up a full cargo of gasoline in New Orleans on August 10, 1918, and headed across the Gulf of Mexico. Then she rounded the Florida keys and moved up the east coast toward Norfolk. Despite the absence of the Diamond Shoals Lightship, she passed Cape Hatteras in safety soon after noon on August 16 and proceeded north toward Wimble Shoals.

The wind was light, from the northeast; the sea comparatively calm. When opposite Wimble Shoals Light Buoy a terrific explosion rocked the ship, wrecking the engine room and putting the lights and wireless out of commission. Captain W. R. Williams ordered his lifeboats made ready for lowering and attempted to reach the beach. He reported later that his vessel was torpedoed, but he did not actually see a torpedo and the absence of enemy submarines in the area (the *U-117*, only German sub on this side of the Atlantic at the time, was several hundred miles further north engaged in other nefarious activities) makes it quite certain that the *Mirlo* struck one of the mines.

The original explosion was witnessed by the lookout in the

Chicamacomico Coast Guard Station, seven miles northeast of the light buoy. The keeper of the station, Captain John Allen Midgett, was summoned and ordered out his power lifeboat. (Though keepers of Coast Guard stations along the coast are generally addressed as "captain," in almost all cases they are chief bosun mates, noncommissioned officers equivalent in rank to Army master sergeants).

While the lifesavers were making preparations to put to sea, a second explosion took place on board the *Mirlo*, her cargo of gasoline caught fire, and Captain Williams, having given up all hope of beaching the ship, ordered his lifeboats lowered away.

The port lifeboat, first to be lowered, fouled the stays and capsized, but the sixteen men aboard, thrown into the sea by the accident, all managed to reach the overturned boat and hang on momentarily. The other two boats got overboard safely, one containing the Captain and sixteen men, and the other, Boatswain Donalds and eighteen men.

It was then that the third and final explosion took place, cutting the ship in half and spewing its cargo of highly inflammable gasoline over the water in all directions.

One boat, the Captain's, was soon clear of the sea of fire; the second, without oars, drifted aimlessly before the wind which was steadily increasing in velocity; while the third, the one that had capsized, remained near the sinking vessel, in the very path of the burning fuel still gushing from her hold. The men clinging to her sides were themselves covered with gasoline, their clothes and their hair and even their bodies on fire. Only by remaining under water for as long as breath would hold out, then coming up again for a hurried breath of air and submerging once more, were they able to remain alive; even so, in short order ten of them disappeared from view, leaving only six still holding on to the overturned boat.

Captain John Allen Midgett of Chicamacomico Station, with six experienced surfmen in his motor surfboat, came through the breakers without accident and headed for the towering cloud of smoke and flames rising from the sea on Wimble Shoals. En route he met the Captain's lifeboat and gave Captain Williams instructions to proceed in close to shore and wait there for his return, for the wind had freshened almost to gale intensity, the waves were building up in size and force, and under those conditions only a self-bailing surfboat in experienced hands could safely pass through the breakers.

Midgett learned from Captain Williams that two other boats had been launched, and that one of these had capsized near the sinking ship. Leaving the Captain's boat he proceeded within a few hundred yards of the *Mirlo*, which by now was on the verge of disappearing beneath the surface. There he was confronted by a veritable sea of fire. The entire surface of the ocean seemed to be covered with burning gasoline. Flames shot up in patches, and above them the great cloud of black smoke rose skyward. Midgett circled the cloud, coming up on the lee side and finding, at last, an opening in the blazing surface of the sea. And down this opening he saw the overturned lifeboat, with figures still clinging to it.

Men do strange things in an emergency—strange and brave and foolish things. Captain John Allen Midgett's next action was all of these, and more, for without a moment's hesitation he turned his wooden boat toward that blazing sea, ordered the crew to man their oars. He skillfully maneuvered her down that narrow open passage, moving directly through great sheets of fire at times, constantly enveloped in black smoke, hardly able to see for the darkness around him. The overturned surfboat was reached at last; the six men, exhausted, burned and blackened, hysterical and unbelieving, were pulled into the surfboat. One of his own men collapsed in the bow and had to be replaced. And then, his mission completed, he turned about and headed toward the open sea.

Only the rising wind, and resultant high waves, had saved the six men clinging to the port lifeboat; for though the gasoline had stilled the water to a great extent, there was still enough wind and splashing water to keep the full force of the heat from them; but that same wind had almost proved the downfall of the nineteen men aboard Boatswain Donalds' boat.

His was the smallest of the three boats, but it carried the most men. The gunwales were almost level with the water, and she shipped water with every wave. Flame, blown by the wind, seared the flesh of the men huddled in the tiny boat and set fire to the sides of the craft. Shirts were taken off and used to beat at the fire, then trousers and all other clothing, until the men were naked; and still the boat burned, and their flesh was singed, and they could see nothing for the black cloud of smoke which enveloped them.

Captain Midgett, having cleared the inferno with the six survivors of the port boat, still was not finished. Again he circled the burning mass but could find no trace of the third boat until at dusk he saw it, drifting helplessly before the wind with its cargo of nude and blackened humanity.

The lifesavers hurried toward the boat, passed a line aboard, and headed back for the beach where Captain Williams was still waiting. Midgett left both boats there, landing the first load of survivors through the surf while other lifesavers on shore shone powerful lights on the ever larger breakers. Then he returned a second time, and still a third, until all of the survivors—seventeen in the Captain's boat, nineteen in the Bosun's, and the six he had picked up from the sea, in all forty-two of the fifty-two who had been aboard the *Mirlo*—were landed safely on shore.

Soon afterwards Captain Midgett and his crew (Zion S. Midgett, A. V. Midgett, Prochorns L. O'Neal, L. S. Midgett, and C. E. Midgett) received Gold Lifesaving Medals from the United States government, and Victory Medals from the British. Then, their burns healed, they returned again to their lonely vigil on the coast.

As for the cause of all this trouble—the German submarine *U-117* —she had moved out to sea off Cape Hatteras, where two days later she attacked and sank the 2,846-ton Norwegian bark *Nordhav*, loaded with linseed oil for New York, and then, her mission done, she headed home.

Before the *U-117* reached Germany still another submarine raider left Kiel en route for our coast. This was the *U-152*, commanded by Kapitänleutnant Franz, and her priority assignment was to lay mines southeast of Currituck; but the *U-152* had not yet reached our coast when, on October 20, she received orders to return to Germany.

That order, if earlier actions can be used as a basis for speculation, was a godsend to our shipping and coastal residents. For whereas the three submarine commanders who had attacked our shores—Korvettenkapitän Von Nostitz in the *U-151*, Fregattenkapitän Kophamel in the *U-140*, and Kapitänleutnant Droscher in the *U-117*—in most cases exhibited genuine concern for the safety of the human beings aboard the vessels they attacked, Kapitän-leutnant Franz of the *U-152* was as ruthless and unmerciful a man as ever sailed the seas.

Franz failed to reach his destination, and en route he sank only two ships, totalling less than 7,000 tons. The first of these he raked with shellfire, ignoring a white flag of surrender, firing at the occupants of the only lifeboat which was launched, and in all killing 215 of the 239 men on board. The second, a small bark, he attacked soon after receiving specific orders from the German high command to engage only warships, since the merchant war had ended. And after sinking the bark he set the nineteen survivors adrift in two small open boats 1,200 miles from land. In those two attacks in mid-ocean he killed more men than did all of the other German subs which visited our waters.

Such was the nature of the man who was en route to the Carolina coast when the submarine war ended. And for all the horror attending the sinking of the *Mirlo* and the other sub victims, maybe we were fortunate after all, that Kapitänleutnant Franz never reached our shores.

EWER VESSELS were lost along the North Carolina coast between the two world wars than in most comparable periods of the past, but when figured on the basis of tonnage lost, or human lives lost, or thrilling rescues and attempted rescues, it was a period that will long be remembered.

CARROLL A. DEERING

Of the hundreds of ships which have been lost in the Graveyard of the Atlantic, none has commanded more attention than the five-masted schooner *Carroll A. Deering*, which fetched up on Diamond Shoals in the darkness of a stormy winter night in 1921.

At sunset, January 30, there was no sign of the *Deering* or any other vessel on the shoals; just the ocean rollers, coming in from two directions, crashing together above the Diamond's sand bars, dropping more sand to form new shoals and move the old ones. But at dawn the next morning, January 31, there was something else out there on the Diamond, a schooner, tall and stately, sails set on her five masts, abandoned by her crew, with no sign then or later as to what had happened to the men who once sailed on her. The *Carroll A. Deering*—Ghostship of The Diamond.

There have been rumors aplenty; repeated rumors of mutiny and murder and piracy. Hardly a year passes that some new theory is not advanced, new clues supposedly uncovered. But what happened to the crew of the *Carroll A. Deering* remains as much a mystery today as it was January 31, 1921, and with the following facts at hand you are welcome to draw your own conclusion.

The *Deering* was launched in 1919 at Bath, Maine, the last of many large schooners constructed for the G. G. Deering Company. Named for the owner's son, she was described as "a tremendous sailing ship," measuring 255 feet in length, 44.3 feet across the beam, and registered as being 1,879 tons.

Under command of Captain F. Merritt the five-master sailed from Boston in September, 1920, bound for Buenos Aires. When off the Delaware Capes, Captain Marritt became ill, so he put in at Lewes, Delaware, and was relieved of his command by a veteran retired ship master, Captain W. T. Wormell.

The *Deering* then proceeded to South America, apparently making several calls there, and leaving Rio de Janeiro on December 2, 1920, en route home to Norfolk, Virginia. She carried no cargo and made one stop on the return journey, at Barbados in the West Indies.

At 6:30 A.M., January 31, 1921, Surfman C. P. Brady, on lookout duty at the Cape Hatteras Coast Guard Station, sighted a five-masted schooner "with all sails set" on Diamond Shoals. At the time the wind was from the southwest, the sea was rough, the tide, strong.

In two boats, lifesavers from four stations—Big Kinnakeet, Cape Hatteras, Creeds Hill, and Hatteras Inlet—put to sea, reaching the vicinity of the stranded vessel in midmorning.

In his official report Keeper C. R. Hooper of Big Kinnakeet Station stated that she was "driven high up on the shoal . . . in a boiling bed of breakers . . . with all sails standing, as if she had been abandoned in a hurry." Keeper J. C. Gaskill of Creeds Hill reported that "she had been stripped of all life-boats and no sign of life on board. . . crew had apparently left in own boats, as ladder was hanging over side."

Because of the breakers surrounding the vessel the lifesavers could get no closer than one-quarter of a mile to the schooner, and at that distance they were unable to make out her name.

The next day the sea continued rough and the Coast Guard cutter *Seminole* was dispatched to the scene from Wilmington; and the day after that the cutter *Manning* and the wrecking tug *Rescue* joined the *Seminole* from Norfolk. Not until February 4, however —four full days after the five-master was first discovered aground— was it possible to board the schooner. Waves had been breaking over her deck, and when the wreckers reached her, water filled her hold. Her seams were so badly ripped apart that there was no hope of floating the vessel. Her steering gear was disabled, charts were scattered about the master's bathroom, and food was set out in the galley and on the stove.

Subsequently the wreckers removed what they could from the vessel, and following a severe storm three weeks later she was dynamited. A small section of her bow drifted ashore on Ocracoke and for years was a tourist attraction, but in a recent hurricane it floated free, taking up on the beach near Hatteras.

So much for the facts; now for the theories, rumors, and speculation.

Mutiny—Investigation revealed that Captain Wormell had confided to a friend in Barbados that he was ill, and that he had no faith in his crew, especially his first mate. It was further reported that the vessel had passed Cape Lookout Light Vessel the day before she stranded, and that a crewman (not the Captain) had shouted through a megaphone that the vessel had lost her anchors in a storm off Cape Fear and needed assistance. This led to the conclusion in some quarters that "Old Man" Wormell had been murdered by the mate or other crewmen, but it offers no explanation of what happened to the survivors.

Piracy—Several other ships disappeared at sea at about the same time (though thousands have disappeared off the Atlantic coast with no trace in years gone by) and there were reports that they had been captured by Russian pirates. At about this time a resident of Buxton claimed he had found a bottle on the beach with a note inside indicating that pirates had boarded the *Deering* and murdered the crew. It was later reliably determined that the man who reported finding the message had written it himself.

Abandoned at Sea—The most frequently voiced opinion—and the one given most credence by the Coast Guard and other agencies which investigated—was that the *Deering* had encountered a storm off the lower Carolina coast, drifting toward Diamond Shoals in a disabled state, and that her eleven crewmen, certain that she would strand on treacherous Diamond, had abandoned her in panic, drifting to sea and certain death in their open boats.

Mutiny, piracy, abandonment by the crew. Take your choice. And if you ever get to Ocracoke examine the remnants of her bow, as thousands of others have, so that you too may become an authority on the fate of the five-master *Carroll A. Deering*.

VIRGINIA and NEW JERSEY

Not all ships lost on our coast were wrecked by the forces of nature; some were purposely sunk by man.

September 5, 1923, two United States battleships, the *Virginia* and the *New Jersey*, were sent to the bottom within a mile of the Diamond Shoals Light Vessel by Army airmen under command of Brigadier General Billy Mitchell. The sinkings were the first step in the scrapping of American war craft, as required under the naval limitations treaty drawn up after World War I. They proved, also, that the mightiest battleships could be sunk by air attack.

The two battleships were sisterships. Construction was started on them in 1902 and completed in 1906 at a cost of six million dollars each. The 435-foot long vessels were listed as having 14,949 tons displacement, and each carried four twelve-inch and eight eight-inch rifles in six turrets.

Most of the Army planes participating in the attack on the two vessels took off from a temporary field set up on the beach near Hatteras. The *New Jersey* was attacked first that morning from a height of over one mile. She soon listed badly but did not sink, so the attack was switched to the *Virginia*, with eight planes, flying at 3,000 feet, dropping a total of thirteen 1,100-pound bombs on her. At 11:54 A.M., just thirty minutes after the attack began, the *Virginia* sank, and at 3:30 that afternoon three bombers returned to finish off the crippled *New Jersey*. She, too, went to the bottom off Diamond Shoals.

SANTIAGO

The Ward Line freighter *Santiago*, loaded with 32,000 bags of sugar, left Cienfuegos on the southern coast of Cuba, March 4,

1924. She had accumulated her cargo at several Cuban ports, including Matanzas on the northern coast, where she had run ashore the week before. This had necessitated discharging some 129 tons of sugar into lighters before she floated free; then the sugar was put back on board again, the *Santiago* proceeded around the island to Cienfuegos, and on March 4, fully loaded and apparently undamaged, she sailed for New York.

Three days out, the 5,000-ton freighter ran into a severe storm, and for the next seventy hours she plowed through heavy seas while the wind increased steadily in intensity. The end came Tuesday night, March 11, at a point approximately sixty miles south of Cape Hatteras. It was precipitated when one of the hatches broke open, letting great quantities of water pour into the holds.

The men were then set to her pumps but were driven from her hold after several hours by the inrushing water. Two officers—the first and third mates—perceiving that the open hatch cover was still intact though swept back and forth across the deck with every roll of the vessel, attempted to move forward to retrieve it. Even as they reached the hatch cover, however, a huge wave poured over the deck, a terrified cry rang out in the darkness, and the two officers disappeared.

By then the holds were practically filled with water, the pumps were inoperative, the engines had stopped, and the vessel was unmanageable. Captain J. S. Baldwin had rockets sent up as signals of distress, ordered the boats launched, and gave the command to abandon ship, meanwhile lashing himself to the mast.

In the mad scramble for the boats three more men were washed overboard, but the first lifeboat was finally lowered over the side, filled with human beings. Before it could be moved into the open, however, the boat was thrown against the huge steel hull and crushed, the water swallowing up the men who had been in it.

A second boat then went over successfully, with eleven men aboard. "There was no attempt to man the oars," a survivor said later, for all the occupants could do was "to cling desperately to the gunwales."

This boat drifted clear of the sinking freighter. Shortly afterwards, with Captain Baldwin still lashed to the mast, the *Santiago* rolled over and disappeared.

For three more hours the lifeboat drifted in the tumultuous sea, half-filled with water, the helpless men able only to hang on for their lives. Suddenly the boat capsized, and the eleven men were thrown into the water. Ten managed to regain holds on the over-turned craft. The eleventh failed to come up again.

Early the next morning the wireless station at Charleston picked up a message from the Norwegian steamer *Cissy*, which read: "Picked up life-boat containing six sailors, three firemen, one carpenter from the steamer *Santiago* which sank 60 miles south of Hatteras. No other life-boats seen. Proceeding to Baltimore."

That marked the end for the Ward liner *Santiago*. Ten saved. Twenty-five lost. One more vessel consigned to the depths off the North Carolina coast.

KYZIKES

"Come at once if you can. We are badly in need of assistance."

The wireless operator of the Greek tank steamer *Kyzikes* tapped out this message shortly after noon, Saturday, December 3, 1927. Other messages followed: The *Kyzikes* was approximately two hundred miles off the Virginia Capes. She had been battered by storm winds and was leaking badly. Water was pouring into her holds from stem and stern. Most of her deck gear had been carried away. She needed help immediately.

After that the messages stopped. The *Kyzikes*' wireless antenna had been carried away. But those brief words had been enough to set in motion extensive attempts at rescue.

Less than sixty miles away from the position given by the *Kyzikes* the steamer *Harvester* had picked up the message, quickly altered her course, and was steaming toward the scene. At Norfolk the tug *Carrabasset*, the only large Coast Guard vessel available, was immediately dispatched to the aid of the tanker. The motor ship *East Indian*, the steamer *City of Atlanta*, the tanker *William M. Irish*, and the steamer *Baron Herries* also were proceeding toward the distressed vessel.

The *East Indian*, considerably farther away than the other vessels, turned back when she learned that assistance was at hand. The *Harvester* and *City of Atlanta* failed to locate the sinking ship. The

Baron Herries sighted distress rockets, stood by momentarily, then lost the tanker in the darkness. The *William M. Irish* damaged her hull and broke her steering gear and had to send out her own calls for assistance; and the *Carrabasset*, encountering northeast winds of better than seventy miles per hour, turned about and almost foundered before regaining the safety of Hampton Roads.

Thus, that night, the battered and leaking *Kyzikes* was as much alone as before, despite the attempts of half a dozen vessels to assist her.

The *Kyzikes* was a craft of 2,627 gross tons, measuring 227 feet in length. Built at Lorain, Ohio, in 1900, and originally named *Paraguay*, she had served under American registry for a number of years before being transferred to the Greek flag and renamed *Kyzikes*. With twenty-eight crewmen on board she had left Baltimore November 28 with a cargo of crude oil destined for Seville, Spain, had begun to leak the third day out, and was en route back to port when the northeaster struck her Friday night. By Saturday, when her distress signals were sent out, Captain Nickolas Kantanlos held almost no hope of saving his vessel; his one thought was to get his crew aboard a passing ship or on shore.

Saturday night, while drifting before the northeaster, the crew made fruitless efforts to pump out the deeply laden vessel. During the process four men were washed overboard and drowned, the tanker's fires were extinguished, her engines stopped, and her lights went out. In the inky blackness of the storm-swept Atlantic, thereafter, the *Kyzikes* drifted—"We were like a piece of bark on the ocean," Captain Kantanlos said—until, at 4:35 Sunday morning, she struck the beach.

"The seas pounded the side of the ship with terrific force," Captain Kantanlos recounted later. "She rocked and shook like a leaf. Then she began to break up. We could hear the tearing of her iron sides, the creaking of the tanks. It was terrible."

Second Mate Evangelos Palamario took up the narrative then. "We had been expecting her to break but the pounding had been so heavy that we didn't realize it when it happened. Day had not begun to break, and it was still inky dark when we saw what we thought was a ship alongside. We immediately signalled with our lights for a rescue, and were answered by similar signals."

Thus, after drifting helplessly throughout the night, after striking an obstruction of unknown form or location, and after crouch-
ing there on the bow of their ship while the horrible sounds of her
own disintegration came to them above the wind, there suddenly
appeared this hope of rescue. Again and again and again the lights
were flashed. Once, twice, three times the answering lights came
back. And then, suddenly, the full truth dawned on them.

This was no rescue vessel at their side. Rather, according to Mate
Palamario, "It was the stern of our own ship, which had swung
around almost alongside, and the men answering our signals were
five of our own men who had also mistaken us for another ship
and were seeking rescue!

"It was evident that the portion of the ship would soon break
away and sink," the Mate continued. "I found a signboard of the
Prudential Oil Company, the only thing available, and put it across
the intervening space of about six feet as a gang plank and saved
the five men marooned on the stern."

In this last statement Mate Palamario was a bit optimistic. He
had saved the five men from going down on the stern, but there
was still before them the prospect of being swept from the battered
bow.

On shore, meanwhile, there was activity of another kind. Ex-
lifesaver Joe Partridge, waking that morning at his home back of
the huge sand dune known as Kill Devil Hills, noticed a peculiar
odor in the air: Oil! And at about the same time Coastguardsman
Jep Harris of Kill Devil Hills Station, on the north patrol, spotted
a dim shape through the rain and spray. Both Partridge and Harris
hurried to the station to spread the word that a vessel was ashore.

Keeper Will H. Lewark mustered his crew, called for assistance
from near-by Kitty Hawk and Nags Head stations and proceeded
to the wreck. The coastguardsmen reached the scene in quick order
but had great difficulty landing a line within reach of the twenty-
four men on the *Kyzikes*, who by this time were all assembled on
the bridge. Contact was finally made, however, the hawser and
whip line were attached to the mast, the breeches buoy was sent
out, and the first man was brought ashore.

It was a tough operation from start to finish, for the *Kyzikes*, or
what remained of her, rolled with every sea, now pulling the line

high in the air, then dumping it down almost in the breakers. Further, it was necessary for the survivors, waiting an opportunity, to dash down on the lower deck between the bridge and the mast in order to reach the spot where the line was tied; and more than one of the twenty-four was almost swept overboard in the process.

As it was, Surfman Will Dough, manning the whip line throughout the rescue, wore the skin completely off his hands, and his fellow coastguardsmen were about as exhausted as the survivors when the last of the twenty-four was brought ashore in the breeches buoy at seven o'clock that night.

For successfully directing the rescue operation Chief Bosun Mate Will H. Lewark of Kill Devil Hills and Chief Bosun Mate Walter G. Etheridge, Keeper of Nags Head Station, were promoted to the rank of Warrant Officer. And in the months that followed repeated efforts were made to salvage the crude oil remaining on the tanker, first by means of pipes to shore, and later by the use of a barge and pump anchored near by. Some oil was saved, but most of it, like the twenty-four crewmen, was thoroughly soused with salt water.

CIBAO

The Norwegian steamer *Cibao*, loaded with 17,000 bunches of Jamaican bananas, ran into the same storm that drove the *Kyzikes* ashore at Kill Devil Hills and stranded seventy-five miles to the south, at a point off the mouth of Hatteras Inlet, two miles from shore and in the midst of a sea of breakers.

Whereas the rescue of the twenty-four survivors of the *Kyzikes* was a breeches buoy operation from first to last, the rescue of the crew of the *Cibao*, which took place at the same time and involved the same number of men, was strictly a job for surfboats.

The *Cibao* was discovered Sunday morning by the lookout at Hatteras Inlet Station, and within thirty minutes the coastguardsmen had launched their power lifeboat, passed through the inlet, and approached within half a mile of the wreck. They found, however, that it was impossible to effect a rescue with the powerboat, and they returned through the inlet once more for their smaller self-bailing surfboat. The keeper and crew of Ocracoke Station, and the keepers of Cape Hatteras, Creeds Hill, and Durants stations, were on hand by then, and all of them had a part in the thrilling rescue that followed.

The surfboat was towed out through the inlet and cast loose just beyond the first bar. With a picked crew aboard, the boat was then rowed in close to the *Cibao*, but so turbulent was the water surrounding her that even the self-bailing boat stood no chance of getting up alongside the stranded vessel.

Through speaking tubes the coastguardsmen shouted instructions to the castaways. Each of the twenty-four was to put on a life belt; each was to tie a separate line about his body and then jump overboard. The instructions were quickly followed. The first man jumped, disappeared beneath the churning surf, bobbed up, then disappeared again, as the swirling sea swept him toward shore. Into this mass of rampaging water the surfboat came and passed by the sailor; a coastguardsman reached over, grasped the line tied around his body, and the craft swept on, through and then beyond the breakers, dragging the *Cibao* crewman behind. When calmer waters were reached the oarsmen held up on their powerful strokes, the surfboat came to a brief standstill, and the soaked and miserable, but living, crewman was hauled aboard.

Back they went again, and time after time the process was repeated, until one boatload was transferred to the larger power lifeboat, and then a second boatload, and finally with the surfboat filled for the third time, the job was done. Twenty-four more seamen pulled from the clutches of the death-dealing surf. A total of forty-eight lives saved in one day. And as in the case of the *Kyzikes*, the leaders here were rewarded—Chief Bosun Mates Charles O. Peel, Bernice R. Ballance, and William H. Barnett—all promoted to Warrant grade.

CARL GERHARD

The spot where the *Kyzikes* came ashore in 1927 is approximately one mile north of the Kill Devil Hills Coast Guard Station. On numerous occasions this writer has fished there, wearing a pair of water-tight goggles and armed with a home-made spear, diving down beneath the surface, into the open hatches of the twisted and rust-covered Greek tanker, in quest of the giant sheepshead and other fish which make their home there in the bowels of the ship.

The bow of the *Kyzikes* remains on the outer reef, covered over with sand except for her engine, which juts up fifteen feet or better from the sandy bottom almost to the surface of the sea. On the inner reef, canted sharply over on one side, is the larger stern section of the tanker; a mass of warped decking and tanks, of ladders, anchors, winches, pipes, cables and machinery, all under water except for one small section which shows above the surface at extreme low tide.

To the south of the battered remains of the *Kyzikes*—which most people call *Paraguay*, her former name—is the even sand bottom, stretching away toward Kill Devil Hills and Nags Head; but to the north there is more wreckage still, for the *Kyzikes* is not alone out there. Parallel with the stern of the tanker—actually touching it at one point—is the equally battered, equally rusted, sand-covered and eerie looking hull of the once proud Swedish steamer *Carl Gerhard*.

As this is written the ocean spray, driven by strong winds from the northeast, clouds up the window panes beside the typewriter, so that the white caps are barely visible out there beyond the beach. The muffled sound of the crashing waves comes through, however, and peering through those spray-shrouded panes at the exact spot where the sunken steamer rests, it is easy to picture the scene that confronted Surfman Ellsworth Baum as he walked his patrol along this same beach, peered through the spray thrown up by just such a northeaster, and saw, in the early morning haze, the looming shape of the steamer aground there beside the *Kyzikes*.

It was September 23, 1929, less than two years after the loss of the *Kyzikes*. The *Carl Gerhard*, 265 feet long, 1,504 tons, loaded with 2,000 tons more of plaster rock, had been buffeted about in the North Atlantic for five days. She was bound from Mabou, Nova Scotia, to Tampa, Florida, and had stranded in the mud off Mabou soon after sailing. It was reported then that she had sustained no damage on the Canadian mud bank, but when the storm winds hit her off the New England coast she began to ship water. To add to the difficulty, the weather was so overcast that sights could not be taken, and according to a later statement by Captain A. Ohlsson, he was lost for five days, looking in vain for stars or

sun above, or the warning beams of lighthouses on the shore; thinking, however, that he was at least fifty miles at sea until the very
moment when the *Gerhard* grated to a stop on the outer bar off
Kill Devil Hills, bumped over the sand reef, and then struck the
sunken hull of the *Kyzikes*.

It was nearly dawn, then, and Surfman Baum sighted the vessel
soon after. His mates were quickly summoned, and four Coast
Guard crews under command of veteran Keeper Herman Smith
of Bodie Island Station, methodically went about the business of
saving life. The sea was too high and too rough for boat service,
so the Lyle gun was placed in position, and a friendly shot was sent
across the deck. Lucky for the *Gerhard*'s crew that the coastguardsmen arrived so quickly, and that Smith's shot was true, for
in the words of Captain Ohlsson, "the seas, lashed for days by the
strong northeast winds, pounced upon her like a lion upon its
prey," and the vessel began to go to pieces as soon as she struck.

There was a woman on board the *Gerhard*, Mrs. Ethel Adehard,
wife of the mate. A crewman came ashore first to test the breeches
buoy, then Mrs. Adehard, and after her the twenty men remaining.
Clothing and other personal belongings were left behind, some to
be recovered later; but as the breeches buoy made trip after trip
other living things beside the human beings appeared there on the
beach; first a dog, pet of one of the crewmen, then a second dog,
and finally a cat.

By afternoon the rescue was completed, and soon thereafter
Mate and Mrs. Adehard and the Swedish crewmen left the beach
at Kill Devil Hills to return to their native land or seek berths on
other ships; but the *Carl Gerhard*, almost completely submerged
now, remains there on the bar off Kill Devil Hills, keeping close
company with the Greek tanker *Kyzikes*.

ANNA MAY

Disastrous shipwrecks and thrilling rescues are not necessarily
confined to large vessels. Few men, for example, have come closer
to death and yet lived to tell about it than the five fishermen on
board the little trawler *Anna May*, which went to pieces on

Diamond Shoals at the height of a severe storm, December 9, 1931.

The *Anna May*, loaded with fish, headed out of Hatteras Inlet at 2:30 that morning, her destination, Hampton, Virginia. Twenty-two-year-old Ralph Carmine was captain of the seventy-foot vessel. His crew consisted of his father, J. E. Carmine, Sr.; a brother, J. E. Carmine, Jr.; a brother-in-law, Rideout Lewis; and a fifth man, M. R. Johnson.

Long before they passed out of Hatteras Bight the trawler's gasoline engine stopped, and for the next hour and a half the five crewmen took turns at trying to remedy the trouble, while the *Anna May* drifted slowly toward Diamond Shoals. As well as Captain Carmine could remember, they were all five bent over the engine box when the craft lurched to a stop, and they looked up to find themselves in the midst of towering breakers. Almost as quickly as it takes to tell it the vessel swamped, filled with water and settled on the shoal, leaving only her single mast above the breakers. Somehow, in that brief moment of decision, all five of them reached the mast and climbed to safety, but they were without distress signals, or life jackets, or lifesaving facilities of any kind. Just the five of them, thinly clad, clinging to the swaying mast in the darkness above the wild surf of Diamond Shoals.

Soon after dawn that morning the lookout at Cape Hatteras Station sighted the trawler's mast and the men hanging to it. Repeated attempts were made to launch a surfboat from the beach, but it was thrown back each time. At two o'clock that afternoon a mist settled over Diamond Shoals, completely obscuring what remained of the craft. By then the power lifeboat from Hatteras Inlet Station had finally managed to pass through the inshore breakers but on reaching Diamond Shoals could find no trace of the wrecked trawler. Newspaper headlines the following day proclaimed: "Fishing Trawler Is Believed Lost In Hatteras Quicksands, Entire Crew Going To Deaths."

As the sky slowly brightened over Diamond Shoals that next morning, however, Coast Guard binoculars were trained on the spot where the wreck had last been seen. Slowly a vague shape came in view, a tall thin pole sticking up out of the breakers. The mast still stood; and human beings yet clung to it!

A picked crew under Keeper B. R. Ballance of Cape Hatteras launched their surfboat from the beach there at the point. The crew of Hatteras Inlet Station, under Keeper Levene Midgett, boarded their power boat once more and moved out through the inlet. Ballance and Midgett were veteran lifesavers, both heroes of other dramatic rescues in days gone by.

Meanwhile, after thirty hours on the constantly swaying mast, young Captain Carmine and his four crewmen had about given up hope. Soaked to the skin, nearly frozen by the December cold, they began that second day with little thought that they had been seen, let alone that they might be saved. Then, suddenly, two boats appeared near by, one coming out from the cape, the other, the larger lifeboat, moving up the coast from Hatteras Inlet. The castaways shouted, waved their arms wildly, for at last there was hope. But even as they attempted to attract the attention of the coastguardsmen the mast swayed far over to one side, dipped lower and lower, and toppled into the chaotic surf.

Under other conditions the two boats would have stayed away from the breakers, anchoring to one side, attempting to rescue the five men by lines and life buoys. But that possibility was gone now, and without hesitation both Ballance and Midgett turned their boats toward the breakers, pressed on, into the midst of the tumultuous sea in which the five men struggled for their lives.

"We came down once between two giant waves, striking the bare sand," Midgett says, but this did not deter the surfmen. Midgett's boat, larger and faster, swept in, picked up one man, then a second, finally a third. Ballance's surfboat was right beside, reached the other two, turned about even as they were dragged aboard. Then both boats passed out of the breakers, into calmer water behind; three men in one, two in the other. All five of the castaways saved at the very moment when death seemed certain.

G. A. KOHLER

For almost ten years after she came ashore in the hurricane of August 23, 1933, the four-masted schooner *G. A. Kohler*, bulking majestically in her last resting place high above the shore, was one of the showpieces of the outer banks. Then, early in World War II she was burned for her scrap iron content, and today there is nothing left on the beach below Salvo to mark the spot where she rested.

The *Kohler*, one of the last of the large sailing vessels, was reported as "wallowing helplessly in the breakers a mile south of Gull Shoal Station," when the full fury of the storm struck the Carolina banks that August morning. Throughout the day and night she remained there, showing distress signals, while the coastguardsmen stood by helplessly waiting for a break in the storm. But the following morning the crews from Gull Shoal and Chicamacomico soon put a line aboard the vessel and succeeded in rescuing the eight men and one woman on board. And when the storm tides subsided the *Kohler* was sitting there, far up on the beach, beyond the reach of all except the highest tides.

For almost ten years she survived the worst that the sea could throw at her, the strong oak timbers as solid as ever; then war clouds formed across the ocean, the oak timbers were set afire, and all that remained was a pile of scrap iron.

TZENNY CHANDRIS

The *Eastern Packet* was little different from many of the other American freighters tied up at the James River anchorage during the depression of the 1930's. Built at Kobe, Japan, in 1920, she had served a period of usefulness while the postwar boom lasted; then, like many another craft, she was towed up the James, anchored at the head of the long line of idle ships, and left there to rust or rot.

In a sense the *Eastern Packet* was more fortunate than many of her idle neighbors, for in the summer of 1937 tugs again appeared at the anchorage, cut out the *Eastern Packet*, hauled her into deep water, and towed the listless freighter down to Norfolk for repairs.

The *Eastern Packet* had been sold. Her purchaser: John Chandris, of the Greek company bearing his name. The price: $64,000.

The first positive step was to change the *Eastern Packet's* name. Henceforth, Chandris announced, she would be known as the *Tzenny Chandris*. After that the shipyard workers came aboard, a Greek crew appeared, and together they swarmed over the vessel, chipping away rust, painting, and putting her machinery in working order. Her engines, overhauled, were made to run again; her

wireless, never of the best, was put in working order but not
modernized; her lifeboats, rust covered, were patched up after a
fashion.

With these hurried repairs completed the *Tzenny Chandris* was
once more ready to put to sea. Captain George Couhopadelis
was her new master. Of the twenty-eight men in her crew all except
Joseph Corrie, a forty-six-year-old English coal passer, were of
Greek extraction. Many of them had not been to sea for several
years. Her wireless operator was young and inexperienced.

The *Tzenny Chandris* took on several thousand tons of scrap iron
before leaving Norfolk, then moved across Hampton Roads to
Newport News for still more cargo. Additional scrap awaited her
at Morehead City before she could begin the long voyage across the
Atlantic to Rotterdam.

She left Newport News, October 27, 1937, and took on the last
of her 9,010 tons of scrap and junk at Morehead City on November
11. When an attempt was made to move her away from the pier at
Morehead City, however, it was discovered that the weight of the
added scrap had caused her to "bump the bottom," and she had to
wait there for high tide before floating free. Finally, Friday morning, November 12, 1937, the *Tzenny Chandris*, deeply laden, sailed
from Morehead City.

By the time the *Chandris* had passed Cape Lookout she was already
taking water perceptibly. "We begged the Captain to turn back to
some port when we found she was leaking," coal-passer Corrie
stated later, "but he said the pumps would take care of the water."

Meanwhile the first winds of an impending storm had ruffled up
the water between Lookout and Hatteras, and already the *Chandris*
was having tough going. "She commenced listing to starboard before
we got into the storm," Corrie said. "When the storm hit us Friday
afternoon water came pouring in from somewhere in the coal bins,
shooting through a little door that coal fell through. When I went
on watch Friday night I didn't want to go down in that place, but
the Captain persuaded me to go. I couldn't swim and when the water
came rushing in that place again, I went on deck. About that time
the engine went off fix, and all lights went out."

By then the seas were sweeping over the boat deck, several of the lifeboats had been carried away, and the cargo had begun to shift so that the vessel was canted over at a fifteen degree angle.

Kostas Palaskas, twenty-five-year-old third engineer, said later that he and others of the crew had been "pleading with the captain for five hours," to send an S.O.S. And when finally the Captain did order the S.O.S. sent out, the operator became confused and was unable to send promptly. Palaskas said that he finally had to threaten the operator at the point of a knife before he got the message off. "I told him I would kill him if he didn't send that S.O.S.," Palaskas said.

The S.O.S. finally went out at 4:06 A.M., Saturday, and though it was repeated several times and was picked up both by shore stations and ships in the vicinity, at no time was the position of the sinking ship given, with the result that one ship passed so close in the darkness that Captain Couhopadelis tried to signal for help with a flashlight.

In the end the Captain ordered all hands to put on life belts, and then sent them over the side into the storm-ravaged seas tossed up off Hatteras. The position of the *Chandris* at that time was approximately forty miles northeast of Diamond Shoals Lightship.

Coal-passer Corrie was the last man to leave the sinking vessel. "The rain and wind made so much noise you couldn't hear anybody yell," he said. "I waited there on deck. I didn't want to jump because I had seen some of the fellows jump and they looked like they got hurt. Then the ship lurched once and went over on her side. She lurched again and went over flat on her side, level as a floor. Then is when I walked down and jumped. I was caught in the suction but I had to open my mouth to breathe and every time I did I took in sea water. It seemed like a year before I came back up."

Twenty-eight human beings and miscellaneous sheep, hogs, and fowl which had been carried along to provide fresh meat on the voyage were left foundering there in the open sea as the *Tzenny Chandris* went to the bottom. Six of the men located a floating lifeboat, battered and water-filled, and managed to climb aboard. Fifteen others were grouped rather closely together, clinging to pieces of wreckage. The remainder were scattered near by, supported by life belts and debris.

At 9:30 that morning, approximately five hours after the *Chandris* sank, the tanker *Swiftsure* sighted the floating lifeboat and rescued the six men who had sought safety in it. The *Swiftsure* wirelessed news of the rescue and its position, and cruised in the area for several hours without sighting other survivors. Then she proceeded on her way to Boston.

Throughout that day and night the other crewmen drifted in the open sea. Two men drowned during the day. A third went crazy, lunged at Captain Couhopadelis in maniacal fury and bit the Captain's nose before being subdued by shipmates. He died that afternoon.

During the night three more men died from exposure, and one young crewman, able to control his thirst no longer, drank salt water, went berserk, tried to choke Palaskas, and finally swam off alone in the night to disappear forever. At dawn Sunday, surrounded by dead and bloated animals and fowl, and with the bodies of their deceased comrades still floating in their life belts near by, the survivors were faced with a new threat—sharks.

Meanwhile, one of the most intensive and methodical rescue attempts in history was being carried out. Four Coast Guard vessels were patrolling the area in systematic sweeps. Seven Navy planes and one Coast Guard plane were combing an assigned area of 19,200 square miles in search of survivors.

At 10:30 A.M. Sunday, Lieutenant (j.g.) A. C. Keller, piloting a Navy patrol plane, sighted the survivors about ninety miles east of Kitty Hawk. Diving low he dropped a smoke bomb to mark the spot, then flew back to the near-by Coast Guard cutter *Mendota*, and directed the surface vessel to the scene. When picked up soon afterwards, the *Chandris* crewmen said the sound of the plane had driven the sharks away.

At this point nineteen survivors had been taken from the spume and spray-filled waters, six by the *Swiftsure*, and thirteen by the *Mendota*. The bodies of four others had also been recovered. Still not accounted for were five more crewmen, including coal-passer Corrie, but by then the Naval planes had nearly exhausted their fuel and were forced to return to Norfolk, leaving only the Coast Guard patrol plane, piloted by Lieutenant R. L. Burke, to continue the search.

Soon afterwards, however, Burke sighted two more men and the bodies of the other three near by. He, too, dropped smoke bombs and guided the *Mendota* to the scene, and so, after more than thirty hours in the sea, Joseph Corrie, last of the twenty-eight to leave the sinking freighter, was picked up and the saga of the *Tzenny Chandris* was ended.

URING THE first six months of 1942 residents of coastal North Carolina were closer to war than were most of our troops then on overseas duty, and the coastal Carolina war, during that period, was a one-sided affair, with the odds strictly on the other side.*

* Little was published at the time concerning these stupendous losses so close to home, and not much more has been published since. In fact, in the preparation of this book, material on World War II ship sinkings has been harder to dig out—and less detail has been available—than for any other period since the War of 1812.

This is due, mainly, to the existence of strict censorship at the time of the sinkings; to the fact that all information on ship sinkings was considered classified material by the armed forces until long after the cessation of hostilities (and some of it still is not available for this reason); and to a recently inaugurated system whereby all of the material compiled by the various governmental commands which had jurisdiction over the North Carolina coast has been transferred to Washington, there to be stored in secret and inaccessible files, or placed on microfilm in the national archives (usually without regard to chronological or geographical arrangement), or destroyed. Unfortunately, a large amount of the factual material relating to ship sinkings seems to have been disposed of in this last manner.

There have been newspaper articles published recently in which it was stated that Navy figures show a specific number of lives lost and a specified amount of cargo destroyed off the North Carolina coast during World War II. These figures are taken from the Navy press release of Sept. 17, 1945, which states that 79 ships were sunk, 843 merchant seamen and gun crew lost their lives, and 425,850 tons of shipping went down within the waters of the Fifth Naval District. However, the report (the only official compilation this writer has been able to uncover) gives information in such sketchy fashion that it is impossible to determine where 11 of the ships were sunk, and of the balance, 12 are shown to have reached port safely, 28 others were sunk off Virginia, Maryland, New Jersey, and New York, and of the 79 ships only 29 are definitely listed as having been sunk off the North Carolina coast.

The compilation of ship losses for World War II comes from this and other sources, mainly from the wreck information lists and card file of the United States Hydrographic Office, which has determined the definite location of the sunken ships as an aid to navigation.

Simply stated, the reason for this early success by Nazi submarine raiders was that the Germans had concentrated on the development of U-boat warfare while this phase of naval preparedness was relegated to a comparatively unimportant status by the United States. Thus, the outbreak of the war in December, 1941, found Hitler with a large and fully trained underseas fleet, and when this fleet attacked shipping along our coast it had about as hard a time of it as a hunter shooting into a pond full of tame ducks.

The amazing thing is that we were able, during that otherwise disastrous six-month period, to so perfect our antisubmarine defenses as to almost completely thwart the underseas raiders throughout the remainder of the war; for the records show that more than 90 per cent of the ship sinkings on our coast during the nearly four years of submarine attacks, occurred in those six months between January and July in 1942.

One of Hitler's first actions after Pearl Harbor had been to order a submarine attack on our east coast shipping, and six of his five-hundred-ton U-boats had been assigned to the job. These five-hundred-tonners, constituting the bulk of the Nazi sub fleet, were 220 feet long and 20.3 feet in width; their top speed was 7½ knots submerged and 17½ knots on the surface; each had four torpedo tubes forward and one in the stern, carried a total of fourteen torpedoes plus deck guns, and was fueled for an average voyage of six weeks duration.

Other U-boats were shortly dispatched to the aid of the six sent out originally, and by January of 1942 some nineteen German underseas craft were operating in the western half of the Atlantic. To guard against them we had five sub-chasers, a nondescript collection of miscellaneous small craft, and a handful of shore-based airplanes. The situation, with one exception, was directly comparable to that in the early part of World War I. The sole exception was that this time the enemy had many times the number of subs to throw into the battle.

The war came to our coast in explosive fashion in the early morning darkness of January 18, 1942. Sixty miles off Cape Hatteras the Standard Oil Company of New Jersey tanker *Allan Jackson*, a single-screw vessel of 4,038 net tons, was proceeding northward in a calm sea. She was loaded with 72,870 barrels of crude oil, nearly capacity, which she had picked up a week earlier at Cartagena, Colombia, for delivery to New York. The crew of the 453-foot vessel consisted of thirty-five officers and men.

At 1:30 that morning Captain Felix W. Kretchmer was in his bunk, resting. Second Mate Melvin A. Rand had the duty on the bridge, Seaman Randolph H. Larson was at the wheel, Boatswain Rolf Clausen was in the messroom playing cards, and Seaman Gustave Nox was en route to the foc'sle head to relieve Seaman Hamon Brown of the lookout duty there.

At 1:35 A.M. two torpedoes struck the *Jackson* in quick succession. The first, hitting the forward tank on the vessel's starboard side, exploded beneath an empty cargo hold and caused only minor damage; the second struck even closer to the bow, exploding with such force that the tanker was split completely in two, her cargo of crude oil spewing out in all directions.

The second explosion threw Captain Kretchmer to the floor, and though flames filled his quarters he managed to escape through a porthole, falling to the boat deck on the lee side. Meanwhile both Rand and Larson were knocked overboard by the force of the explosion, Boatswain Clausen rushed on deck in search of a lifeboat, and seamen Nox and Brown, closer than the others to the actual point where the torpedo made contact, already were dead.

The scene, at that time, was one of despair for the crewmen yet alive, for in addition to the flames engulfing the sinking ship the entire surface of the water surrounding the vessel was covered with fiercely burning oil.

Boatswain Clausen, in his frantic search for a lifeboat, discovered that the No. 1 boat was a total wreck, the No. 2 boat was jammed in its chocks and could not be budged, the No. 4 boat was surrounded by wind-driven flames, and only the No. 3 boat remained serviceable. This was immediately lowered away, and even before it struck the water Clausen and seven others jumped inside.

"When the boat was in the water and held in position by the painter we were 3 to 4 feet from the ship's side," Clausen said. "Around us, within a short distance, were the flames of crude oil burning on the surface of the sea. What saved us was the strong discharge from the condenser pump. The outlet happened to be just ahead of the lifeboat, and the force of the stream of water, combined with the motion of the ship, pushed the burning oil away.

"I unhooked the falls and cut the painter," Clausen continued. "At that time, the broken-off bow of the *Allan Jackson* was listing to port and the main part of the vessel was listing to starboard, over our lifeboat. After cutting the painter, I found in the excitement no one had unlashed the oars. By the time I cut the lashings and the oars were manned, the boat was being sucked toward the propeller."

The prospect of drowning or of being burned to death was bad enough, but now the eight men faced a third and even greater danger. For they were pulled directly beneath the great propeller and with each revolution the huge blades struck the boat, threatening not only to crush the small craft, but to grind to pieces its human occupants as well. For seconds that lasted interminably the men stood helplessly while this giant grinder spiralled, with sickening regularity and force just above them. But finally, pushing against the stern of the ship with oars, the men managed to get clear of the propeller, were suddenly caught in its backwash, and driven this time straight at the great mass of burning oil astern.

Once again luck was with them, for this backwash from the propeller forced a clear path through the burning mass, and with oars properly manned at last the boat proceeded down this turbulent path to safety.

Within ten minutes both sections of the tanker sank from view, but the men in the lifeboat remained near by, searching for other survivors, and they rescued one man, a radio operator, Stephen Verbonich.

"Then we saw a white light, low over the sea, which undoubtedly was on a submarine," Clausen said. "Putting up sails, we steered for shore in a westerly direction."

Two and a half hours later a second light was seen, a blueish searchlight, east of the lifeboat. Clausen started signalling with a flashlight, turning the beam on the white sail and beginning a message in Morse code, but his companions feared the light might be from a submarine, and he stopped signalling. For the remainder of the night the nine men—eight who had pulled away from the sinking ship in Boat No. 3, and Radioman Verbonich—proceeded westward under sail without incident. The night was comparatively warm and the Gulf Stream wind moderate; under other circumstances theirs could have been an enjoyable outing.

Captain Kretchmer was not having as easy a time of it. Finding himself on the boat deck after escaping through the porthole, he looked around for signs of life. He could locate none of his crew and so started up the ladder leading to the bridge. "The decks and ladders were breaking up and the sea was rushing aboard," he said. "As the vessel sank amidships, the suction carried me away from the bridge ladder. After a struggle I came to the surface, on which oil was afire a short distance away." He then managed, somehow, to grasp a couple of small boards and supported his weight on these throughout the remainder of the night as he drifted away from the scene of the disaster.

Meanwhile, both Second Mate Rand and Seaman Larson had also located pieces of wreckage large enough to keep them afloat, though in the immediate confusion they became separated. Rand later sighted another small raft, to which Third Mate Boris A. Voronsoff and Junior Third Mate Francis M. Bacon were clinging, and joined forces with them; but Bacon began to get cramps and lashed himself to the wreckage, where he died soon after.

Thus, as the first light of false dawn appeared in the sky that morning the tanker *Allan Jackson* had disappeared completely, with only an oil slick to mark her burial place beneath the waters of the Gulf Stream; nine of her crew were in the No. 3 lifeboat a considerable distance to the west; Captain Kretchmer was clinging to his two tiny boards; Mates Rand and Voronsoff were together on their comparatively seaworthy raft, and Seaman Larson was floating near by on a small piece of wreckage.

They might all have remained thus until they either floated ashore or drowned had it not been for Boatswain Clausen's brief attempt to signal with his flashlight against the sails. For his signals had been seen by a friendly vessel, the U.S. Destroyer *Roe*, which remained near by until morning, picking up all of the survivors in turn.

That first submarine attack on the Carolina coast had proven costly in lives as well as cargo; for of the thirty-five crewmen on board the *Allan Jackson* only the thirteen listed above were saved.

But the *Allan Jackson* was just one of many ships, and her crewmen but the first of many merchant seamen lost in what has since been referred to as the Battle of Torpedo Junction.

Eight more ships went to the bottom off the North Carolina coast by the end of January, including the British tanker *Empire Gem* and the American-owned combination ore and oil carrier *Venore*, both of which were sunk southeast of Diamond Shoals on January 23 with considerable loss of life. Only the captain and one crewman survived the sinking of the *Empire Gem*, and twenty-one men were lost on the *Venore*.

Another eight went down in February; four freighters, three tankers, and the Brazilian passenger ship *Buarque*. Of the survivors of these eight sunken ships none were subjected to a more harrowing experience than the six crewmen from the Norwegian cargo ship *Blink*, who were picked up in a lifeboat at sea February 14. Twenty-three persons had left the sinking ship in the lifeboat three days earlier but seventeen had died as the small craft floated on the wintry Atlantic.

The U-boat attacks in January and February had been relatively haphazard affairs, but by the first of March the Nazis had effectively organized their forces. For one thing, instead of operating singly as they had in World War I, they now cruised in packs, exchanging information as to convoy locations by wireless and banding together, especially at night, for their lethal attacks. In addition, two or three were permanently stationed off Diamond Shoals in all but the roughest weather, resting on the sandy bottom during the daytime, then surfacing at night as our ships attempted to dash around Cape Hatteras.

Night was most frequently the time of attack, not only because it was more difficult for the subs to be seen, but because our authorities had not yet ordered a blackout along the coast. Consequently, the subs were able to surface beyond the shipping lanes, thus silhouetting the unwary tankers and freighters against the lights on shore.

These tactics paid off in royal fashion, for during the month of March the subs sank an average of almost one ship daily along the North Carolina coast.

One of the ships sunk during March was the American freighter

Caribsea, which went down on the eleventh with a valuable cargo of manganese ore. On the *Caribsea*, as on most merchantmen, the licenses of her officers were prominently displayed in a special glass case, and one of the licenses thus exhibited was that of Engineer James Baugham Gaskill, whose birthplace was listed as Ocracoke, North Carolina.

Gaskill was one of the crew members killed when the *Caribsea* was sunk that night southeast of Ocracoke. On the island, today, the inhabitants will tell you that the glass case, with Gaskill's license prominently displayed, came ashore a few days later near the village; and if you visit the Ocracoke Methodist Church they will undoubt edly point out a special cross behind the altar, a cross said to have been made from the nameplate of the *Caribsea*, which the island residents claim drifted through Ocracoke Inlet and was found opposite Gaskill's birthplace on the sound shore.

Of all the merchant seamen set adrift off our coast during World War II, Seamen Jules Souza of the American cargo carrier *Alcoa Guide* was the luckiest. For the *Alcoa Guide* was sunk March 16, some three hundred miles off Hatteras, and from then until late April—more than a month—Jules Souza drifted on an improvised raft. Three companions on the raft with him died long before help came, but amazingly Souza stuck it out and lived to tell of his experience.

On the night of March 18 the U-boats really hit the jackpot. They sank five ships then: the tankers *Papoose*, *W. E. Hutton*, and *E. M. Clark*, all at about the same time near Cape Lookout (the survivors of the *Papoose* rowed to shore in the glare from the burning *Hutton*) and the freighters *Liberator* and *Kassandra Louloudis* off Cape Hatteras. These vessels were in convoy and the *Louloudis* was attacked while going to the assistance of the torpedoed tanker *Acme*, which, ironically, was towed to Newport News and saved; and the *Liberator* went down within a hundred feet of the larger and more valuable *Esso Baltimore*, a tanker which was overlooked by the underseas raiders.

The record for March 23 shows that one and two-thirds ships were sunk off our shore. The one ship was the American tanker *Naeco*, a 3,258-ton vessel loaded with kerosene, which went down, off Cape Lookout. The two-thirds of a ship was the three-hundred-foot bow section of the tanker *Esso Nashville*, torpedoed two days earlier some sixteen miles northeast of Frying Pan Shoals.

The *Esso Nashville*, less than three years old at the time, was originally 463 feet in length, 64 feet in breadth, and built to carry 106,718 barrels of oil. At Bayway, New Jersey, March 4, 1942, thirty-eight lifesaving suits had been placed aboard the vessel, one for each officer and crewman; on the sixteenth she cleared from Port Arthur, Texas, with a full cargo of fuel oil for New Haven, Connecticut; at 12:20 A.M., March 21, having passed Cape Fear a short time before, a dull thud-like noise resounded throughout the vessel, awakening the members of the crew who were asleep and alerting those on duty.

Third Mate John Kerves had just been relieved of his watch and was descending from the bridge when he felt and heard the thud. He hurried to the starboard side to investigate. "I looked around for perhaps a minute, and then I saw a streak in the water coming toward us rapidly," he said. "When I realized it was a torpedo I turned around and started to go inside, but it hit before I managed this. It struck within three seconds. Flames shot in the air and oil was thrown everywhere. Some of the hot oil was blown in my face."

Ever since he had taken over command of the *Esso Nashville* Captain Edward V. Peters had insisted on holding frequent and unexpected lifeboat drills, and this preparation, plus the timely installation of the lifesaving suits at the beginning of the voyage, helped save lives on the *Esso Nashville*.

As soon as the torpedo struck, the vessel keeled over so far that Captain Peters said he "feared she was going to turn over." But she righted herself, and then with her bow and stern sections practically cut apart by the force of the explosion, began to settle at the point of impact. The result was that within minutes her bow and stern were so high in the air that her masts almost touched, looking for all the world like a broken and splintered matchstick floating upright in the water.

Captain Peters immediately ordered all hands to abandon ship, and her four lifeboats were soon in the water. The No. 4 boat, with twenty-one men on board, was so crowded that it could not be moved away from the side of the ship, so six of the occupants—those who had been able to don their lifesaving suits—slipped overboard, and with the load thus lightened the others managed to row clear.

Abandoning ship had been accomplished with a minimum of time and with only one casualty. Captain Peters had slipped on the oily deck and had fallen between a lifeboat and the side of the vessel, breaking his leg as he did so. Occupants of the lifeboat attempted to pull him on board, but he was so covered with slimy oil that they found it impossible, and he ordered them to shove off before the boat was crushed. Despite his fractured leg Captain Peters remained afloat for three-quarters of an hour, finally reaching the point where the torpedo had struck the ship and managing to crawl aboard. He bandaged his leg, hoisted the ensign upside down, and tied a white flag to the rail. Helpless to do anything else, he just waited there, alone on his stricken vessel, hoping and praying that she would remain afloat until dawn. She did!

The occupants of the four boats were picked up early that morning by small naval vessels operating in the vicinity, and soon after Captain Peters was removed from the tanker. Tugs were then dispatched to the scene but before they could take the vessel in tow she broke completely in two. The large bow section, already very low in the water, was left there to sink, which it did two days later. The tugs managed to tow the smaller 163-foot after section—with the engine room still intact—into Morehead City, and from there it was taken to Baltimore where her original builders prefabricated a new bow, and ten months later she was christened again and put back into active service.

Two of the more serious losses to submarine attack in late March were the tanker *Dixie Arrow*, in which eleven lives were lost on the twenty-sixth, including all of her deck officers, and the Panamanian freighter *Equipoise*, sunk the following day with a loss of thirty-eight lives.

It was the sinking of the American passenger ship *City of New York* forty miles southeast of Cape Hatteras on March 29, however, which resulted in one of the most unusual incidents of the war. The *City of New York* (the second ship of this name sunk in the same general vicinity; the other, a Civil War transport, was sunk at Hatteras Inlet) was a 5,025-ton vessel, en route from Capetown to New York with 41 passengers, 88 crewmen and 9 gunners. This made a total of 138 people on board the steamer when she sank, and of this number 33 perished, leading to the natural conclusion, based on simple arithmetic, that 105 survived. The fact is, however, that when the survivors were finally picked up from her four lifeboats the number totalled one more than this, or 106. For the Navy Department says this was the only case ever recorded of a baby being born in a lifeboat, and the success of the delivery under such trying circumstances was due largely to the fact that the ship's doctor happened to be in the same lifeboat with the expectant mother. The U.S. Destroyer *Roper* picked up the mother, child, doctor, and their companions; and in appreciation the child was named Jesse Roper Noharovic.

The submarines kept up their one-a-day pace well into April. On the first the freighter *Rio Blanco* sank two minutes after she was struck by a torpedo east of Cape Hatteras, and nine members of her crew were adrift for two weeks before being rescued. On April 3 a total of thirty-seven crewmen and gunners were lost when the armed freighter *Otho* was torpedoed 180 miles off the coast, and the same day the officers of the American tanker *Byron D. Benson* vanished in a lifeboat in a sea of blazing oil when the vessel was sunk off Caffeys Inlet. Eight more tankers went down between then and April 14, including the *British Splendour*, sunk off Diamond Shoals with twelve deaths April 6, and the *San Delfino*, torpedoed off Chicamacomico three days later with twenty-eight persons losing their lives when their lifeboat drifted into a mass of burning fuel.

For almost three months the Nazi subs had been going about their deadly business. In less than ninety days they had sunk some fifty large ships, most of them loaded with valuable cargo, yet there had not been a single documented instance of one of the attacking U-boats being destroyed. By mid-April, however, a change was in prospect, for we finally had started blacking out our coastal communities, the British had transferred a number of armed trawlers to submarine patrol duty off North Carolina, additional planes and patrol vessels had been made available, and a more efficient convoy system had been put in practice.

In addition, a mined and protected anchorage was being provided at Cape Lookout, making it possible for almost all coastal shipping to proceed at night, blacked out. For most ships could make it from

Lookout to Hampton Roads (closest protected port to the north) or Charleston (closest to the south) between dusk and dawn.

Pinning it down to actual dates, April 14, 1942, was the day when the tide of battle changed. For early that morning the destroyer *Roper* encountered a submarine south of Wimble Shoals, dodged one torpedo, and then opened fire with her deck guns at three hundred yards range (so close that her searchlights were played on the target). The gunfire seriously damaged the sub while she was in the process of submerging, and the destroyer's depth charges finished her off. A number of bodies were recovered from the sunken sub that morning, and the craft was definitely identified as the five-hundred-ton *U-85*. Thus the first submarine kill of the war off the North Carolina coast was recorded.

For a time it looked as if the *Roper*'s success had been little more than an accident, for certainly the overconfidence of the submarine commander had been a contributing factor to the loss, and his cohorts, becoming more wary as a result, were able to elude our defenders for the remainder of the month. During this period eight more vessels were sunk, including the British freighter *Empire Thrush*, loaded with phosphates and TNT. The *Empire Thrush* was torpedoed off Cape Hatteras the same day that the *U-85* went down, but fortunately for her fifty-five crewmen the explosive cargo did not ignite, and all reached port safely. Another vessel lost at about the same time was the British freighter *Harpagon*, loaded with planes, tanks, and 2,602 tons of explosives. The *Harpagon* was sunk off Cape Hatteras, April 19, and the following day the Panamanian freighter *Chenango*, bound from Rio de Janeiro to Baltimore, went down off Dare County with the loss of all hands except an Irish fireman named James Terrence Bradley, who was picked up from a raft twelve days later with a dying companion.

The record for May demonstrates in the most dramatic fashion how effectively our antisubmarine defenses had been developed in such a short time. During the month the subs sank but three vessels, all British; two of them were armed trawlers serving on convoy or patrol duty. Meanwhile, during the same period, the Navy credited a destroyer with sinking a German submarine off Cape Fear on May 2; the Coast Guard cutter *Icarus* chased the *U-352* ashore near Cape Lookout, May 9, capturing most of her crew; and the Navy claimed two other kills, one on the eleventh and the other on the nineteenth. A four to three score, if the Navy claims can be accepted, with our side at last on top.

Between the end of May and the middle of July twelve more of our ships went down, several from striking mines, while the Nazis were losing one of their own number in exchange. Among the vessels lost was the sugar-laden freighter *Manuela* which was torpedoed, remained afloat for several days, and was being towed into Morehead City when it was torpedoed a second time and finally sank; and the tug *Keshena* which struck a mine while towing a torpedoed vessel into port July 19.

From then until the end of the war the subs had poor pickings, getting only a handful of ships during the next three years; the most noteworthy were the Cuban freighter *Libertad,* sunk off Lookout on December 4, 1943, with a loss of twenty-five crewmen, and the freighter *Belgian Airman,* torpedoed eighty miles east of Nags Head, April 14, 1945, with the loss of one life.

The totals for the four years of war show eighty-seven vessels lost on the North Carolina coast, not including the German submarines. Of these, better than two-thirds were sunk by Nazi raiders, the remainder going down as the result of striking mines, stranding, or foundering at sea. In size and numbers of vessels sunk, lives lost, and cargo destroyed the period from 1942 through 1945 was the worst on record; but it could have been multiplied many times had we not come up with effective antisubmarine facilities in 1942.

UNLESS WE BECOME em-
broiled again in full-scale war, replete with submarine attacks on
coastal shipping, there probably will be comparatively few shipwrecks to add to those covered in this book.

The basic causes of the countless ship losses in bygone years are
still here. The treacherous submerged sand bars on Diamond and
Lookout and Frying Pan Shoals are as unpredictable in their move-
ments now as they were when the brigantine of Lucas Vasquez de
Ayllon foundered off Cape Fear in 1526. The North Carolina coast
still is a prime target for the death dealing hurricanes which swirl
into being in the heat of the tropics during the late summer of
each year. The Gulf Stream still sweeps northward past our coast,
tangling with the cold Arctic waters off Hatteras; and the strong
and ever changing winds continue to buffet the unprotected sand
banks which stretch out to form a barrier reef beyond the inland
sounds.

These dangers were here when European settlers first came to our
shores. They will no doubt remain at least as long as the settlers do.
But other changes have taken place in the meantime—man-made
changes which tend to lessen the awesome threat of the shifting
shoals, the hurricanes, the currents, and the constant winds.

Ship construction shows, as well as anything, how these changes have eliminated much of the danger and the romance from the work of the mariners who ply our coastal trade. For it was one thing to sail before the mast, with the wind alone providing locomotion; with only the sound of creaking rigging about you, and the sight of billowing sails above; and with the knowledge, always, that the next day, or the next hour, or the next moment, the wind and current might conspire to tear your masts away, or rip off your rudder, or force you on the near-by shoals. But it is another thing, today, to stand on the hot deck of a freighter; to listen to the steady, tiresome thump of the engines; to see and feel the black clouds of soot-laden smoke belching from the stacks; and to wonder, because it is all so simple and automatic now, just why it was the oldtimers were so in fear of the Graveyard of the Atlantic.

This shift from sail to steam is just one manifestation of the slow and hardly noticeable change that has caused the word shipwreck, already, to be primarily associated in man's mind with the dim past, rather than with the present or future. For the men and methods of lifesaving have undergone great changes since the days when Spencer Gray and Malachi Corbel and Rasmus Midgett and their compatriots walked lonely patrols along the bleak and barren surfside at the height of tempests, rowed their flimsy motorless surfboats through breakers so high that even they did not honestly think it could be done, and braved the full fury of Outer Diamond at storm-height in a craft powered alone by sail and by their own strong arms and backs.

Today, shore-based lifesaving facilities have been so improved and so modernized that most of the stations on the North Carolina coast have been abandoned; jeeps have replaced the horse and foot patrol; amphibious ducks, blimps, airplanes, and helicopters have taken over much of the work of the surfboat; radio, radar, loran, and ship-to-shore telephone have simplified communication and warnings; and the men themselves, younger, less experienced hands, are now more concerned, through no doing of their own, with dummy drills, polishing brass, and pulling stuck cars from the sand ruts. And if the trend toward modernization continues the time may yet come when one man, seated before a huge panel of instruments, could keep watch over the entire coast of North Carolina.

The effects of past shipwrecks will long be remembered on the outer banks, however, for many of the people now populating Carolina's coastal communities are direct descendants of men and women who went there when their ships were cast away in the surf; and like the ships themselves, they stayed on indefinitely. Most of the Haymans of eastern North Carolina, for example, stem from two brothers who washed ashore at Kitty Hawk almost 150 years ago, married in Currituck and Tyrrell counties, and raised families there. Today there are sixth generation Haymans who can trace their ancestry back to the two brothers.

There still is an occasional shipwreck along our coast; several ships have been lost since the end of World War II. One of these was a small sailing yacht, *Nautilus*, which stranded at Big Kinnakeet; two others were wartime LST's, cast ashore at Chicamacomico in a hurricane while being towed south for salvage; a fourth was the small freighter *Southern Isles*, which broke in two and sank off Hatteras at the height of a severe storm; a fifth was the Panamanian freighter *Miget*, which drifted ashore at Portsmouth and went to pieces in the surf in early 1952. And wherever the remnants of such a vessel can be seen, the tourists flock in ever increasing numbers.

There undoubtedly will be other shipwrecks in the years to come, but the glamor has gone out of it—the glamor, and the romance, and most of the mystery and suspense. And the chances are slim that a lifesaver will ever again face a task comparable to that of Dunbar Davis in August, 1893, or of the people of Ocracoke in the hurricane of 1842, or that a single storm will wreak the havoc of San Ciriaco in 1899.

VESSELS TOTALLY LOST ON THE
NORTH CAROLINA COAST

The following listing of vessels totally lost along the coast of North Carolina has been arranged to correspond with those chapters of the book which deal with periods rather than specific shipwrecks. As a means of simplification, locations are general rather than specific. For example, a vessel lost two and a quarter miles south of Nags Head Station would be listed as wrecked at Nags Head; one sunk twenty-five miles east-southeast of Cape Fear would be listed as lost off Cape Fear; one stranded in the vicinity of the Virginia-North Carolina border would be listed as wrecked at Wash Woods.

By the same token it has been difficult to determine the exact date when certain vessels were lost. The barge *J. R. Teel*, for example, broke loose from the tug *Wellington*, November 8, 1913, drifted ashore near Cape Lookout on the ninth, but was not declared a total loss until she broke up on November 10. Thus the *J. R. Teel* is listed as having been lost at Cape Lookout, November 10, 1913.

A number of listings of shipwrecks and marine disasters exist, but in no cases have vessels been taken from these listings without further substantiation, since double checking revealed numerous vessels listed as lost which were, in reality, towed into port or salvaged.

Except in unusual cases vessels of less than fifty tons, and those lost in inland waters, are not included in this listing. Neither are hundreds more which disappeared at sea off the North Carolina coast or are presumed to have been lost in the area.

For the use of persons interested in checking further on this subject, an additional list of vessels probably lost off the North Carolina coast has been made available to various libraries, including those of the Mariners' Museum, Newport News, Virginia, and the University of North Carolina, Chapel Hill, North Carolina.

1526-1814 (See pages 1-8)

NAME	TYPE	DATE	PLACE	LIVES LOST
(?)	Brigantine	June, 1526	Cape Fear	?
Tiger	(?)	June 29, 1585	Ocracoke Inlet	?
(?)	Fly-boat	1665	Cape Fear	0
(?)	Sloop	1666	Cape Lookout	2
Nuestra de Solidad	Ship	Aug. 18, 1750	Drum Inlet	0
(?)	(?)	Aug. 18, 1750	Cape Hatteras	?
El Salvador	(?)	Aug. 18, 1750	Topsail Inlet	?
(?)	(?)	Aug. 18, 1750	Currituck Inlet	?
Tyrrel	Brig	July 3, 1759	Off Hatteras	16
Aurora	Brigantine	Sept. 19, 1776	Portsmouth	0
(?)	(?)	1778	Roanoke Inlet	?
Betsy	Sloop	Sept. 6, 1797	Currituck Inlet	?
* Patriot	Pilot boat	Jan. 1813	Nags Head	?
† # 140	Gunboat	Sept. 23, 1814	Ocracoke	?

1815-1838 (See pages 9-26)

NAME	TYPE	DATE	PLACE	LIVES LOST
Voucher	Ship	Nov. 19, 1817	Chicamacomico	0
William Carlton	Ship	May 15, 1818	Kill Devil Hills	0
Georgia	Brig	July 15, 1818	Currituck Inlet	0
Revenue	Sloop	Dec. 1818	Currituck Inlet	0
Henry	Sloop	Dec. 5, 1819	Ocracoke	6
Islington	Ship	Mar. 16, 1820	Cape Hatteras	0
Horatio	Ship	Apr. 2, 1820	Diamond Shoals	8
Enterprize	Schooner	Oct. 27, 1822	New Inlet	0
Emulous	Schooner	Jan. 22, 1825	Kitty Hawk	0
Diomede	Schooner	Jan. 23, 1825	Kitty Hawk	?
Harvest	Schooner	Nov. 18, 1825	Bodie Island	?
Victory	Schooner	1825	Kitty Hawk	?

* This vessel, discovered ashore at Nags Head, was thought to be the *Patriot*.

† In recent years there has been considerable speculation over the identity of a small vessel found buried in the sands on Bodie Island. So much interest was manifested in the find that a crew of CCC boys and other volunteer workers was recruited for the express job of uncovering the hulk, and when this was done a number of specialists, representing museums and government agencies, were called in to inspect the rotting vessel. First reports published in the newspapers were that it was a Viking ship, then that it was a crompster, and finally that it was a type known as a pinkie, used in coastal trade in colonial days. According to a detailed study published by the National Park Service in 1939, however, it was concluded that the vessel was one of 176 small gunboats built for the United States government between 1805 and 1807. One of these, gunboat # 140, is definitely known to have exploded and burned near Ocracoke Inlet in 1814, and the Bodie Island craft was found to have the same dimensions, the same type of workmanship and the same pointed bow and stern. The Bodie Island vessel is not included in the above listing, nor is it mentioned in the text of this volume, since no information has been made available as to the time it was wrecked or the circumstances surrounding its loss. This note is appended, however, so that those who have read the Viking stories will know that much of the tale is false.

NAME	TYPE	DATE		PLACE	LIVES LOST
Cape Hatteras	Lightship	Aug.	1827	Ocracoke	2
William Gibbons	Steamer	Oct.	10, 1836	New Inlet	0
Premium	Sloop	Jan.	8, 1837	Ocracoke	0
Hiram	Schooner	Jan.	19, 1837	Wash Woods	0
Victory	Schooner	Feb.	6, 1837	Bodie Island	0
Carroll	Brig	Feb.	8, 1837	Cape Lookout	0
Seaman	Schooner	Mar.	5, 1837	New River Inlet	0
Aurora	Schooner	June	1837	Ocracoke	0
Hunter	Schooner	Aug.	19, 1837	Kitty Hawk	2
Alhambra	Schooner	Aug.	26, 1837	Bodie Island	0
William	Schooner	Aug.	29, 1837	Cape Lookout	?
Cumberland	Schooner	Oct.	8, 1837	Core Bank	0
Enterprize	Brig	Oct.	9, 1837	Bodie Island	1
Home	Steamer	Oct.	9, 1837	Ocracoke	90
Oran Sherwood	Sloop	Oct.	29, 1837	Currituck Beach	0
Wave	Schooner	Dec.	9, 1837	Currituck Beach	0
Indus	Brig	Dec.	18, 1837	Hatteras Inlet	0
Ralph	Brig	Dec.	22, 1837	Wash Woods	0
Horse	Schooner	Jan.	31, 1838	Currituck Beach	0

1838-1860 (See pages 27-49)

NAME	TYPE	DATE		PLACE	LIVES LOST
Pulaski	Steamer	June	14, 1838	Off New River	100
Milledgeville	Packet	Aug.	30, 1839	Chicamacomico	9
Mary	Schooner	Dec.	22, 1839	Ocracoke	0
Escambia	Brig	Mar.	25, 1840	Frying Pan Shoals	?
Flora	Ship	Mar.	28, 1840	Frying Pan Shoals	?
North Carolina	Steamer	July	25, 1840	Off Cape Fear	0
William J. Watson	Schooner	Nov.	15, 1840	Bodie Island	0
Lambert Tree	Schooner	Feb.	17, 1841	Off Ocracoke	0
American Trader	Schooner	Aug.	24, 1841	Currituck Beach	0
Alonzo	Schooner	Aug.	24, 1841	Currituck Beach	0
Heroine	Schooner	Oct.	1841	Whales Head	0
Astoria	Bark	Jan.	29, 1842	Hatteras Inlet	0
Ashley	Brig	June	2, 1842	Cape Fear	0
D.W. Hall	Brig	June	14, 1842	Hatteras Inlet	0
Trident	Schooner	June	14, 1842	Bodie Island	0
Kilgore	Brig	Aug.	24, 1842	Wash Woods	0
Pioneer	Brig	Aug.	24, 1842	Ocracoke	1
Congress	Ship	Aug.	24, 1842	Cape Hatteras	7
Leroy	Schooner	Oct.	5, 1842	Big Kinnakeet	0
Marion	Brig	Nov.	4, 1842	Bodie Island	2
F. A. Tupper	Schooner	Mar.	27, 1843	Chicamacomico	0
Driver	Schooner	Jan.	17, 1844	Cape Hatteras	0
Danube	Schooner	May	14, 1844	Bodie Island	0
McDonough	Schooner	June	13, 1844	Kitty Hawk	0
Argon	Schooner	Dec.	1844	Cape Lookout	0
Moon	Brig	May	8, 1845	Nags Head	0
Victoria	Ship	Oct.	23, 1845	Currituck Beach	0
Ontario	Bark	Dec.	1, 1845	Diamond Shoals	0
Emilie	Bark	Dec.	3, 1845	Wash Woods	7
Regulus	Schooner	Jan.	5, 1846	Hatteras Shoal	0
Comet	Schooner	Jan.	7, 1846	Ocracoke Inlet	?

1838-1860 (See pages 27-49)—*Continued*

NAME	TYPE	DATE	PLACE	LIVES LOST
James T. Hatfield	Schooner	Jan. 18, 1846	Wash Woods	o
C. C. Thorn	Schooner	June 2, 1846	New Inlet	?
Howell (or Howard)	Ship	July 30, 1846	Nags Head	o
Mary Anna	Schooner	Sept. 8, 1846	Off Hatteras	o
Antilla	Schooner	Nov. 6, 1846	Nags Head	?
Pennsylvania	Brig	Sept. 24, 1847	Diamond Shoals	o
Rodney	Brig	June 20, 1848	Off Cape Fear	o
R. W. Brown	Schooner	Dec. 11, 1848	New Inlet	?
Evergreen	Schooner	Jan. 9, 1849	Currituck Beach	o
J. P. Bickley	Schooner	Mar. 1849	Cape Hatteras	o
Fanny Gray	Schooner	Mar. 1849	Ocracoke	?
Margaret	Brig	July 24, 1850	Diamond Shoals	o
Ocean	Brig	July 1850	Diamond Shoals	o
Belle	Brig	July 1850	Diamond Shoals	o
Racer	Schooner	July 1850	Diamond Shoals	3
Mary Ellen	Brig	July 1850	Diamond Shoals	o
Franklin	Steamer	Sept. 14, 1850	Currituck Beach	?
Edward Wood	Schooner	Nov. 23, 1850	Currituck Inlet	o
John Boushell	Schooner	Jan. 28, 1851	Albemarle Sound	4
America	Steamer	Jan. 30, 1851	Off Hatteras	o
Rich'd H. Wyatt	Schooner	Jan. 31, 1851	Off Hatteras	o
Monterey	Schooner	Mar. 7, 1851	Cape Lookout	o
Aid Harrington		May 23, 1851	Caffeys Inlet	o
Jane	Schooner	June 1851	Hatteras	o
P. B. Savery	Schooner	Aug. 11, 1851	Chicamacomico	o
Walter J. Doyle	Schooner	Mar. 1852	Beaufort Bar	?
Magnolia	Schooner	Dec. 3, 1852	Chicamacomico	1
Mary Turcan	Brig	Dec. 13, 1852	Off Currituck	o
Mountaineer	Steamer	Dec. 25, 1852	Kitty Hawk	o
Henrietta Pierce	Schooner	Jan. 16, 1853	Kitty Hawk	o
Augustus Moore	Schooner	Apr. 15, 1853	Kitty Hawk	o
Bladan McLaughlin	Steamer	May 6, 1853	Kitty Hawk	o
Albemarle	Brig	Sept. 7, 1853	Off Hatteras	?
Eliza	Bark	Nov. 28, 1853	Wash Woods	1
Rattler	Clipper	Dec. 8, 1853	Currituck Beach	o
Rio	Schooner	Dec. 1853	Bodie Island	o
Sun	Schooner	Jan. 13, 1854	Beaufort Inlet	?
Cassius	Schooner	Feb. 12, 1854	Off Hatteras	o
Orline St. John	Bark	Feb. 21, 1854	Off Hatteras	4
Robert Walsh	(?)	Mar. 8, 1854	Off Hatteras	11
Sam Berry	Steamer	Jan. 12, 1856	Masonboro Inlet	1
Mary Varney	Bark	Apr. 5, 1856	Off Hatteras	1
A. S. Willers	Schooner	Sept. 1857	Cape Hatteras	?
Baltic	Schooner	Nov. 1857	Currituck Beach	?
Amanda Coons	Brig	Nov. 11, 1858	Currituck Beach	?
Agamemnon	Ship	Mar. 25, 1859	Currituck Beach	?
Mary	Schooner	Oct. 26, 1859	Ocracoke	?
Charles	Schooner	Nov. 1859	Nags Head	?
Lady Whidbee	Schooner	Jan. 17, 1860	New Inlet	o
Chansfield	Schooner	Feb. 1860	Albemarle Sound	?
Jane Henderson	Ship	June 21, 1860	Wash Woods	o
Vera Cruz	Steamer	1860	Bodie Island	?

1861-1865 (See pages 50-65)

NAME	TYPE	DATE	PLACE
Black Squall	Brig	April 8, 1861	Ocracoke
B. T. Martin	Brig	July 24, 1861	Chicamacomico
York	Conf. privateer	Aug. 9, 1861	Cape Hatteras
Governor	Fed. transport	Oct. 31, 1861	Off Hatteras
Peerless	Fed. transport	Oct. 31, 1861	Off Hatteras
City of New York	Fed. transport	Jan. 15, 1862	Hatteras Inlet
Curlew	Conf. gunboat	Feb. 7, 1862	Roanoke Island
Sea Bird	Conf. gunboat	Feb. 10, 1862	Elizabeth City
Appomattox	Conf. gunboat	Feb. 10, 1862	Elizabeth City
Fanny	Conf. gunboat	Feb. 10, 1862	Elizabeth City
Forrest	Conf. gunboat	Feb. 10, 1862	Elizabeth City
Black Warrior	Conf. schooner	Feb. 10, 1862	Elizabeth City
R. B. Forbes	Fed. steamer	Feb. 25, 1862	Currituck Banks
Oriental	Fed. transport	May 8, 1862	Bodie Island
Modern Greece	Blockade runner	June 27, 1862	Cape Fear
Pickett	Fed. gunboat	Sept. 6, 1862	Washington
Volant	Brig	Sept. 1862	New Inlet
Ellis	Fed. gunboat	Nov. 25, 1862	New River
Monitor	Fed. gunboat	Dec. 30, 1862	Cape Hatteras
Frying Pan Shoals	Conf. lightship	Dec. 31, 1862	Cape Fear River
Columbia	Fed. gunboat	Jan. 14, 1863	Masonboro Inlet
Golden Liner	Blockade runner	Apr. 27, 1863	Cape Fear River
Kate (2nd)	Blockade runner	July 12, 1863	Smiths Island
Hebe	Blockade runner	Aug. 18, 1863	Near Cape Fear
Bainbridge	Federal brig	Aug. 21, 1863	Off Hatteras
Alexander Cooper	Blockade runner	Aug. 22, 1863	Near Cape Fear
Arabian	Blockade runner	Sept. 15, 1863	Near Cape Fear
Phantom	Blockade runner	Sept. 23, 1863	Rich Inlet
Elizabeth	Blockade runner	Sept. 24, 1863	Lockwoods Folly
Douro	Blockade runner	Oct. 11, 1863	Wrightsville
Venus	Blockade runner	Oct. 21, 1863	Near Cape Fear
Beauregard	Blockade runner	Dec. 11, 1863	Carolina Beach
Antonica	Blockade runner	Dec. 19, 1863	Frying Pan Shoals
Bendigo	Blockade runner	Jan. 4, 1864	Lockwoods Folly
Vesta	Blockade runner	Jan. 10, 1864	Tubbs Inlet
Iron Age	Fed. gunboat	Jan. 11, 1864	Lockwoods Folly
Ranger	Blockade runner	Jan. 11, 1864	Lockwoods Folly
Wild Dayrell	Blockade runner	Feb. 1, 1864	Stump Inlet
Underwriter	Fed. gunboat	Feb. 2, 1864	New Bern
Nutfield	Blockade runner	Feb. 4, 1864	New River Inlet
Dee	Blockade runner	Feb. 6, 1864	Near Cape Fear
Fanny & Jenny	Blockade runner	Feb. 9, 1864	Wrightsville
Emily of London	Blockade runner	Feb. 9, 1864	Wrightsville
Spunkie	Blockade runner	Feb. 9, 1864	Near Cape Fear
Southfield	Fed. gunboat	Apr. 19, 1864	Plymouth
Raleigh	Conf. gunboat	May 7, 1864	Cape Fear River
Georgiana McCaw	Blockade runner	June 2, 1864	Cape Fear
Pevensey	Blockade runner	June 9, 1864	Bogue Inlet
Florie	Blockade runner	Sept. 10, 1864	Cape Fear Bar
Badger	Blockade runner	Sept. 10, 1864	Cape Fear Bar
North Carolina	Conf. gunboat	Sept. 1864	Cape Fear River
Condor	Blockade runner	Oct. 1, 1864	Near Cape Fear

1861-1865 (See pages 50-65)—*Continued*

NAME	TYPE	DATE	PLACE	LIVES LOST
Albemarle	Conf. ram	Oct. 27, 1864	Plymouth	
Ella	Blockade runner	Dec. 3, 1864	Cape Fear	
Louisiana	Fed. gunboat	Dec. 24, 1864	Fort Fisher	
Tallabassee	Conf. gunboat	Jan. 15, 1865	Near Cape Fear	
Cape Fear	Blockade runner	Jan. 1865	Cape Fear River	
North Heath	Blockade runner	Jan. 1865	Cape Fear River	

1866-1877 (See pages 66-85)

NAME	TYPE	DATE	PLACE	LIVES LOST
Andrew Johnson	Steamer	Oct. 5, 1866	Currituck Inlet	?
Geo. E. Maltby	Brig	Jan. 7, 1867	Off Hatteras	0
Martha	Schooner	Jan. 10, 1867	Currituck Beach	0
Alfred Thomas	Schooner	Mar. 10, 1867	New Inlet	?
Flambeau	Steamer	Mar. 1867	New Inlet	0
Quick	Brig	Mar. 1867	Oregon Inlet	5
Jonas Sparks	Schooner	Apr. 14, 1867	Beaufort Bar	?
Vesta	Schooner	Apr. 1867	Hatteras Inlet	?
G. W. Carpenter	Schooner	Apr. 1867	Creeds Hill	?
Daniel Chase	Schooner	Nov. 4, 1867	Ocracoke Inlet	?
Adamantine	Schooner	Nov. 1867	Bodie Island	?
Oneota	Steamer	Nov. 1867	Off Cape Lookout	?
Francis	Steamer	Dec. 30, 1867	Carolina Beach	0
Nevada	Steamer	June 4, 1868	Hatteras Shoal	1
Istria	Bark	June 1868	Diamond Shoals	23
Patapsco	Steamer	Sept. 12, 1868	Cape Lookout	0
Samuel Eddy	Schooner	Feb. 1869	Frying Pan Shoals	0
Alliance	Steamer	Mar. 4, 1869	Hatteras Inlet	?
Thames	Steamer	Apr. 6, 1869	Off Cape Hatteras	?
Gulf City	Steamer	June 11, 1869	Lookout Shoals	22
Ezra	Bark	Sept. 1869	Bodie Island	?
Eleanor T.	Schooner	Feb. 4, 1870	Carolina Beach	5
Eagle	Steamer	Mar. 4, 1870	Bodie Island	0
M. A. Forbes	Bark	May 1870	Currituck Beach	?
Key West	Steamer	Oct. 1870	Cape Hatteras	0
Fairbanks	Steamer	Dec. 9, 1870	Hatteras Inlet	0
Kensington	Steamer	Jan. 27, 1871	Off Chicamacomico	0
La. Republique	Steamer	Feb. 1871	Off Cape Lookout	0
Pontiac	Ship	Feb. 1871	Cape Lookout	?
William Muir	Brig	Apr. 1, 1871	Currituck Beach	0
Harriet N. Rogers	Schooner	Jan. 15, 1873	Bodie Island	0
Annie McFarland	Brig	Jan. 30, 1873	Currituck Beach	0
Faugh-A-Ballagh	Brigantine	Feb. 2, 1873	Currituck Beach	0
William	Schooner	Feb. 6, 1873	Chicamacomico	?
Ariadne	Steamer	Feb. 7, 1873	Nags Head	0
Volunteer	Steamer	Feb. 23, 1873	Nags Head	0
R. B. Thompson	Schooner	July 3, 1873	Off Cape Hatteras	9
Spellbourne	Schooner	Oct. 1873	Off Cape Hatteras	0
Henrietta	Clipper	Nov. 4, 1873	Frying Pan Shoals	14
Waltham	Brig	May 4, 1874	Bodie Island	0
J. Means	Schooner	Oct. 12, 1874	Bodie Island	0

NAME	TYPE	DATE	PLACE	LIVES LOST
Blaisdell	Schooner	May 1875	Off Hatteras	?
Clara Davidson	Schooner	Feb. 7, 1876	Hatteras Inlet	?
Nuova Ottavia	Bark	Mar. 1, 1876	Currituck Beach	16
Shiloh	Schooner	Mar. 17, 1876	Durants	2
Lotta Lee	Schooner	Mar. 1876	Hatteras Inlet	0
Henry G. Fay	Schooner	Apr. 1, 1876	Caffeys Inlet	0
Electric	Schooner	Aug. 21, 1876	Off Cape Fear	0
S. S. Lewis	Wrecking Schooner	Sept. 1876	Cape Hatteras	?
J. H. Lockwood	Schooner	Nov. 20, 1876	Chicamacomico	0
America	Bark	Dec. 24, 1876	Chicamacomico	0
Iona	Schooner	Apr. 9, 1877	Chicamacomico	?
Benj. W. Robinson	Schooner	Apr. 10, 1877	Chicamacomico	0
Hattie L. Fuller	Schooner	Apr. 13, 1877	Oregon Inlet	0
Western Star	Schooner	Sept. 11, 1877	Bodie Island	0
Huron	Steamer	Nov. 24, 1877	Nags Head	103

1878-1893 (See pages 86-132)

NAME	TYPE	DATE	PLACE	LIVES LOST
E. B. Wharton	Schooner	Jan. 31, 1878	Ocracoke	?
Metropolis	Steamer	Jan. 31, 1878	Currituck Beach	85
C. C. Overton	Brig	Feb. 1, 1878	Ocracoke	?
Success	Bark	Jan. 15, 1879	Bodie Island	0
Ida B. Silsbee	Schooner	Aug. 18, 1879	Cape Hatteras	0
M & E Henderson	Schooner	Nov. 30, 1879	Pea Island	4
Whitney Long	Schooner	Dec. 20, 1879	Creeds Hill	0
Benjamin Dickerman	Bark	Oct. 18, 1880	Off Hatteras	1
L & D Fisk	Schooner	Nov. 23, 1880	Diamond Shoals	6
A. B. Goodman	Schooner	Apr. 4, 1881	Diamond Shoals	1
Mary J. Fisher	Schooner	Aug. 24, 1881	Off Lockw'ds Folly	4
Sandusky	Ship	Aug. 28, 1881	Off Hatteras	3
Mary Bear	Schooner	Sept. 9, 1881	New Topsail Inlet	1
Thomas J. Lancaster	Schooner	Oct. 5, 1881	New Inlet	7
H. W. McColly	Schooner	Oct. 5, 1881	Gull Shoal	0
F. L. Carney	Bark	Jan. 22, 1882	Hatteras Inlet	10
Stampede	Schooner	Feb. 4, 1882	Off Cape Fear	1
Mary L. Vankirk	Schooner	Feb. 5, 1882	New Inlet	0
Minnie	Schooner	Apr. 12, 1882	Cape Fear	0
Mercy T. Trundy	Schooner	Apr. 24, 1882	Cape Fear	0
James W. Haig	Schooner	Sept. 26, 1882	Durants	0
Robbie L. Foster	Schooner	Oct. 14, 1882	Cape Fear	0
Edna Harwood	Schooner	Nov. 31, 1882	Off Hatteras	1
Enterprise	Steamer	Dec. 4, 1882	Off Mauls Point	3
John Floyd	Schooner	Dec. 14, 1882	Diamond Shoals	0
Thomas J. Martin	Schooner	Jan. 9, 1883	Caffeys Inlet	0
Eugene	Schooner	Jan. 22, 1883	Ocracoke	0
Dulcimer	Bark	Feb. 12, 1883	Durants	0
Angela	Barkentine	Mar. 4, 1883	Paul Gamiels Hill	0
Luola Murchison	Schooner	Oct. 3, 1883	Kitty Hawk	0
Florence	Schooner	Jan. 5, 1884	Chicamacomico	0
John N. Parker	Schooner	Jan. 8, 1884	Hatteras Inlet	0
Emma C. Rommell	Schooner	Jan. 8, 1884	Gull Shoal	0

1878-1893 (See pages 86-132)—*Continued*

NAME	TYPE	DATE	PLACE	LIVES LOST
Dos Hermanos	Steamer	Sept. 13, 1884	Frying Pan Shoals	2
Isaac L. Clark	Schooner	Dec. 17, 1884	Diamond Shoals	0
Ephraim Williams	Barkentine	Dec. 22, 1884	Big Kinnakeet	0
Ario Pardee	Schooner	Dec. 29, 1884	Wash Woods	0
A. F. Crockett	Schooner	Feb. 17, 1885	Ocracoke	0
Wave	Steamer	Mar. 5, 1885	Cape Fear River	3
Ada F. Whitney	Schooner	Sept. 22, 1885	Poyners Hill	0
Thomas Sinnickson	Schooner	Oct. 12, 1885	Hatteras Inlet	0
Vapor	Schooner	Nov. 5, 1885	Cape Fear Bar	0
Harkaway	Bark	Nov. 30, 1885	Caffeys Inlet	0
Nellie Wadsworth	Schooner	Dec. 6, 1885	Hatteras Inlet	0
Crissie Wright	Schooner	Jan. 11, 1886	Lookout Shoals	6
Jennie Beasley	Schooner	Jan. 26, 1886	Currituck Inlet	0
Codorus	Bark	Aug. 4, 1886	Diamond Shoals	0
Kate Wentworth	Schooner	Nov. 18, 1886	Bogue Banks	1
George S. Marts	Schooner	Apr. 16, 1887	Off Hatteras	2
Samuel Welsh	Barkentine	Feb. 25, 1888	Whales Head	0
Rachel A. Collins	Schooner	Mar. 12, 1888	Off Hatteras	4
Annchen	Brigantine	July 17, 1888	Creeds Hill	0
Lena Breed	Schooner	Dec. 4, 1888	Diamond Shoals	0
Walter S. Massey	Barkentine	Jan. 18, 1889	Diamond Shoals	0
Allie R. Chester	Schooner	Jan. 20, 1889	Diamond Shoals	5
James B. Anderson	Schooner	Jan. 21, 1889	Durants	0
Josie Troop	Bark	Feb. 22, 1889	Chicamacomico	11
John S. Wood	Schooner	Apr. 7, 1889	Wash Woods	0
Parrott	Schooner	Apr. 7, 1889	Albemarle Sound	2
Hattie Lollis	Schooner	Apr. 7, 1889	Nags Head	0
Wolseley	Bark	Apr. 11, 1889	Big Kinnakeet	0
N. Boynton	Barge	Apr. 17, 1889	Poyners Hill	0
John Shay	Schooner	Apr. 17, 1889	Cape Hatteras	6
Aberlady Bay	Steamer	May 10, 1889	Lookout Shoals	0
Viola W. Burton	Schooner	May 27, 1889	Big Kinnakeet	0
Frank M. McGear	Schooner	Oct. 23, 1889	Whales Head	0
Henry P. Simmons	Schooner	Oct. 23, 1889	Wash Woods	7
Francis E. Waters	Schooner	Oct. 24, 1889	Nags Head	6
Lizzie S. Haynes	Schooner	Oct. 24, 1889	Pea Island	5
Annie E. Blackman	Schooner	Oct. 24, 1889	New Inlet	6
Busiris	Schooner	Oct. 24, 1889	Poyners Hill	0
Pioneer	Steamer	1889	Ocracoke	?
San Antonio	Bark	Jan. 21, 1890	Cape Fear River	0
Mary A. Trainer	Schooner	Jan. 28, 1890	Durants	0
St. Johns	Schooner	Mar. 17, 1890	Durants	1
Sue Williams	Schooner	Mar. 22, 1890	Chicamacomico	0
Joseph Rudd	Schooner	Mar. 22, 1890	Lookout Shoals	0
William H. Keeney	Schooner	Mar. 28, 1890	Little Kinnakeet	0
Hattie S. Clark	Schooner	May 15, 1890	Off Cape Fear	5
Mignon	Steam yacht	Sept. 9, 1890	Cape Fear	0
Blanche	Schooner	Dec. 17, 1890	Ocracoke	0
Joseph H. Neff	Schooner	Dec. 17, 1890	Oak Island	1
Charles C. Lister, Jr.	Schooner	Jan. 22, 1891	Ocracoke	0
Nathaniel Lank	Schooner	Jan. 22, 1891	Gull Shoal	:

NAME	TYPE	DATE	PLACE	LIVES LOST
J. W. Gaskill	Schooner	Feb. 16, 1891	Pea Island	0
Strathairly	Steamer	Mar. 24, 1891	Chicamacomico	19
Vibilia	Bark	May 25, 1891	Poyners Hill	0
William H. Hopkins	Schooner	June 21, 1891	Big Kinnakeet	0
A. L. & M. Townsend	Schooner	July 7, 1891	Cape Lookout	0
Annie E. Pierce	Schooner	Feb. 22, 1892	Little Kinnakeet	1
Freddie Hencken	Schooner	Feb. 26, 1892	Gull Shoal	0
Bronx	Sloop	June 21, 1892	Beaufort Harbor	0
Casket	Bark	Sept. 13, 1892	Frying Pan Shoals	0
Mattie E. Hiles	Schooner	Oct. 30, 1892	Currituck Inlet	0
Irene Thayer	Schooner	Nov. 19, 1892	Oregon Inlet	0
Formosa	Bark	Feb. 20, 1893	Diamond Shoals	0
Nathan Esterbrook, Jr.	Schooner	Feb. 20, 1893	Little Kinnakeet	1
Alphild	Bark	Feb. 27, 1893	Cape Fear	0
Martha	Schooner	Mar. 4, 1893	Cape Hatteras	0
Lillie F. Schmidt	Schooner	Mar. 9, 1893	Ocracoke	0

1893-1899 (See pages 133-60)

NAME	TYPE	DATE	PLACE	LIVES LOST
Wustrow	Brig	Aug. 29, 1893	Oak Island	0
Kate E. Gifford	Schooner	Aug. 30, 1893	Oak Island	0
Enchantress	Schooner	Aug. 31, 1893	Oak Island	0
Emma J. Warrington	Schooner	Oct. 4, 1893	Paul Gamiels Hill	0
Ravenwood	Barkentine	Oct. 13, 1893	Chicamacomico	0
Charles C. Dame	Schooner	Oct. 14, 1893	Cape Fear	0
Mary W. Morris	Schooner	Oct. 27, 1893	Oak Island	0
* Gertrude	Schooner	Nov. 29, 1893	Cape Fear	?
Wetherby	Steamer	Dec. 2, 1893	Diamond Shoals	0
Clythia	Bark	Jan. 22, 1894	Wash Woods	0
(?)	Schooner	Feb. 4, 1894	Diamond Shoals	?
Florence C. Magee	Schooner	Feb. 26, 1894	Bodie Island	0
A. P. Richardson	Schooner	Sept. 26, 1894	Ocracoke	0
Elizabeth A. Baizley	Schooner	Sept. 28, 1894	Cape Fear	0
Ogir	Bark	Oct. 10, 1894	Oak Island	0
Richard S. Spofford	Schooner	Dec. 27, 1894	Ocracoke	1
Hester A. Seward	Schooner	Jan. 6, 1895	Ocracoke	0
Etta M. Barter	Schooner	Feb. 27, 1895	Portsmouth	0
Edward S. Stearns	Schooner	Mar. 4, 1895	Durants	0
Sallie Bissell	Schooner	Mar. 4, 1895	Portsmouth	0
Laura Nelson	Schooner	Mar. 30, 1895	Bodie Island	0
Addie Henry	Schooner	Apr. 14, 1895	Ocracoke	0
J. W. Dresser	Barkentine	July 23, 1895	Cape Hatteras	0
Martin S. Ebel	Schooner	Nov. 5, 1895	Big Kinnakeet	0
Emma C. Cotton	Schooner	Dec. 27, 1895	Pea Island	0
James Woodall	Steamer	Jan. 12, 1896	New Inlet	0
William H. Allison	Schooner	Feb. 3, 1896	Cape Fear	0
Maggie J. Lawrence	Schooner	Feb. 10, 1896	Pea Island	0
Glanayron	Steamer	May 22, 1896	Cape Hatteras	0
Henry Norwell	Barkentine	July 7, 1896	Gull Shoal	0
E. S. Newman	Schooner	Oct. 11, 1896	Pea Island	0
Levi Davis	Tug	Nov. 29, 1896	Oak Island	0

* Not definitely identified.

1893-1899 (See pages 133-60)—*Continued*

NAME	TYPE	DATE	PLACE	LIVES LOST
George M. Adams	Schooner	May 1, 1897	Nags Head	0
Hesperides	Steamer	Oct. 9, 1897	Cape Hatteras	0
Mathilda	Ship	Oct. 27, 1897	Bodie Island	0
Samuel W. Hall	Schooner	Dec. 24, 1897	Chicamacomico	0
William	Schooner	Jan. 23, 1898	Oak Island	0
Samuel W.Tilton	Schooner	Feb. 17, 1898	Chicamacomico	0
S. Warren Hall	Schooner	Apr. 5, 1898	Portsmouth	0
Milton	Schooner	Apr. 27, 1898	Bodie Island	0
George L. Fessenden	Schooner	Apr. 27, 1898	Chicamacomico	4
S. G. Hart	Schooner	Aug. 10, 1898	Little Kinnakeet	0
Charmer	Schooner	Mar. 4, 1899	Portsmouth	0
Alfred Brabrook	Schooner	Mar. 7, 1899	Gull Shoal	0
J. C. McNaughton	Schooner	Apr. 8, 1899	Durants	0
June	Sloop	Aug. 11, 1899	Oregon Inlet	0

August, 1899 (See pages 161-69)

NAME	TYPE	DATE	PLACE	LIVES LOST
Aaron Reppard	Schooner	Aug. 16, 1899	Gull Shoal	5
Florence Randall	Schooner	Aug. 16, 1899	'Big Kinnakeet	0
Fred Walton	Hulk	Aug. 17, 1899	Portsmouth	0
Lydia A. Willis	Schooner	Aug. 17, 1899	Portsmouth	2
Robert W. Dasey	Schooner	Aug. 17, 1899	Little Kinnakeet	0
Priscilla	Barkentine	Aug. 17, 1899	Gull Shoal	4
Minnie Bergen	Schooner	Aug. 18, 1899	Chicamacomico	0

1899-1918 (See pages 170-92)

NAME	TYPE	DATE	PLACE	LIVES LOST
Henrietta Hill	Schooner	Aug. 24, 1899	Portsmouth	0
Roger Moore	Schooner	Oct. 30, 1899	Big Kinnakeet	0
Ariosto	Steamer	Dec. 24, 1899	Ocracoke	21
Mary C. Ward	Schooner	Jan. 26, 1900	Pamlico Sound	5
Three Friends	Schooner	Feb. 9, 1900	Portsmouth	0
Jane C. Harris	Schooner	Feb. 25, 1900	Oregon Inlet	0
Lizzie S. James	Schooner	Mar. 12, 1900	Ocracoke	0
William H. Kenzal	Schooner	Apr. 5, 1900	Cape Hatteras	?
Virginia	Steamer	May 2, 1900	Cape Hatteras	6
Hettie J. Dorman	Schooner	May 5, 1900	Cape Hatteras	0
Palestro	Steamer	Aug. 9, 1900	Cape Hatteras	0
George R. Congdon	Schooner	Jan. 31, 1901	Cape Hatteras	0
General S. E. Merwin	Schooner	Mar. 4, 1901	Gull Shoal	0
Seabright	Steamer	Sept. 18, 1901	Oak Island	0
Leading Breeze	Schooner	Nov. 23, 1901	Portsmouth	0
Ea	Steamer	Mar. 15, 1902	Cape Hatteras	0
Ida C. Schoolcraft	Schooner	July 1, 1902	Core Bank	0
Ida Lawrence	Schooner	Dec. 4, 1902	Ocracoke	0
Olive Thurlow	Barkentine	Dec. 5, 1902	Cape Lookout	1
Wesley M. Oler	Schooner	Dec. 5, 1902	Hatteras Inlet	10
Nineveh	Bark	Jan. 24, 1903	Off Cape Fear	0
Wm. H. Shubert	Schooner	Feb. 16, 1903	Bodie Island	0
C. S. Glidden	Schooner	Mar. 17, 1903	Cape Lookout	0
John A. Buttrick	Schooner	Mar. 30, 1903	Cape Fear	1

NAME	TYPE	DATE	PLACE	LIVES LOST
J. F. Becker	Schooner	Apr. 26, 1903	Oregon Inlet	0
Vera Cruz VII	Brig	May 8, 1903	Portsmouth	1
Lucy Russell	Schooner	June 21, 1903	Gull Shoal	0
James H. Hamlen	Barkentine	Aug. 28, 1903	Cape Lookout	0
Mabel Rose	Schooner	Oct. 11, 1903	Wash Woods	0
J. B. Holden	Schooner	Oct. 11, 1903	Paul Gamiels Hill	0
Clarance H.	Schooner	Dec. 9, 1903	Oak Island	5
Joseph W. Brooks	Schooner	Jan. 17, 1904	Cape Lookout	0
Benjamin M. Wallace	Schooner	Mar. 26, 1904	Chicamacomico	0
Kate Spencer	Schooner	Oct. 7, 1904	Cape Lookout	0
Montana	Schooner	Dec. 11, 1904	Pea Island	1
Northeastern	Steamer	Dec. 27, 1904	Cape Hatteras	0
Emma C. Middleton	Schooner	Jan. 4, 1905	Cape Fear	0
Cordelia E. Hays	Schooner	Jan. 15, 1905	Cape Hatteras	0
Sarah D. J. Rawson	Schooner	Feb. 9, 1905	Cape Lookout	1
Blanche Hopkins	Schooner	Apr. 11, 1905	Gull Shoal	0
D. D. Haskell	Schooner	May 9, 1905	Core Bank	0
Clara E. Bergen	Schooner	June 26, 1905	Durants	0
Thomas A. Goddard	Barge	Dec. 9, 1905	Nags Head	0
Robert H. Stevenson	Schooner	Jan. 13, 1906	Cape Hatteras	12
Jennie Lockwood	Schooner	Feb. 13, 1906	Pea Island	0
Myrtle Tunnell	Schooner	Mar. 9, 1906	Cape Fear	0
Raymond T. Maull	Schooner	Mar. 21, 1906	Gull Shoal	0
Matilda D. Borda	Schooner	July 16, 1906	Gull Shoal	0
Nellie Floyd	Schooner	Sept. 18, 1906	Off Cape Fear	1
John I. Snow	Schooner	Jan. 14, 1907	Portsmouth	0
Hilda	Schooner	Feb. 6, 1907	Cape Hatteras	7
Oriente	Bark	Apr. 28, 1907	Poyners Hill	0
Harry & Ralph	Sloop	June 26, 1907	Cape Fear	0
Saxon	Barge	Oct. 12, 1907	Gull Shoal	3
Leonora	Schooner	Jan. 8, 1908	Cape Hatteras	5
Anne Comber	Schooner	Jan. 17, 1908	Pamlico Sound	0
Melrose	Schooner	Feb. 15, 1908	Core Bank	0
Orient	Schooner	Apr. 18, 1908	Cape Lookout	0
Governor Safford	Steamer	July 24, 1908	Bogue Inlet	0
Flora Rogers	Schooner	Oct. 23, 1908	Bodie Island	0
Charles S. Hirsch	Schooner	Oct. 29, 1908	Paul Gamiels Hill	2
Arleville H. Peary	Schooner	Oct. 31, 1908	Wash Woods	0
Belle O'Neill	Schooner	Feb. 3, 1909	Cape Lookout	0
Eleazer W. Clark	Schooner	Nov. 17, 1909	Cape Fear	0
Brewster	Steamer	Nov. 29, 1909	Cape Hatteras	0
Marie Palmer	Schooner	Nov. 30, 1909	Cape Fear	0
Governor Ames	Schooner	Dec. 13, 1909	Off Chicamacom'o	11
Frances	Schooner	Feb. 1, 1910	Big Kinnakeet	8
Arroyo	Steamer	Feb. 20, 1910	Portsmouth	0
Thomas G. Smith	Schooner	Apr. 10, 1910	Core Bank	0
Catherine M. Monohan	Schooner	Aug. 24, 1910	Off Ocracoke	0
Wm. H. Davidson	Schooner	Dec. 12, 1910	Paul Gamiels Hill	0
Martha E. Wallace	Schooner	Dec. 21, 1910	Cape Lookout	0
Spero	Bark	Dec. 24, 1910	Hatteras Inlet	0
Harriet C. Kerlin	Schooner	Feb. 6, 1911	Cape Hatteras	0
Wellfleet	Schooner	Mar. 6, 1911	Cape Hatteras	0
Willie H. Child	Schooner	Aug. 17, 1911	Gull Shoal	0

1899-1918 (See pages 170-92)—*Continued*

NAME	TYPE	DATE	PLACE	LIVES LOST
James Davidson	Schooner	Aug. 26, 1911	Cape Fear	0
Charles H. Valentine	Schooner	Aug. 29, 1911	Cape Fear	0
Lizzie H. Patrick	Schooner	Nov. 27, 1911	Cape Lookout	0
Charles J. Dumas	Schooner	Dec. 27, 1911	Pea Island	0
Thistleroy	Steamer	Dec. 28, 1911	Cape Lookout	0
Mary S. Eskridge	Schooner	Dec. 31, 1911	Big Kinnakeet	0
Harry Prescott	Schooner	Jan. 18, 1912	Cape Hatteras	0
Elm City	Schooner	Mar. 25, 1912	Little Kinnakeet	?
John Maxwell	Schooner	Nov. 2, 1912	New Inlet	6
Savannah	Schooner	Dec. 27, 1912	Cape Fear	0
Montrose W. Houck	Schooner	Feb. 18, 1913	Paul Gamiels Hill	0
Zaccheus Sherman	Schooner	Feb. 28, 1913	Gull Shoal	0
Richard F.C. Hartley	Schooner	Sept. 2, 1913	Chicamacomico	2
George W. Wells	Schooner	Sept. 3, 1913	Ocracoke	0
J. R. Teel	Barge	Nov. 10, 1913	Cape Lookout	1
Helen H. Benedict	Schooner	Feb. 6, 1914	Nags Head	0
Isle of Iona	Steamer	Dec. 13, 1914	Ocracoke	0
George N. Reed	Schooner	Jan. 20, 1915	Pea Island	0
Mindora	Steamer	Jan. 22, 1915	Cape Fear	0
Idler	Yacht	Jan. 24, 1915	Cape Hatteras	12
Sylvia C. Hall	Schooner	Mar. 17, 1915	Cape Lookout	0
Prinz Maurits	Steamer	Apr. 3, 1915	Off Cape Hatteras	49
The Josephine	Schooner	Apr. 3, 1915	Kill Devil Hills	3
William H. Macy	Barge	Apr. 3, 1915	Wash Woods	0
Loring C. Ballard	Schooner	Apr. 3, 1915	Gull Shoal	0
Col. Thomas F. Austin	Schooner	Feb. 24, 1916	Cape Fear	0
Elsie A. Bayles	Schooner	Apr. 5, 1916	New Inlet	2
M. B. Davis	Schooner	Dec. 8, 1917	Bogue Inlet	0
Lulu M. Quillin	Schooner	Dec. 11, 1917	Little Kinnakeet	0
Veturia	Steamer	Feb. 20, 1918	Cape Hatteras	0

1918 (See pages 193-208)

NAME	TYPE	DATE	PLACE	LIVES LOST
* Harpathian	Steamer	June 5, 1918	Off Currituck	0
* Vinland	Steamer	June 5, 1918	Off Currituck	0
* Vindeggen	Steamer	June 8, 1918	Off Currituck	1
* Pinar del Rio	Steamer	June 9, 1918	Off Nags Head	0
Nat Meader	Schooner	June 26, 1918	Cape Hatteras	0
Hattie Gage	Tug	June 29, 1918	Nags Head	1
Luna	Schooner	July 29, 1918	Portsmouth	0
Elizabeth T. Doyle	Schooner	July 30, 1918	Cape Hatteras	0
* O. B. Jennings	Tanker	Aug. 4, 1918	Off Wash Woods	1
* Stanley M. Seaman	Schooner	Aug. 5, 1918	Off Cape Hatteras	0
* Merak	Steamer	Aug. 6, 1918	Little Kinnakeet	0
* Diamond Shoals	Lightship	Aug. 6, 1918	Cape Hatteras	0
† Mirlo	Tanker	Aug. 16, 1918	Chicamacomico	10
* Nordhav	Bark	Aug. 17, 1918	Off Bodie Island	0
Proteus	Steamer	Aug. 19, 1918	Off Hatteras	?

* Sunk by German submarine.
† Sunk by contact with German mine.

1919-1940 (See pages 209-27)

NAME	TYPE	DATE	PLACE	LIVES LOST
Gracie D. Chambers	Schooner	Feb. 13, 1919	Poyners Hill	0
Black Hawk	Yacht	Nov. 6, 1919	Oregon Inlet	0
Explorer	Tug	Dec. 12, 1919	Nags Head	0
Sunbeam	Schooner	Dec. 17, 1919	Off Currituck	18
Momie T.	Schooner	Jan. 27, 1920	Caffeys Inlet	0
Powel	Steamer	Apr. 6, 1920	Off Hatteras	0
Maside	Steamer	Dec. 14, 1920	Fort Macon	0
Carroll A. Deering	Schooner	Jan. 31, 1921	Diamond Shoals	11
Louise Howard	Schooner	Apr. 14, 1921	Fort Macon	0
Mary J. Haynie	Schooner	May 24, 1921	Ocracoke	0
Laura A. Barnes	Schooner	June 1, 1921	Bodie Island	0
U.S.S. New Jersey	Battleship	Sept. 5, 1923	Diamond Shoals	0
U.S.S. Virginia	Battleship	Sept. 5, 1923	Diamond Shoals	0
Santiago	Steamer	Mar. 11, 1924	Off Hatteras	25
Dorothea L. Brinkman	Schooner	Mar. 22, 1924	Oregon Inlet	?
Irma	Schooner	Apr. 29, 1925	Kill Devil Hills	0
Victoria S.	Schooner	Aug. 23, 1925	Ocracoke	0
Isabella Parmenter	Schooner	Nov. 1, 1925	Chicamacomico	0
Morris and Cliff	Schooner	Jan. 16, 1926	Bogue Inlet	0
Adelaide Day	Schooner	Nov. 8, 1927	Off Hatteras	0
Kyzikes	Tanker	Dec. 4, 1927	Kill Devil Hills	4
Cibao	Steamer	Dec. 4, 1927	Hatteras Inlet	0
George W. Truitt, Jr.	Schooner	Feb. 20, 1928	Ocracoke Inlet	0
Bainbridge	Schooner	Feb. 5, 1929	Nags Head	0
A. Ernest Mills	Schooner	May 3, 1929	Currituck Beach	3
Carl Gerhard	Steamer	Sept. 23, 1929	Kill Devil Hills	0
Lavinia M. Snow	Schooner	Mar. 7, 1930	Durants	0
Catherine G. Scott	Schooner	Oct. 14, 1930	Off Hatteras	3
Anna May	Trawler	Dec. 9, 1931	Diamond Shoals	0
St. Rita	Trawler	Jan. 13, 1932	Paul Gamiels Hill	0
Ella Pierce Thurlow	Schooner Barge	Mar. 23, 1932	Cape Fear	0
Cities Service Petrol	Tanker	July 14, 1933	Off Cape Lookout	2
G. A. Kohler	Schooner	Aug. 23, 1933	Gull Shoal	0
Glory	Steamer	Aug. 1933	Nags Head	?
Nomis	Schooner	Aug. 16, 1935	Hatteras Inlet	0
Mount Dirfys	Steamer	Dec. 26, 1936	Cape Fear	?
Tzenny Chandris	Steamer	Nov. 13, 1937	Off Kitty Hawk	7
Albatross	Trawler	Feb. 21, 1940	Ocracoke Inlet	?

1942-1945 (See pages 228-39)

NAME	TYPE	DATE	PLACE
Allan Jackson	Tanker	Jan. 18, 1942	Cape Hatteras
Brazos	Cargo	Jan. 18, 1942	Cape Hatteras
Norvana	Cargo	Jan. 18, 1942	Cape Hatteras
City of Atlanta	Cargo	Jan. 19, 1942	Cape Hatteras
Ciltvaira	Tanker	Jan. 20, 1942	Gull Shoal
Empire Gem	Tanker	Jan. 23, 1942	Creeds Hill
Venore	Cargo	Jan. 23, 1942	Creeds Hill
York	Cargo	Jan. 1942	Kill Devil Hills
Amerikalund	(?)	Feb. 2, 1942	Wash Woods
Victolite	Tanker	Feb. 10, 1942	Caffeys Inlet

1942-1945 (See pages 228-39)—*Continued*

NAME	TYPE	DATE	PLACE
Blink	Cargo	Feb. 11, 1942	Cape Hatteras
Buarque	Passenger	Feb. 15, 1942	Kill Devil Hills
Olympic	Tanker	Feb. 23, 1942	Kill Devil Hills
Norlavore	Cargo	Feb. 24, 1942	Cape Hatteras
Cassimir	Tanker	Feb. 26, 1942	Cape Fear
Marore	Cargo	Feb. 26, 1942	Gull Shoal
Raritan	Cargo	Feb. 28, 1942	Cape Fear
Anna R. Heidritter	Schooner	Mar. 1, 1942	Ocracoke
Arabutan	Cargo	Mar. 7, 1942	Cape Hatteras
Chester Sun	Tanker	Mar. 10, 1942	Big Kinnakeet
Caribsea	Cargo	Mar. 11, 1942	Cape Lookout
John D. Gill	Tanker	Mar. 12, 1942	Cape Fear
Ario	Tanker	Mar. 15, 1942	Cape Lookout
Ceiba	Cargo	Mar. 15, 1942	Nags Head
Resource	(?)	Mar. 15, 1942	Kill Devil Hills
Alcoa Guide	Cargo	Mar. 16, 1942	Cape Hatteras
Olean	Tanker	Mar. 16, 1942	Cape Lookout
Tenas	Barge	Mar. 17, 1942	Creeds Hill
Australia	Tanker	Mar. 17, 1942	Diamond Shoals
Papoose	Tanker	Mar. 18, 1942	Cape Lookout
W. E. Hutton	Tanker	Mar. 18, 1942	Bogue Inlet
E. M. Clark	Tanker	Mar. 18, 1942	Ocracoke
Liberator	Cargo	Mar. 19, 1942	Cape Hatteras
Kassandra Louloudis	Cargo	Mar. 19, 1942	Cape Hatteras
Teresa	Cargo	Mar. 21, 1942	Cape Hatteras
Naeco	Tanker	Mar. 23, 1942	Cape Lookout
Empire Steel	Tanker	Mar. 24, 1942	Wash Woods
Narraganset	Tanker	Mar. 25, 1942	Cape Hatteras
Dixie Arrow	Tanker	Mar. 26, 1942	Ocracoke
Carolyn	Cargo	Mar. 27, 1942	Nags Head
Equipoise	Cargo	Mar. 27, 1942	Caffeys Inlet
City of New York	Passenger	Mar. 29, 1942	Cape Hatteras
Malchase	Cargo	Mar. 29, 1942	Cape Lookout
Rio Blanco	Cargo	Apr. 1, 1942	Cape Hatteras
Otho	Cargo	Apr. 3, 1942	Cape Hatteras
Byron D. Benson	Tanker	Apr. 3, 1942	Caffeys Inlet
Ensis	Tanker	Apr. 4, 1942	Cape Hatteras
British Splendour	Tanker	Apr. 6, 1942	Cape Hatteras
Lancing	Tanker	Apr. 7, 1942	Cape Hatteras
Kollskegg	Tanker	Apr. 7, 1942	Cape Hatteras
San Delfino	Tanker	Apr. 9, 1942	Cape Hatteras
Atlas	Tanker	Apr. 9, 1942	Cape Lookout
Tamaulipas	Tanker	Apr. 10, 1942	Cape Lookout
Tennessee	Tanker	Apr. 11, 1942	Cape Lookout
U-85	German sub	Apr. 14, 1942	Nags Head
Empire Thrush	Cargo	Apr. 14, 1942	Cape Hatteras
Desert Light	Cargo	Apr. 16, 1942	Oregon Inlet
Empire Dryden	Cargo	Apr. 19, 1942	Oregon Inlet
Harpagon	Cargo	Apr. 19, 1942	Cape Hatteras
Agra	Tanker	Apr. 20, 1942	Cape Hatteras
Chenango	Cargo	Apr. 20, 1942	Kill Devil Hills
Bris	Cargo	Apr. 21, 1942	Cape Lookout

NAME	TYPE	DATE	PLACE
Ashkabad	Cargo	Apr. 29, 1942	Cape Lookout
Lady Drake	Cargo	May 5, 1942	Oregon Inlet
Senateur Duhamel	Trawler	May 6, 1942	Fort Macon
U-352	German sub	May 9, 1942	Cape Lookout
Bedfordshire	Trawler	May 1942	Cape Lookout
West Notus	Cargo	June 1, 1942	Cape Hatteras
Manuela	Cargo	June 5, 1942	Cape Lookout
Pleasantville	Cargo	June 8, 1942	Cape Hatteras
F. W. Abrams	Tanker	June 10, 1942	Ocracoke
U.S.S.Y.P. 389	Antisub	June 19, 1942	Cape Hatteras
Ljubica Matkovic	Cargo	June 24, 1942	Core Bank
Nordal	Cargo	June 24, 1942	Ocracoke
William Rockefeller	Tanker	June 28, 1942	Cape Hatteras
City of Birmingham	Cargo	June 30, 1942	Cape Hatteras
U-701	German sub	July 7, 1942	Cape Hatteras
Keshena	Tug	July 19, 1942	Cape Hatteras
Mayfair	Schooner	Nov. 9, 1942	Carolina Beach
Louise	Cargo	Dec. 16, 1942	Kinnakeet
Parkins	Trawler	Dec. 19, 1942	Cape Lookout
Portland	Cargo	Feb. 11, 1943	Cape Lookout
Wellfleet	Tug	Mar. 4, 1943	Cape Hatteras
Suloide	Cargo	Mar. 26, 1943	Bogue Banks
Panam	Tanker	May 4, 1943	Cape Lookout
Libertad	Cargo	Dec. 4, 1943	Cape Lookout
Belgian Airman	Cargo	Apr. 14, 1945	Nags Head

REFERENCES FOR "THE OUTER BANKS"

Bolton, Herbert. *The Spanish Borderlands.* New York, 1921. Vol. 23.

Borreson, Thor. "Final Report on the Remains of the Old Ship Found on Bodie Island, Dare County, North Carolina." National Park Service, Richmond, May 3, 1939.

Colonial Records of North Carolina, The. Vols. 1-13.

Hawks, Francis L. *History of North Carolina.* (From Hakluyt, Vol. 3.) Fayetteville, N. C., 1857.

Herrera, Antonio de. *History of America.* (Trans. Captain John Stevens.) Vol. 3.

Norfolk Weekly Journal, Sept. 20, 1797.

Pidgin, Charles Felton. *Theodosia.* Boston, 1907.

Pool, Bettie Freshwater. *The Eyrie.* New York, 1905.

Regional Review. National Park Service, Richmond, 1939.

Thomas, R. *Interesting and Authentic Narratives of the Most Remarkable Shipwrecks, Fires, Famines, Calamities, Providential Deliverances, and Lamentable Disasters on the Seas, in Most Parts of the World.* Columbus, n. d.

Winsor, Justin (ed.). *Narrative and Critical History of America.* Cambridge, 1886. Vol. 2, Part 1.

REFERENCES FOR "SHIPWRECKS BECOME NEWS"

American Beacon (Norfolk), Jan.-Dec., 1837; Jan.-Feb., 1838.

Emmerson, J. C., Jr. (comp.). *The Steamboat Comes to Norfolk Harbor.* Portsmouth, Va., 1947.

————. *Steam Navigation in Virginia and Northeastern North Carolina Waters.* Portsmouth, Va., 1949.

Ellms, Charles. *The Tragedy of the Seas.* Philadelphia, 1848.

Florida Law Journal, May, 1935.

Howland, S. A. *Steamboat Disasters and Railroad Accidents in the United States.* Worcester, Mass., 1840.

New York Daily Express, Oct. 7, 1837.

Norfolk Beacon & Portsmouth Advertiser, 1817-1836.

Norfolk Herald, 1818-1822.

Norfolk and Portsmouth Herald, Jan.-Dec., 1837.

Regional Review. National Park Service, Richmond, Aug., 1939.

Surfside News (Kill Devil Hills, N. C.), Nov., 1950.

Tannehill, Ivan Ray. *Hurricanes: Their Nature and History*. Princeton, 1938.

REFERENCES FOR "THE STEAM PACKET PULASKI"

American Beacon and Norfolk and Portsmouth Advertiser, Feb. 3, 1838; June 22-29, 1838.

Brown, H. H. (pub.). *A Minute and Circumstantial Narrative of the Loss of the Steam Packet Pulaski, which burst her boiler, and sunk on the coast of North Carolina, June 14, 1838*. (Pamphlet) Providence, 1839.

Charleston Courier, Jan., 1838.

Howland, S. A. *Steamboat Disasters and Railroad Accidents in the United States*. Worcester, Mass., 1840.

Wilmington Advertiser, June 20, 1838.

REFERENCES FOR "THE TOLL MOUNTS"

Howland, S. A. *Steamboat Disasters and Railroad Accidents in the United States*. Worcester, Mass., 1840.

Nautical Magazine, 1854-1857.

Norfolk Beacon & Portsmouth Advertiser, 1839-1854.

Norfolk Ledger, Dec. 13, 1877.

Ocracoke Beacon, Dec. 15, 1941.

Preble, George H. *A Chronological History of the Origin and Development of Steam Navigation*. Philadelphia, 1883.

Redfield, W. C. *Cape Verde and Hatteras Hurricane*. New Haven, 1854.

Southern Argus (Norfolk), 1854-1860.

Tannehill, Ivan Ray. *Hurricanes: Their Nature and History*. Princeton, 1938.

REFERENCES FOR "IRONCLADS AND BLOCKADE RUNNERS"

Ammen, Daniel. *The Navy in the Civil War—Atlantic Coast*. New York, 1905.

Battles and Leaders of the Civil War. Vols. 1 and 4.

Century Magazine, May, 1888.

Harper's Monthly, Dec., 1864; Sept., 1866; Dec., 1870.

Moore, Frank. *The Rebellion Record*. New York, 1861-1868. Vols. 3 and 4.

News and Observer (Raleigh), April 14, 1951.

Norfolk Virginian-Pilot, Dec. 3, 1950; April 22, 1951.

Parker, W. R. *Recollections of a Naval Officer*. New York, 1885.

Poore, Benjamin Perley. *The Life and Public Services of Ambrose E. Burnside.* Providence, 1882.

Porter, David Dixon. *The Naval History of the Civil War.* New York, 1886.

Roe, Alfred S. *The Twenty-fourth Regiment, Massachusetts, Volunteers, 1861-1866.* Worcester, 1907.

Robinson, William M., Jr. *The Confederate Privateers.* New Haven, 1928.

Sprunt, James. *Derelicts.* Wilmington, 1920.

Times (London), 1863.

United States Naval Institute Proceedings, Oct. and Nov., 1918.

REFERENCES FOR "CATCHING UP ON LOST TRADE"

Annual Report of the United States Life-Saving Service, 1876-1878. Washington, 1876-1878.

Norfolk Journal, 1867-1877.

Norfolk Landmark, 1874-1877.

Norfolk Virginian, 1868-1871.

Original wreck reports of the United States Lifesaving Service.

World Almanac & Book of Facts, 1950.

Personal Interviews:

    Miss Jeanette Gray, Church's Island, N. C.

    Mr. Russell Griggs, Church's Island, N. C.

    Mrs. B. Hampton Griggs, Church's Island, N. C.

REFERENCES FOR "THE HURON"

Annual Report of the United States Life-Saving Service, 1878. Washington, 1878.

Baltimore American, Nov., 1877.

Baltimore Sun, Nov., 1877.

Blasius, William. "Causes of the Huron Disaster" (paper read before the American Philosophical Society), Dec. 7, 1877.

Coastland Times (Manteo, N. C.), June 24, 1949.

New York Herald, Nov., 1877.

Norfolk Landmark, Nov.-Dec., 1877.

Norfolk Ledger, Nov.-Dec., 1877.

United Services, a Quarterly Review of Military and Naval Affairs, The. Vol. 1. Philadelphia, 1879.

REFERENCES FOR "THE METROPOLIS"

Annual Report of the United States Life-Saving Service, 1878. Washington, 1878.

Baltimore Bulletin, Feb., 1878.
Coastland Times (Manteo, N. C.), Jan. 26, 1951.
Forbes, R. B. *Notes on Some Few of the Wrecks and Rescues During the Present Century*. Boston, 1889.
New York Herald, Feb., 1878.
New York Star, Feb., 1878.
New York Times, Feb., 1878.
New York World, Feb., 1878.
Norfolk Landmark, Feb., 1878.
Norfolk Ledger, Feb., 1878.
Philadelphia Times, Jan.-Feb., 1878.

REFERENCES FOR "EACH MAN A HERO"

Annual Report of the United States Life-Saving Service, 1778-1893. Washington, 1878-1893.
Coastland Times (Manteo, N. C.) miscellaneous issues, 1936-1950.
Dare County Times (Manteo, N. C.) miscellaneous issues, 1936-1950.
North Carolina, A Guide to the Old North State. Chapel Hill, 1939.
Original wreck reports of the United States Lifesaving Service.
Surfside News (Kill Devil Hills, N. C.), Oct., 1950.
Personal Interviews:
    Chief Bosun Mate Levene Midgett, Rodanthe, N. C.
    A. W. Drinkwater, Manteo, N. C.
    T. S. Meekins, Manteo, N. C.

REFERENCES FOR "THE LONG DAY OF DUNBAR DAVIS"

Annual Report of the United States Life-Saving Service, 1894. Washton, 1894.
Norfolk Journal, March 12, 1871.
Original wreck reports of the United States Lifesaving Service.
Personal Interviews:
    Will D. Davis (son of Dunbar Davis), Southport, N. C.
    Mrs. Martha Davis Aspinwall (daughter of Dunbar Davis), Southport, N. C.

REFERENCES FOR "SHIPWRECKS AS A BUSINESS"

Annual Report of the United States Life-Saving Service, 1893-1899. Washington, 1893-1899.
Original wreck reports of the United States Lifesaving Service.
Personal Interviews:
    A. W. Drinkwater, Manteo, N. C.
    T. S. Meekins, Manteo, N. C.

REFERENCES FOR "SAN CIRIACO"

Annual Report of the United States Life-Saving Service, 1900. Washington, 1900.

Original wreck reports of the United States Lifesaving Service, 1899.

Tannehill, Ivan Ray. *Hurricanes: Their Nature and History.* Princeton, 1938.

REFERENCES FOR "FROM SAIL TO STEAM"

Annual Report of the United States Life-Saving Service, 1899-1914. Washington, 1899-1914.

Annual Report of the United States Coast Guard, 1915-1920. Washington, 1915-1920.

Norfolk Virginian-Pilot, April 4-14, 1915.

Original wreck reports of the United States Lifesaving Service, 1899-1914.

Original assistance rendered reports of the United States Coast Guard, 1915-1920.

REFERENCES FOR "UNGUARDED SHORES"

Annual Report of the United States Coast Guard, 1920. Washington, 1920.

Brown, Riley. *Men, Wind and Sea.* New York, 1939.

Chaffee, Allen. *Heroes of the Shoals.* New York, 1935.

David, Evan J. *Our Coast Guard.* New York, 1937.

James, Henry J. *German Subs in Yankee Waters: First World War.* New York, 1940.

Merchant Vessels of the United States. Washington, 1917, 1918, 1919.

Report of the United States Coast Guard Cutter *Gentian,* Norfolk, 1944.

Wreck Information List, United States Hydrographic Office, Washington, 1945.

Personal Interviews:

Captain Walter Barnett, Buxton, N. C.

Chief Bosun Mate Levene Midgett, Rodanthe, N. C.

REFERENCES FOR "PEACETIME ENEMY"

Annual Report of the United States Coast Guard, 1920-1932. Washington, 1920-1932.

Baarslag, Karl. *Coast Guard to the Rescue.* New York, 1937.

Brown, Riley. *Men, Wind and Sea.* New York, 1939.

Chaffee, Allen. *Heroes of the Shoals*. New York, 1935.

Coastland Times (Manteo, N. C.), Nov. 7, 1947.

Daily Advance (Elizabeth City, N. C.), Oct. 15, 1950.

Wreck Information Card File, United States Hydrographic Office, Suitland, Md.

Original assistance rendered reports of the United States Coast Guard, 1919-1940.

Merchant Vessels of the United States. Washington, 1929, 1931, 1932.

News and Observer (Raleigh), Feb. 2, 1950.

Norfolk Virginian-Pilot, Feb., 1921; Sept., 1923; March, 1924; April, 1925; Dec., 1927; Feb., 1929; Sept., 1929; Dec., 1931; Jan., 1932; March, 1932; Aug., 1933; Nov., 1937; March, 1950.

Report of the United States Coast Guard Cutter *Gentian*, Norfolk, 1944.

Wreck Information List, United States Hydrographic Office, Washington, 1945.

Personal Interviews:

    Lt. W. L. Lewark, Kill Devil Hills, N. C.

    Chief Bosun Mate Levene Midgett, Rodanthe, N. C.

    Surfman Marvin Midgett, Kitty Hawk, N. C.

    Chief Bosun Mate Jep Harris, Kill Devil Hills, N. C.

    A. W. Drinkwater, Manteo, N. C.

    T. S. Meekins, Manteo, N. C.

REFERENCES FOR "THE U-BOATS RETURN"

Baltimore Sun, Sept. 17, 1945.

"Battle of Torpedo Junction, The," Fifth Naval District press release, Sept. 17, 1945.

Fifth Naval District Wreck List, Norfolk, Aug. 2, 1944.

Morison, Samuel E. *History of United States Naval Operations in World War II*. Boston, 1947. Vol. 1.

Norfolk Virginian-Pilot, Sept. 16, 1945.

Report of the United States Coast Guard Cutter *Gentian*, Norfolk, 1944.

Ships of the Esso Fleet in World War Two. New Jersey, 1946.

Wreck Information Card File, United States Hydrographic Office, Suitland, Md.

Wreck Information List, United States Hydrographic Office, Washington, 1945.

CHART of SHIP, MAST, and RIGGING TYPES

SKYSAILS
ROYALS
TOPGALLANTS
TOPSAILS
COURSES

FORE AND AFT SAIL

SQUARE SAIL

SLOOP

2 1
TWO MAST SCHOONER

3 2 1
THREE MAST SCHOONER

4 3 2 1
FOUR MAST SCHOONER

4 5 3 2 1
FIVE MAST SCHOONER

6 4 5 3 2 1
SIX MAST SCHOONER

BRIGANTINE

SHIP

TYPES OF MASTS

1. FOREMAST
2. MAINMAST
3. MIZZENMAST
4. SPANKERMAST
5. JIGGERMAST
6. PUSHERMAST

BRIG

FOUR MAST BARK

JACKASS BARK

FOUR MAST BARKENTINE

Wilmington

Wrightsville

Shallotte

Southport

R
MAS
MASON INL

CORNCAKE (FORMER

LOCKWOODS FOLLY INLET
SHALLOTTE INLET
TUBBS INLET
LITTLE RIVER INLET

Cape Fea

Frying P

William K. Hubbell